The Pilot's Manual

Multi-Engine Flying

The Pilot's Manual

Multi-Engine Flying

All the aeronautical knowledge required to earn
a multi-engine rating on your pilot certificate

Mark Dusenbury
Shayne Daku
Robert Laux

Aviation Supplies & Academics, Inc.
Newcastle, Washington

The Pilot's Manual: Multi-Engine Flying
Mark Dusenbury • Shayne Daku • Robert Laux

Aviation Supplies & Academics, Inc.
7005 132nd Place SE • Newcastle, Washington 98059-3153
(425) 235-1500
Email: asa@asa2fly.com
Internet: www.asa2fly.com

Acknowledgments and photography credits: The publisher and authors wish to thank
those who contributed illustration material for this volume, specifically Piper Aircraft, Inc.
for the use of the Piper Seminole *PA44-180 Pilot's Operating Handbook* in performance charts
and more; Cessna Aircraft Company *Cessna 421C Pilot's Operating Handbook*; NASA-Glenn
Research Center, for SLD icing photo, Figure 7-2; Avidyne Corporation, images from the
Avidyne Entegra PFD/MFD manuals (for Chapter 9); FAA AeroNav Products approach
and sectional charts, and FAA-H-8083-25A *Pilot's Handbook of Aeronautical Knowledge*
illustrations and photos (including Chapter 7 image of Teledyne Controls *90004 TAS/Plus
Air Data Computer*). Cover photo at bottom right ©iStock.com/NNehring. Unless noted in
this preceding list, all other photography in this volume is by and belongs to the authors.

Printed in the United States of America

2018   2017   2016   2015   9 8 7 6 5 4 3 2 1

ASA-PM-ME
ISBN 978-1-61954-266-2 (hardcover)

Library of Congress Cataloging-in-Publication Data
Dusenbury, Mark, author.
  The pilot's manual : multi-engine flying / Mark Dusenbury, Shayne Daku, Robert Laux.
    pages cm — (The pilot's manual series)
  Includes bibliographical references and index.
  ISBN 978-1-61954-266-2 (hardcover : alk. paper) — ISBN 1-61954-266-8 (hardcover :
alk. paper)
 1. Multi-engine flying—Handbooks, manuals, etc. 2. Airplanes—Piloting—Handbooks,
manuals, etc. I. Daku, Shayne, author. II. Laux, Robert, author. III. Title.
  TL711.T85D84 2015
  629.132'52—dc23
                          2015007908

Contents

Personal Progress Table

I. Multi-Engine Systems

Text	Review

II. Aerodynamics

Text	Review

Text	Review

Foreword

Congratulations! You are entering the world of multi-engine flying, which will open up new opportunities for you to utilize an airplane for personal or professional transportation. A multi-engine airplane allows you to cruise faster, carry more passengers or cargo, and in most cases, fly higher. Since most are larger and more capable, you and your passengers can fly in greater comfort as well.

With this greater capability comes a greater complexity of the aircraft systems, their operation, aircraft performance, and their effect on your decision-making. A multi-engine airplane with two or more engines adds to the performance and redundancy of the aircraft, so it imposes more duties upon you as the pilot when one of those engines fail.

For these reasons, it is essential that you have a thorough understanding of the aircraft's systems and performance in both normal and abnormal situations so that you make proper decisions to ensure safety of flight. Proper aeronautical decision making is driven in part by a full understanding of how each system operates, what factors are affected in aircraft controllability and performance when an engine fails, and proper performance planning.

Section I of this book provides a thorough investigation of the aircraft systems of multi-engine airplanes. The systems found in cabin-class, pressurized multi-engine aircraft covered here are those of the typical light-twin trainer. Yet this solid foundation also touches on some advanced systems, in order to give you a boost toward future preparations for the more complex multi-engine aircraft that you'll encounter later on.

Sections II and III cover the aerodynamics knowledge, aircraft controllability, and proper performance planning that will be necessary for operating and making proper decisions when flying multi-engine airplanes.

The Pilot's Manual: Multi-Engine Flying is written to give you the insight into all these aspects in order to lay a strong foundation in your preparation to become a multi-engine pilot. The chapters include scenarios and questions so you can apply your understanding.

If you want to better prepare yourself through in-depth learning about multi-engine flying, *The Pilot's Manual: Multi-Engine Flying* is definitely for you.

Kent Lovelace
Professor, Department of Aviation
University of North Dakota

Multi-Engine Flying

About the Authors

Mark Dusenbury is an Associate Professor for the John D. Odegard School of Aerospace Sciences at the University of North Dakota in Grand Forks, North Dakota. Before coming to the University of North Dakota, Mark was an airline pilot for American Eagle Airlines, and a member of the United States Marine Corps Reserves. He also holds a Commercial Pilot certificate with instrument, single, and multi-engine ratings, and is a Certified Flight Instructor for single, multi-engine, and instrument airplane.

Shayne Daku is an Assistant Professor for the John D. Odegard School of Aerospace Sciences at the University of North Dakota in Grand Forks, North Dakota. Before coming to the University of North Dakota, Shayne was an airline pilot for Air Wisconsin Airlines Corporation. He also holds an Airline Transport Pilot (ATP) certificate with instrument, single, and multi-engine ratings, and is a Certified Flight Instructor for single, multi-engine, and instrument airplane.

Robert Laux is a Lecturer for the John D. Odegard School of Aerospace Sciences at the University of North Dakota in Grand Forks, North Dakota. Before coming to the University of North Dakota, Robert was an airline pilot for Piedmont Airlines and a corporate pilot for SC Aviation Incorporated. He also holds an Airline Transport Pilot (ATP) certificate with instrument, single, and multi-engine ratings, and is a Certified Flight Instructor for single, multi-engine, and instrument airplane.

Multi-Engine Flying

Introduction

Multi-engine aircraft fly faster and farther, and are capable of reaching higher altitudes and carrying more payload—all very desirable characteristics for pilots and owners alike. Along with these characteristics, however, comes an increase in systems complexity and a demand for decision making, problem solving, and flight planning skills. If you are a pilot accustomed to lower speeds, lower altitudes, and the more simplistic systems of single-engine aircraft, adding a multi-engine class rating to your pilot certificate can present a steep learning curve. This book is one tool available to you that will help with that learning curve—being introduced to the concepts and practice of flying multi-engine aircraft.

It doesn't take long to become comfortable with the flight characteristics of multi-engine aircraft, as they fly much the same as their single-engine counterparts. The biggest challenge in becoming a multi-engine pilot is in learning the complexity of the systems, and leveraging that knowledge to maximize aircraft performance and effectively handle abnormalities.

A multi-engine pilot must be prepared for an engine failure at any given point in the flight and have a list of possible alternatives. Preflight planning—performance calculations and airport planning—requires more attention to detail. The pilot of a single-engine aircraft does not have to decide what to do if the engine fails; gravity will limit the options available. The pilot of a multi-engine aircraft is faced with a much more complicated decision if an engine fails in flight—a decision that will vary widely depending on many factors such as aircraft performance, surrounding terrain, and weather conditions.

Section I of this book describes the systems of multi-engine aircraft, focusing on the items that present unique challenges. Multi-engine aircraft aerodynamics and related concerns are covered in Section II. Section III combines the concepts from the first two sections to provide you with a scenario-based example of the problems and challenges that multi-engine pilots must handle. This section provides you with skills to understand and mitigate the risks associated with multi-engine flying, and discusses the regulatory aspects. Multi-engine aircraft are expensive and their owners often want to gain a quick return on their investments. Multi-engine pilots must be aware of the unique regulatory concerns, and the limitations on what they can and cannot do.

It is essential for the multi-engine pilot to be prepared for the challenge of flying these aircraft. This book will provide the foundational knowledge necessary to become a safe and effective multi-engine pilot. By tying together a systems knowledge, checklist protocol, and aeronautical decision making, a multi-engine pilot can be confident of achieving mastery of the aircraft.

Enjoy your journey into the flight levels!

How This Book is Organized

The sections of this book are broken down into multiple parts to aid your comprehension of the material and help you reach mastery of each topic. Key components of each chapter include **objectives**, defining what you need to learn; **key terms** used in the chapter; **detailed descriptions** and discussion of the concepts to provide you with a thorough understanding; and **review questions** designed to deepen your understanding and apply the material.

In addition, the chapters on systems in Section I cover **operation and handling** considerations, providing an overview of how pilots interact with the systems during aircraft operations, as well as possible **emergencies** that pilots may face related to each system.

We recommend that you first read the objective to gain a sense of the desired outcome of each chapter. Next, read through and become familiar with the key terms, referencing the glossary in Appendix 1 for definitions as needed. If you need help identifying the most important concepts, examine the review questions at the end of the chapter before reading or rereading the chapter content. As do the other volumes in "The Pilot's Manual Series," the margins contain notes and sidebars about key terms and concepts to aid you in retention of the material.

Section I

Multi-Engine Systems

In years past, a pilot moving from a high-performance single-engine airplane to a multi-engine airplane would benefit from not only another engine, but also redundancy in aircraft systems. Today's multi-engine aircraft share many similarities with their single-engine counterparts: the systems on multi-engine aircraft function in the same manner but with the added complexity of the interaction and management of multiple, redundant systems operating simultaneously.

In multi-engine flying, you as the pilot need to understand how best to interact with the system and how to appropriately respond to a malfunction of that system. Therefore, a particular challenge lies in the decision-making process as it ties in with the intricacies of the systems—thus, the principles of aeronautical decision making (ADM) are worked into the discussion for each systems chapter in this section.

In each chapter, you will first review system basics and then cover the limited differences between multi-engine and single-engine airplanes, and how to operate within those differences accordingly. At the end of each systems chapter, the discussion will be on examining emergencies and the appropriate pilot response when systems fail or degrade in performance.

For the multi-engine pilot, effectively tying together knowledge of the aircraft's systems with checklist protocol and ADM leads to mastery of the aircraft.

1   **Flight Controls**

2   **Powerplant**

3   **Propeller Systems**

4   **Fuel**

5   **Landing Gear and Hydraulics**

6   **Electrical**

7   **Environmental**

8   **Oxygen**

9   **Flight Instruments, Avionics, and Warning Systems**

Flight Controls

1

🔍 Chapter Focus for Multi-Engine Flight Control Systems

Flight controls on multi-engine aircraft are nearly identical to those used on single-engine aircraft with two exceptions: multi-engine aircraft tend to have larger control surfaces (sometimes requiring powered deflection), and universally require larger rudders and vertical stabilizer surfaces. The reasons for these differences are covered in this chapter.

You will also learn to identify and describe the primary and secondary flight controls found on multi-engine aircraft, and apply that knowledge to the operation and handling of the aircraft. Following that you will learn to apply the appropriate emergency action for the various abnormal and emergency events involving flight controls.

Aircraft flight control systems might seem like an elementary concept, but as aircraft weight and complexity increases so does the complexity of the flight control system. Each multi-engine type's basic flight control system will have its own unique characteristics, so pilots must always review the Pilot's Operating Handbook (POH) and receive competent flight instruction on that aircraft type prior to operating the aircraft.

Primary Flight Controls

The *primary flight controls* are the ailerons, elevator, and rudder. These controls are used to maneuver the aircraft about the vertical, longitudinal, and lateral axis (pitch, roll, and yaw). *See* Figure 1-1.

Ailerons

There are three main types of *aileron*: plain, differential, and Frise. Some aircraft use a combination of these. The purpose of ailerons is simply to roll the aircraft. Most aircraft—both single- and multi-engine—use ailerons for roll; one exception to this is the Mitsubishi MU-2, which uses flight spoilers on the wings to reduce lift asymmetrically, causing the aircraft to roll. More commonly, multi-engine aircraft use flight spoilers and ailerons working together to create more responsive roll authority through all phases of flight. These unique systems utilize an interconnect system to tie-in flight spoiler movement with aileron movement.

On most light multi-engine aircraft, the basic flight control surfaces are mechanically driven using a series of cables, rods, and pulleys connected directly to the flight controls in the cockpit. Some multi-engine aircraft incorporate a system called rudder boost, which helps the pilot apply rudder force during one-engine-inoperative (or, single-engine) operations. Of course, flight control systems can vary greatly from aircraft to aircraft and the specifics for each aircraft you fly will be found in the POH and Aircraft Maintenance Manual (AMM).

Plain ailerons travel the same distance whether deflecting upwards or downwards. They are not designed to compensate for adverse yaw or reduce the likelihood of a wingtip stall at high angles of attack (AOA). Wingtip stalls occur

Key Terms

(in the order they appear in this chapter)

primary flight controls
ailerons
single-engine operations
elevator
rudder
stabilator
spoiler
anti-servo tab
differential ailerons
Frise ailerons
deep stall
secondary flight controls
plain flap
split flap
Fowler flap
slotted flap

single-engine operations: operating a multi-engine aircraft with one engine inoperative

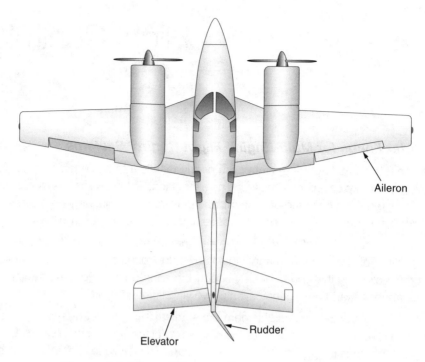

Figure 1-1. Primary flight controls on a multi-engine aircraft.

because the down aileron increases the AOA on the outboard section of the wing, which can cause the tips to stall before the root. This is an undesirable characteristic that is overcome by incorporating a different aileron in aircraft design.

Differential ailerons are designed to reduce the chances of wingtip stalls as well as adverse yaw. This is done by restricting travel of the downward-moving aileron in comparison to the upward moving aileron. The name "differential" refers to the difference in travel distance of upward and downward moving ailerons. This technique is achieved through the rigging of the cable and pulley system used to move the ailerons.

Frise-type ailerons are designed to counteract adverse yaw. With a plain aileron, the downward moving aileron produces more lift as a result of the higher angle of attack. Due to the increase in lift there is an increase in induced drag. In a roll to the left, the right aileron produces more lift than the left; this also produces more drag, yawing the aircraft to the right away from the desired direction of travel. Frise ailerons deflect the upward moving aileron into the slipstream below the wing surface, causing more parasite drag on the descending wing. This will compensate for the induced drag caused by the down-going aileron (Figure 1-2).

Frise-type and differential ailerons do not completely eliminate adverse yaw, they only reduce it. In order to counteract adverse yaw, the pilot must apply rudder in the direction of the turn to maintain coordination. Some multi-engine aircraft utilize a combination of Frise and differential ailerons to maximize the benefits and minimize adverse yaw and wingtip stalling characteristics.

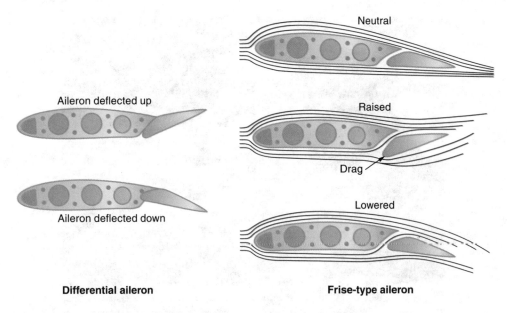

Neutral

Aileron deflected up

Raised

Drag

Aileron deflected down

Lowered

Differential aileron

Frise-type aileron

Down aileron deflects less than up aileron, reducing adverse yaw. On Frise-type ailerons, the upward moving aileron protrudes into the airflow below the wing, increasing drag and reducing adverse yaw.

Figure 1-2. Typical Frise-type and differential ailerons.

Elevator and Rudder

The *rudder* and *elevator* are part of the empennage and are included to provide lateral and longitudinal control and stability. The rudder is hinged off of the vertical tail surface. Some light multi-engine aircraft—including the Piper Seminole (a common multi-engine training aircraft)—have a stabilator instead of an elevator (Figure 1-3).

The rudder on multi-engine aircraft tends to be much larger (heavier and harder to move) than on single-engine aircraft. This is because of the directional control requirements of operating a multi-engine aircraft with one engine failed.

There are four methods of increasing the force that the rudder creates: increase the surface area, increase the deflection, increase the airflow around the rudder, and increase the distance from the rudder to the center of gravity, which affects maximum available rudder force. This will impact the rudder effectiveness when operating a multi-engine airplane with one engine inoperative.

Light twins also incorporate rudder trim. The trim tab is located on the back of the rudder and may also serve as an anti-servo tab. Using the rudder trim wheel in the cockpit, the pilot can relieve rudder pressure. During single-engine operations, the pilot will have to remove any rudder trim applied in cruise before landing. This is to prevent directional control problems when power on the operative engine is reduced to idle.

The rudder's *anti-servo tab* moves with the rudder but travels farther in the same direction, adding control force resistance when the pilot pushes the rudder pedals. This feature is designed to prevent the pilot from overstressing the rudder by making it more difficult to make full and abrupt rudder applications. Alternatively, the pilot can move the anti-servo tab manually using the rudder trim wheel in the cockpit in order to relieve control pressures. In essence, the same surface is used for two completely different purposes, which can cause confusion about the system's function and operation, yet reduces the complexity of the aircraft system. Ultimately, aircraft manufacturers attempt to achieve the most efficient and effective design possible.

stabilator: a single-piece, horizontal tail surface on an airplane that serves as both a horizontal stabilizer and an elevator.

The anti-servo tab moves farther in the same direction as control deflection. The pilot can also manually move the anti-servo tab in the opposite direction, relieving control pressure.

A traditional elevator's trim tab is hinged from the trailing edge of the horizontal stabilizer, and moves independently; a traditional trim tab only relieves control pressure.

Figure 1-3. Stabilator (left) with anti-servo tab compared with a traditional elevator (right).

Stabilator

The Piper Seminole uses a *stabilator* in place of a horizontal stabilizer and elevator system. A stabilator is simply a fully moveable horizontal flight surface in contrast to the fixed horizontal stabilizer and moveable elevator used on other aircraft. The stabilator design provides more maneuverability for aircraft that are longitudinally stable.

Like the rudder, the stabilator includes an anti-servo and trim tab. The anti-servo tab is designed to prevent the pilot from overstressing the aircraft by increasing control pressure progressively as control surface deflection is increased. The anti-servo tab moves in the same direction as the stabilator, but slightly farther. For example, if the stabilator is at +10°, the anti-servo tab would be at +12°. The anti-servo tab on the stabilator can also be moved manually by the pilot (using the trim wheel or electric trim) to relieve control pressures much the same as an elevator trim tab (Figure 1-4).

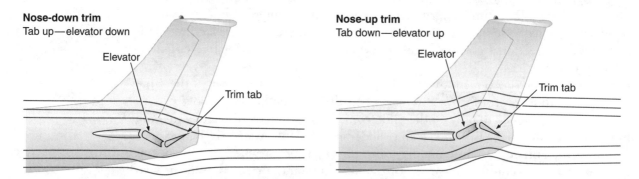

Figure 1-4. Trim operation for an anti-servo tab and a traditional elevator work the same—the pilot moves the tab in the opposite direction of deflection, to relieve control pressure.

Tail Design

Some multi-engine aircraft incorporate a T-tail design, while others use a conventional tail design. Each design has its own benefits and drawbacks.

One benefit of a T-tail design is that in cruise flight the stabilator is located in undisturbed airflow above the effects of the wing downwash. A T-tail aircraft will be less pitch-sensitive during power changes and while adding flaps.

The drawbacks of a T-tail are found at low airspeeds and in a *deep stall* condition. At low airspeeds, the T-tail requires larger control deflection to create a pitch change. The deep stall condition is usually caused by an aft center of gravity (CG) position and a high AOA, and can result in an unrecoverable stall. At a high AOA, the wings and fuselage blanket the horizontal tail surface, reducing the amount of laminar airflow over the elevator or stabilator. This reduces its effectiveness and in extreme cases can make stall recovery impossible (Figure 1-5).

In an attempt to prevent an aircraft from reaching the deep stall condition, aircraft manufacturers have included an elevator/stabilator down spring to the mechanical linkage that controls the elevator/stabilator. When airflow over the tail surface is reduced to the point at which the control surface cannot maintain balance, the down spring drives the stabilator to a nose-down position.

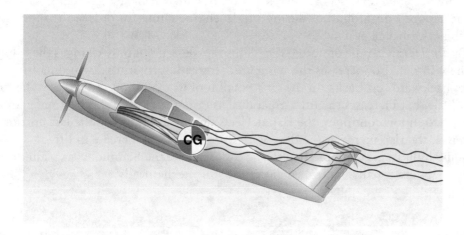

Figure 1-5. T-Tail aircraft with aft CG at a high AOA can lead to a deep stall and make elevators/stabilators less effective control surfaces.

Secondary Flight Controls

Secondary control surfaces allow the pilot to refine control of the aircraft, reduce pilot workload, and maximize aerodynamic effectiveness in slow and high-speed flight. *Secondary flight controls* include flaps, trim, and flight spoilers.

Flaps

The *plain flap* is the simplest of the four types. It increases the airfoil camber, resulting in a significant increase in the coefficient of lift (C_L) at a given angle of attack. The plain flap is a simple hinged portion of the trailing edge. Out of the four types of flaps, the plain flap produces the least amount of C_L for a given AOA. Plain flaps are rarely used in multi-engine aircraft.

The most popular flap on aircraft today is the *slotted flap*. Variations of this design are used for both small and large aircraft. Slotted flaps increase the lift coefficient significantly more than plain or split flaps. On small aircraft, the hinge is located below the lower surface of the flap, and when the flap is lowered, a duct forms between the flap well in the wing and the leading edge of the flap. When the slotted flap is lowered, high energy air from the lower surface is ducted to the flap's upper surface. The high energy air from the slot accelerates the upper surface boundary layer and delays airflow separation, providing a higher coefficient of lift.

Multi-engine aircraft built by Cessna commonly use *split flap* systems. In a split flap system, a portion of the underside of the wing "splits" from the upper portion of the wing (Figure 1-6). This results in a change in the coefficient of lift at low angles of deflection and an increase in interference drag at high angles of deflection. When operating split flaps, the pilot will notice a few important differences in aircraft control. At low angles of deflection the split flap will create an increase in lift, but also a considerable increase in drag. At high deflection angles (higher flap settings) the split flap will create negligible lift but a high amount of drag. For this reason, a split flap system at full flap extension is very effective at slowing the aircraft down, or creating high rates of descent. The pilot must be sure to reduce flap settings promptly in the case of a go-around or during single-engine climbs in order to gain the best climb performance available.

Fowler flaps are a type of slotted flap. This flap design not only changes the camber of the wing, it also increases the wing area. Instead of rotating down on a hinge, it slides backwards on tracks. In the first portion of its extension, it increases the drag very little, but increases the lift a great deal as it increases both the area and camber. As the extension continues, the flap deflects downward. During the last portion of its travel, the flap increases the drag with little additional increase in lift.

Some light twins combine flap types; for example, the Seminole has plain slotted flaps. Flaps are usually controlled electrically or mechanically.

Figure 1-6. Cessna split flap system.

Electric flap systems are commonly used on multi-engine aircraft. Electrically driven flaps offer a few benefits to the pilot: they move the flap panels smoothly and at a constant rate, and they move larger flap panels without amplifying the physical stress to the pilot. An obvious drawback to an electric flap system is that the flaps will be unusable during a complete electrical failure. Other drawbacks include the potential for a flap motor failure or micro-switch failure, and the possibility of asymmetrical flap extensions. Most light multi-engine aircraft use a solid connection between the left and right flap panels to prevent asymmetrical flap extension, but as the aircraft increase in size, this interconnection is difficult to achieve.

Spoilers

Some multi-engine aircraft use high drag devices called *spoilers*, which are deployed from the upper surface of the wings to interrupt the smooth airflow, reducing lift and increasing drag. Spoilers are most often used to control rate of descent without increasing airspeed. Some aircraft use spoilers for roll control, which has the advantage of eliminating adverse yaw. To turn right, for example, the spoiler on the right wing is raised, destroying some of the lift and creating more drag on the right. The right wing drops, and the aircraft banks and yaws to the right. Deploying spoilers on both wings at the same time allows the aircraft to descend without gaining speed. Spoilers are also deployed to help reduce ground roll after landing. By destroying lift, they transfer weight to the wheels, improving braking effectiveness.

Trim

Although an aircraft can be operated throughout a wide range of attitudes, airspeeds, and power settings, it can be designed to fly hands-off within only a very limited combination of these variables. Trim systems are used to relieve the pilot of the need to maintain constant pressure on the flight controls, and usually consist of flight deck controls and small hinged devices attached to the trailing edge of one or more of the primary flight control surfaces. Designed to help minimize a pilot's workload, trim systems aerodynamically assist movement and position of the flight control surface to which they are attached. Common types of trim systems include trim tabs, balance tabs, anti-servo tabs, ground adjustable tabs, and an adjustable stabilizer.

Use of Multi-Engine Flight Controls

A basic test of the flight controls' operation and handling is done during the aircraft preflight and prior to takeoff. Each flight control should be checked for freedom of movement and the correct direction of travel. If a crosswind is present, the flight controls should be deflected in the proper direction during taxi operations and during the takeoff ground run.

The aircraft's rudder pedals control nose-wheel steering. Nose-wheel steering, differential braking, and differential power can be used individually or in combination to turn the aircraft on the ground. When taxiing, you will notice that a multi-engine aircraft may take extra power to start moving, but once it is rolling, it will have a tendency to taxi faster. These taxi characteristics vary widely depending on the aircraft model and weight. It is a good idea to spend a little time getting used to the taxi characteristics of the aircraft before attempting a takeoff. You might need to

Figure 1-7.
Electric elevator trim—split switch.

use brakes while taxiing to prevent taxiing at too high of a speed. Be careful not to hold constant pressure on the brakes (dragging the brakes) as this will heat up the brakes and make them less effective if they are needed for an aborted takeoff.

Trim operation can be electric or manual. Electric trim consists of two rocker switches; one controls the clutch, and the other controls the motor (Figure 1-7). To operate the electric trim, move both parts of the switch at the same time. The purpose of the dual rocker switch is to prevent inadvertent activation of the trim. Test the trim prior to each flight using the procedure outlined in the POH. Additionally, it is good practice to be aware of all of the possible methods of disabling the trim should a trim runaway occur (which is described below in the "Emergencies" section). Know the position of the circuit breaker(s) associated with the electric trim, as well as any electric trim power switch that could be used to deactivate the trim quickly in the case of a trim runaway.

Flight Controls in Emergencies

Electric Trim Malfunction (Runaway Trim)

Runaway trim, a condition in which the electric trim moves without input of the pilot, is one of the most dangerous examples of an electric trim malfunction. In the event of a runaway trim, the pilot should physically take control of the aircraft and then disengage the electric trim system. Typically this is done by pulling the electric trim circuit breaker or powering off the electric trim system—the aircraft POH will provide the specific response items for this condition. Multi-engine pilots must memorize this response.

Another potential trim malfunction is an overall failure of the system, which will lead to the electric trim not functioning. This is significantly less dangerous than runaway trim and more of just a nuisance to the pilot; if this system fails, the pilot will have to revert to manual trim inputs.

Flight Control Failures

Flight control failures are typically limited to structural failures such as a control jamming or a control linkage breaking. This can lead to any number of control problems depending on the severity of the problem and the particular control(s) affected. Below are some of the possible flight control failures along with alternate means for maneuvering the aircraft to a safe landing.

There are multiple methods to roll an aircraft; the most desirable option is to use the ailerons. In the case of an aileron failure, however, the pilot will need to use another method to roll the aircraft. Roll is a result of one wing producing more lift than the other, causing that wing to climb while the other wing descends. This asymmetric wing lift can be produced by increasing its relative wind. Simply applying rudder force will result in a yaw and a roll (known as aerodynamic coupling). A pilot can also increase the thrust on one of the engines to attain the same result. It's also possible to create the yawing force by opening a door on one side of the aircraft or the other, although this should be considered a last ditch effort to control the aircraft.

For pitch control failures, a few basic strategies can be used. In multi-engine aircraft, the manipulation of thrust is generally going to be the most effective method for adjusting pitch attitude. For example, an increase in thrust will cause a pitch change. For aircraft with the centerline of thrust below the center of gravity (CG), an increase in thrust will cause the nose to pitch up. Alternatively, decreasing thrust will cause the nose to pitch down. The reverse is true for multi-engine aircraft that have a centerline of thrust above the CG. Another method of descending is to roll the aircraft, which will cause a loss of the vertical component of lift, resulting in a descent. The pilot can also attempt to operate pitch trim, in some cases the elevator may become jammed while the pitch trim is still operational.

Flap malfunctions can lead the pilot to land in a no-flap or reduced flap condition. In these cases, the pilot must be aware that approach speeds will be higher than normal leading to a longer-than-normal landing distance. Most performance charts do not provide calculations for landing without flaps, or with less than full flaps; these conditions require pilot judgment and awareness of approach speeds and landing performance. Exercise caution during these times, and ensure that you have given yourself extra landing distance.

Asymmetrical flap extension is a problem unique to larger multi-engine aircraft, although aircraft designers try to limit the possibility of this occurring. In systems that use individual flap panels, there is a flap position monitor that measures the position of each flap panel during extension or retraction. If the flap positions are asymmetric, the system will stop flap movement and lock out further flap control. This problem will need to be fixed by maintenance on the ground, and the pilot will be forced to land with the currently selected and locked-in flap position.

Review 1
Flight Controls

Primary Flight Controls

1. What are the primary flight controls on a multi-engine aircraft?

2. What is the difference between an elevator and stabilator?

3. How does an anti-servo tab work?

4. Explain the purpose of the elevator down spring.

5. Describe the difference between differential and Frise ailerons. Can they be combined?

6. How would the pilot respond to a jammed elevator/stabilator?

7. What is "aerodynamic coupling"?

Secondary Flight Controls

8. Explain how to handle a trim runaway malfunction.

9. What are considered secondary flight controls?

10. Explain plain, split, Fowler, and slotted flaps.

11. Explain the difference between high deflection angles and low deflection angles with respect to a split flap system.

12. Explain how flight spoilers could be used to control a multi-engine aircraft.

13. Explain the difference between an approach with full flaps and an approach with partial or no-flaps.

14. How do multi-engine aircraft prevent asymmetric flap deployment?

Answers are provided in Appendix 2.

Powerplant

2

Chapter Focus for Multi-Engine Powerplant Systems

Multi-engine aircraft engines are much like those in single-engine aircraft. Some have carbureted piston engines, such as the Piper Seminole, and others have fuel-injected piston engines, such as the Cessna 421, which also utilizes a turbosupercharger. Of course, there are also multi-engine aircraft that use turbine engines.

This chapter will focus on piston-powered engines and turbocharging. You will learn to identify and describe the components and operation of piston powerplants found on multi-engine aircraft, apply this knowledge to the operation and handling of these aircraft, and identify and understand how to apply the appropriate action in response to various powerplant abnormal and emergency events.

The Four-Stroke Piston Engine Cycle

All piston engines operate under a principle called the *Otto Cycle* which can be broken down into four basic steps: intake, compression, combustion, exhaust. Each step—or stroke—is measured by the movement of the piston from the top position of the cylinder to the bottom. These two positions are referred to as *top dead center* (TDC) and *bottom dead center* (BDC) (Figure 2-1).

The four strokes of the cycle:
1. *Intake stroke*: The piston begins at TDC and moves down the cylinder, drawing a mixture of air and fuel into the cylinder through an opening in the top of the cylinder called the intake valve; in the case of a fuel-injected engine, only air is drawn in on the intake stroke and fuel is added once the air has reached the cylinder. Once the piston reaches BDC, the intake valve closes and the intake stroke is complete.
2. *Compression stroke*: With the intake and exhaust valves closed, the piston now travels back up the cylinder, compressing the mixture of air and fuel. The compression stroke ends when the piston reaches TDC.
3. *Power stroke*: Just before the piston reaches TDC the air fuel mixture is ignited, causing a rapid thermal expansion of the mixture. This "rapid burn" creates a force that pushes the piston back down the cylinder towards BDC. This stroke ends when the piston reaches BDC.
4. *Exhaust stroke*: as the piston reverses its direction and heads back up the cylinder, the exhaust valve opens allowing the spent air fuel mixture to be forced out of the cylinder. This stroke ends when the piston reaches TDC, and the cycle repeats, starting again with the intake stroke.

The pistons are attached to a *crankshaft* that converts the linear action—up and down motion—into a rotational force. This rotational force is then used to spin the propeller, fuel pump, vacuum pump and alternator. This is referred to as the accessory drive. In some cases, the propeller is attached to a reduction gear, which allows the propeller to spin at a slower speed than the crankshaft and all other

Key Terms

(in the order they appear in this chapter)

Otto cycle
top dead center (TDC)
bottom dead center (BDC)
intake stroke
compression stroke
power stroke
exhaust stroke
crankshaft
pushrod
induction
normally aspirated
turbocharging
turbo-normalizing
compressor
waste gate
exhaust bypass valve
deck pressure
manifold (absolute) pressure (MAP)
density controller
differential pressure controller
supercharging
intercooler
carburetor
venturi
power enrichment system
accelerator pump
air bleed
fuel Injection
cylinder head temperature (CHT)
exhaust gas temperature (EGT)
shock cooling
mineral oil
ashless dispersant oil
synthetic oil
oil cooler
magneto

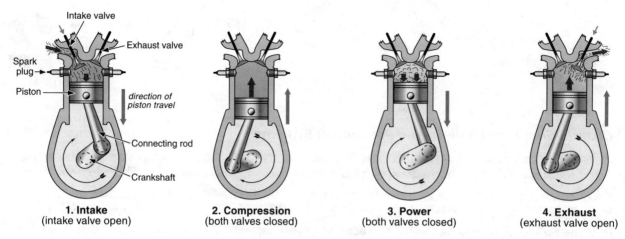

Figure 2-1. The four piston movements of a four-stroke internal combustion engine.

1. Intake
(intake valve open)

2. Compression
(both valves closed)

3. Power
(both valves closed)

4. Exhaust
(exhaust valve open)

components driven by the crankshaft. In most cases the alternator is powered by the crankshaft using a belt drive, and the fuel, oil and vacuum pumps are gear-driven.

Also important in this process is the timing for opening and closing the intake and exhaust valves. These valves are opened mechanically using *pushrods* that are driven up and down by a rotating camshaft. The camshaft is turned by the crankshaft, making the cycle self-sustaining.

Counter-Rotating Engines

Some multi-engine aircraft have counter-rotating engines. An example is the Piper Seminole, which has a Lycoming O-360-A1H6 on its left side and a Lycoming LO-360-A1H6 on its right side (when viewed from the cockpit). These engines are both four-cylinder, carbureted, normally-aspirated (not turbocharged) and are capable of producing 180 brake horsepower (BHP) at the International Standard Atmosphere (ISA). These two engine models are nearly identical, except for the fact that the LO-369-A1H6 on the right side of the aircraft rotates counterclockwise—the opposite direction of most piston engines (Figure 2-2).

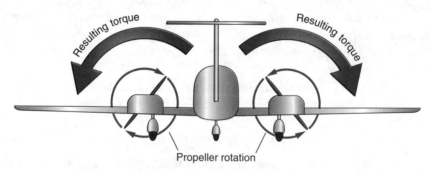

Figure 2-2. Propeller torque reaction.

Induction

In order to produce combustion, a piston engine must draw in air and mix it with fuel. Air used for combustion is called *induction* air. The location where induction air enters the engine is called the intake. The air entering the engine must be clean, so the primary intake for induction air goes through a filter before entering the engine. If this air intake becomes blocked, an alternate intake can be opened to allow unfiltered air into the induction system. (Figure 2-3)

As the pressure and density of the induction air decreases as a result of climbing in altitude or operating in hot temperatures, the engine will produce less power. To combat this, engine manufacturers have incorporated systems to increase the density and pressure of induction air. This process is called mechanical aspiration, better known as *turbocharging*.

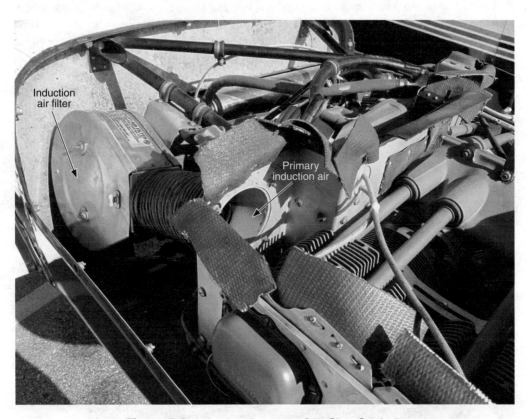

Induction air filter

Primary induction air

Figure 2-3. Induction air system of the Piper Seminole.

Turbocharging

The concept of turbocharging an engine is simple: induction air is routed through a pump that increases the pressure of the air. But unfortunately the simplicity ends there: turbocharged piston aviation engines are complex, intricate systems that vary widely from one engine model to another.

Some general principles that apply across different engine models do exist, and these are explained below. Some of these principles differ from automotive principles and definitions, so be careful in differentiating automotive mechanical aspiration and aviation mechanical aspiration.

Key Components and Principles of Turbocharged Engines

Key components of turbocharged engines:
- *compressor*
- *turbine*
- *waste gate*
- *exhaust bypass valve*
- *intake manifold*
- *density controller*

The key components of a turbocharger are shown in Figure 2-4.

With respect to aviation piston engines and for the purpose of this book, *turbocharging* refers to the process of using exhaust air to drive an intake air pump—called a *compressor*—to increase the pressure of induction air to at or below atmospheric pressure (30 in. Hg). Turbocharging serves two purposes in aviation engines: a turbocharged engine provides higher engine power output for takeoff and it can also serve the purpose of maintaining engine power output as the aircraft climbs to higher altitudes; this latter process is called *turbo-normalizing*. In this case, the turbocharger will not compress the intake air at low altitudes but will gradually increase intake

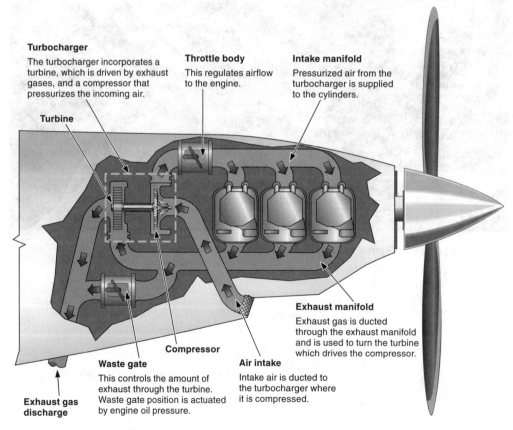

Turbocharger
The turbocharger incorporates a turbine, which is driven by exhaust gases, and a compressor that pressurizes the incoming air.

Turbine

Throttle body
This regulates airflow to the engine.

Intake manifold
Pressurized air from the turbocharger is supplied to the cylinders.

Exhaust manifold
Exhaust gas is ducted through the exhaust manifold and is used to turn the turbine which drives the compressor.

Compressor

Air intake
Intake air is ducted to the turbocharger where it is compressed.

Waste gate
This controls the amount of exhaust through the turbine. Waste gate position is actuated by engine oil pressure.

Exhaust gas discharge

Figure 2-4. Key components of turbocharged engines.

air pressure as the aircraft climbs, to compensate for the decreasing air density. A normalized turbocharger will seek to maintain a constant intake air pressure as the aircraft climbs to higher altitudes.

Compressor

The compressor is the "pump" that increases the pressure of the intake air. In most cases the *compressor* is a round, fan-shaped object that rapidly changes the velocity of the air when it is spun at high speed. There are a few different types of compressors in use today; centrifugal compressors are by far the most common compressors used in modern turbocharged aviation engines.

Turbine

The turbine wheel is connected (by shaft) to the compressor. The purpose of the turbine wheel is to convert accelerated exhaust gases into rotational energy—much like a water wheel converts water current into rotational energy. This rotational energy turns the compressor wheel, which in turn compresses the intake air. The faster the air travels over the turbine, the faster it will spin and the more the intake air will be compressed.

Waste Gate

The *waste gate* is a butterfly valve located inside the exhaust pipe that can direct exhaust gas over the turbine wheel, or direct exhaust gas around the turbine wheel and out the exhaust pipe into the atmosphere. It is the waste gate that controls how fast the turbine wheel is spinning, and by direct association controls how much the intake air gets compressed. The waste gate is typically controlled by oil pressure from the engine, although older turbocharged engines have manually (pilot-controlled) waste gates. Twin Comanche aircraft equipped with Rajay Turbochargers have manually controlled waste gates.

Exhaust Bypass Valve

The *exhaust bypass valve* controls the waste gate. Most exhaust bypass valves are controlled by engine oil pressure. If the exhaust valve opens, the waste gate will open, and vice versa.

Deck Pressure and Manifold Pressure

There are two locations at which it is important to measure the pressure of the intake air. The *deck pressure* is the measurement of the air pressure (in inches of mercury) in the intake manifold prior to the throttle valve.

The *manifold pressure (MAP)* is the measurement of air pressure in the intake manifold just after the throttle valve (measured in inches of mercury). Pilots use this value to set power in large piston-powered aircraft, especially turbocharged engines. The pilot must be careful to stay within operating limitations when setting power for takeoff, particularly on ground-boosted engines, as excessive manifold pressure will cause damage to the engine.

MAP = manifold absolute pressure... or more simply, manifold pressure

Density Controller

The purpose of the *density controller* is to provide the normalizing feature of the turbocharger. As the deck pressure decreases, the density controller will increase the oil pressure to the exhaust bypass valve, which in turn closes the waste gate. As the waste gate closes, the turbine spins faster and the compressor increases the pressure of the intake air which will result in a higher deck pressure and manifold pressure. The density controller is designed to work only during full power.

Differential Pressure Controller

The *differential pressure controller* is designed to limit the boost—increased pressure of intake air—during partial power applications. The differential pressure controller measures the difference between deck pressure and manifold pressure across the throttle valve. A difference of approximately 2 in. Hg is maintained between deck pressure and manifold pressure.

Variable Pressure Controller

Some turbochargers combine the function of the density controller and differential pressure controller into one unit, called the variable pressure controller, and instead of being controlled by air pressure, there is a direct connection between the throttle and the controller. The variable pressure controller is adjusted when the pilot moves the throttle and it adjusts the oil pressure to the waste gate to maintain a certain engine boost.

Supercharging

In general—and for the purposes of this book—*supercharging* refers to the process of increasing the pressure of the induction air to above atmospheric pressure (more than 30 in. Hg) by use of an engine-driven (rather than exhaust-driven) pump. This pump or compressor is most often gear or belt driven by some part of the engine. In general, the goal of supercharging is to increase the overall power output of the engine for increased performance during takeoff and initial climb; this is commonly referred to as *ground-boosting*.

There are two primary types of superchargers: internal and external. Internal superchargers compress the fuel and air mixture together and then deliver the high pressure air to the cylinders. External superchargers compress only the air and then deliver the compressed air to the cylinders, where the fuel is added internally.

Turbo/Supercharging

Some aviation piston engines use a combination of turbocharging and supercharging. The turbocharging compensates for the decreasing pressure with altitude by increasing the pressure of the intake air to at or below 30 in. Hg to maintain engine power output, and the supercharging increases the power output of the engine for takeoff and initial climb by increasing the pressure of the intake air above 30 in. Hg while operating at low altitudes. In most cases this will require two separate compressors, one that is exhaust driven and one that is engine driven (Figure 2-5).

Intercooler

A supercharger is able to increase engine power output by drastically increasing the pressure of the intake air. This increase in pressure causes the intake air to get hot—which decreases its density. To counteract this, most supercharged engines will put the compressed air (and fuel if it has been already mixed) through a heat exchanger. This heat exchanger—or *intercooler* as it is most commonly named—will cool the pres-

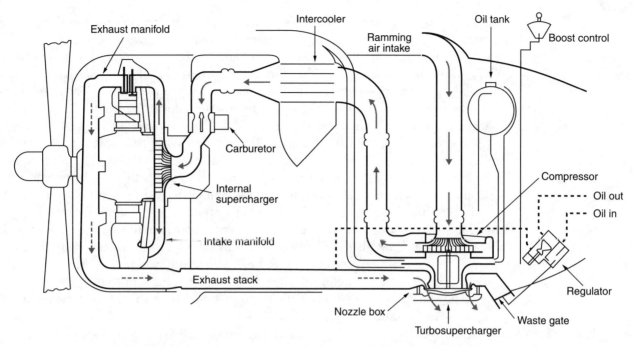

Figure 2-5. Schematic diagram for turbosupercharged engine.

surized air by directing ambient (unpressurized) air over a heat exchanger containing the hot pressurized air.

Engine Protection During Boosting

The presence of high-pressure air in the intake manifold requires some protective devices to prevent engine damage during "boosting." Turbosuperchargers have components to help protect the engine from over-boost.

- The *absolute pressure controller*'s purpose is to relieve deck pressure to prevent damage as a result of over-boosting.
- The *rate-of-change controller* limits the rate of boost to a maximum of 6.4 in. Hg per second, to prevent the system from overshooting the pilot-selected power setting.
- The *pressure ratio controller* limits the deck pressure to 220% of ambient air pressure. This is done to prevent detonation.

Additional key terms:
*absolute pressure
  controller*
rate-of-change controller
pressure-ratio controller

Carburetor

Some light twin-engine aircraft such as the Piper Seminole have carbureted engines. Carbureted engines mix the air and fuel before it is delivered to the cylinders.

The Seminole has a float-type, horizontal draft *carburetor* (Figure 2-6). The float-type carburetor is the most common type of carburetor used in normal category piston-powered aircraft (multi-engine aircraft included). A float-type carburetor consists of two main parts: the float chamber and the venturi.

The float chamber is a very small collector tank that works much like the tank on the back of a toilet. When fuel begins to drain from the float chamber and the fuel level drops, the float—which always stays at the surface of the fuel—will drop and allow fuel to refill the float chamber. Once the fuel level reaches the top of the float chamber, the float will cut off the fuel supply to the chamber. At the bottom of the float chamber is a line that delivers fuel from the chamber to the discharge nozzle (located on the venturi side of the carburetor), where it will be mixed with air as it is traveling to the cylinders. At the opening of this line inside the float chamber is the mixtures needle, which can be adjusted by the pilot using the mixture lever to control the amount of fuel that is sent to the discharge nozzle.

The other half of the carburetor is called the *venturi*, or barrel. It is here that the induction air is mixed with fuel and delivered to the cylinders. Other components found on this side of the carburetor are the throttle valve, discharge nozzle, idle jet and air bleed. The throttle valve is directly connected to the throttle lever, which is what the pilot uses to control the power output of the engine. By moving the throttle lever forward, the throttle valve opens wider and allows a greater volume of air to travel through the venturi; this draws more fuel from the float chamber to mix with the air and travel on to the cylinders, resulting in more engine power output. The throttle lever controls the amount of air being sent to the cylinders, and the carburetor mixes the appropriate amount of fuel with that air to produce more engine power (Figure 2-7).

Figure 2-6. Side-draft carburetor.

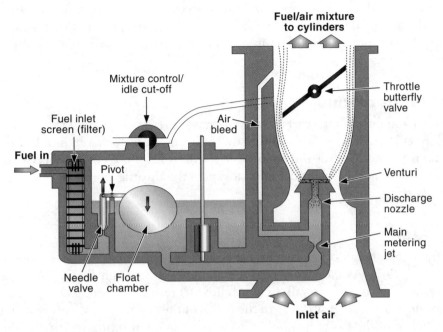

Figure 2-7. Basic operating principles of a carburetor.

Carburetor Idle System

When the pilot sets the throttle to idle, the throttle valve is only slightly open to allow a very small volume of air to be delivered to the cylinders. This creates an imbalance in air pressure on either side of the throttle. The cylinders are trying to draw fuel and air to sustain combustion, but the throttle valve is only slightly open, creating suction on the cylinder side of the throttle valve. However, with very little air flow through the venturi, this means very little fuel is being drawn out of the float chamber, which ultimately would result in the engine quitting. For this reason, carbureted engines have an idle port (sometimes referred to as an idle jet or needle).

The idle jet is located on the cylinder side of the throttle valve and allows a mixture of fuel and air to be drawn in and mixed with the air going to the cylinders. The suction that occurs on the cylinder side of the throttle valve draws air and fuel from the float chamber. The idle jet has an adjustable screw that mechanics can turn to adjust the amount of fuel and air that is delivered during idle. If the throttle lever is brought to idle and the engine RPM is too high or too low, the likely culprit is the idle jet. Almost all of the fuel entering the cylinders during idle power setting is coming from the idle jet; and conversely, almost all of the fuel entering the cylinders during high power settings is coming from the main discharge nozzle (and none from the idle jet).

Power Enrichment System

The Seminole carburetor system also includes a *power enrichment system*, the purpose of which is to enrich the fuel and air mixture (add more fuel to the air) during full-throttle operations. This system helps in cooling the cylinders during high power settings.

An added benefit of cooling the cylinders with the power enrichment system is that the engine can be operated at a more economic mixture for all other power settings. Typically an economic (lean) fuel mixture creates high temperatures and creates the potential for damage to the cylinders. With the power enrichment system, a small amount of vaporized fuel is added to the cylinders to cool the temperature of the cylinders.

Accelerator Pump

Another component of the carburetor system is the *accelerator pump*. This is a mechanical plunger that forces additional fuel through the main discharge nozzle when the throttle is moved towards the open position. This helps the engine accelerate more quickly and smoothly when the pilot advances the throttle from low power to high power settings.

Air Bleed

The final component of the carburetor system to be discussed is the *air bleed* system (see Figure 2-7). As the velocity of the air flowing through the venturi increases (as a result of increased aircraft airspeed, not as a result of opening the throttle), the venturi decreases the air pressure in the barrel of the carburetor, which in turn draws more fuel from the float chamber. This will cause the mixture to enrich when the aircraft airspeed increases, which is not a desired condition. The air bleed line draws air from the float chamber and delivers it to the discharge nozzle to maintain proper fuel air mixture.

Disadvantages of Carbureted Engines

Carbureted engines have a few disadvantages, including:
- Slightly delayed engine response
- Poor cold weather engine acceleration
- Carburetor icing

The slow engine response is a result of the time it takes for the larger volume of air and fuel to travel from the carburetor to all of the cylinders. Because the fuel is mixed with air at the carburetor upstream of the cylinders and then delivered to each cylinder—and pilot throttle control is linked to the carburetor—there is a slight delay between pilot power adjustment and engine response.

The poor engine acceleration during cold air temperatures is due to the increase in air density of cold air. The carburetor is capable of handling varying volume and speed of airflow, but is poorly equipped to handle varying air density. When advancing the throttle from low power settings to high power settings, such as during take-offs or go-arounds, the venturi receives a high volume of dense, cold air, which has insufficient fuel to sustain combustion. This can cause the engine to fail (or at least sputter) at a time when its power is most needed. As a result, pilots operating in very cold ambient air temperatures should advance the throttle slowly and deliberately to prevent inadvertent engine failure. Some operators also suggest turning on carburetor heat prior to large power advancements to help prevent this problem from occurring.

The third problem associated with carbureted engines is by far the most common cause of inadvertent engine failures or loss of power in flight. Carburetor icing can occur when moist air is drawn into the venturi of the carburetor. As air enters the venturi, the static pressure decreases, causing the local temperature of the air to drop. It is highly possible for the moisture in the induction air to reach the freezing point

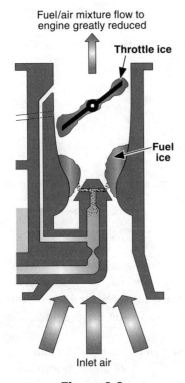

Figure 2-8.
Example of carburetor ice formation.

Fuel/air mixture flow to engine greatly reduced

Throttle ice

Fuel ice

Inlet air

Figure 2-9. Carburetor icing potential regions.

Relative humidity

100%
90%
80%
70%
60%
50%

High carburetor icing potential

Carburetor icing possible

20°F/-7°C   32°F/0°   70°F/21°C   100°F/38°C

Outside air temperature

and turn into supercooled liquid. As soon as this supercooled liquid impacts a hard surface (the throttle valve, for instance) it will turn to ice. At a minimum, this will restrict the amount of air entering the engine and result in a decrease in power output. At worst, carburetor icing will completely block all air and fuel going to the engine and cause the engine to fail (Figure 2-8).

The air temperature and relative humidity ranges for possible carburetor icing are shown in Figure 2-9.

Carburetor Heat

To combat carburetor icing, all carbureted piston aircraft engines are equipped with carburetor heat. This system uses hot air from around the exhaust manifold to heat the induction air before it reaches the carburetor. This serves one of two purposes: to melt any ice that has accumulated in the carburetor, or to prevent ice from forming in the carburetor.

Use carburetor heat when conditions exist that could lead to carburetor icing; days of high relative humidity at nearly any temperature can cause ice to form in the induction system. You will recognize the presence of carburetor icing by a decrease in engine power output or performance, a rough-running engine, or a complete loss of power. If carburetor icing is suspected, it is important to promptly turn on the carburetor heat. You must select full carburetor heat; partial carburetor heat may not completely melt the ice, or may only heat the ice enough for it to re-freeze further downstream. Expect the engine performance to worsen until the resulting water is burned off.

One concern of operating with carburetor heat on is that the air coming from the carburetor heat box is unfiltered. Use of carburetor heat on the ground should be limited to very short periods of time (during run-up) to ensure that foreign objects such as rocks, sand, or grass are kept out of the engine.

Fuel Injection

Another method of mixing the fuel with air for combustion is to directly inject the fuel into the cylinder where the combustion will take place. This is called *fuel injection*. Fuel-injected engines do not require a carburetor, but they do require some unique components in order to function properly (Figure 2-10).

Injector

Fuel-injected engines require a sprayer (nozzle) to spray a mist of fuel into each cylinder. This nozzle is most commonly referred to as the injector. Each cylinder has an injector placed near the top of the cylinder. The injector must spray an even pattern of fuel inside the cylinder at all times to create an even burn inside the cylinder. The process of mixing fuel and air properly is called atomization. The more atomized fuel droplets are, the more even and efficient the combustion will be. In order to maintain proper fuel atomization, the fuel injector must stay clean and free of any contaminants.

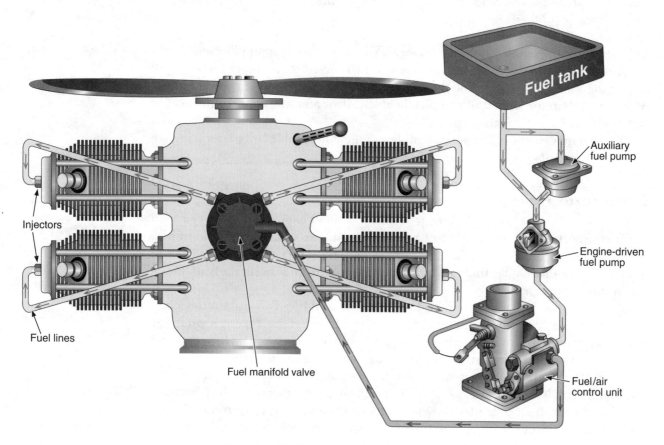

Figure 2-10. Typical fuel injection system.

This can be a challenge because the injector is subjected to high temperatures; in some cases, breakdown of carbons due to high temperatures can cause residual impurities in the fuel that can attach to and eventually block the fuel injector nozzle. For this reason, it is very important that pilots operating fuel-injected aircraft ensure the fuel used is the proper octane and is clean.

Fuel Pump

Another important factor in proper fuel atomization is ensuring that the fuel reaching the nozzle is at a high enough pressure to create a consistent, even spray pattern. For this reason, fuel-injected engines require a fuel pump to deliver the fuel to the injector at a consistent pressure.

Fuel Control Unit

The next key component of a fuel-injected system is the fuel control unit. This is the heart of the fuel injection system. The throttle and mixture levers are connected to the fuel control unit. Older fuel control units were mechanically controlled, while newer units incorporate electronic fuel control to provide more precise fuel delivery to the cylinders. But whether the fuel control unit is mechanical or electronic, it must provide an adequate volume of fuel to mix with the induction air in the cylinders to support combustion. Of course, the pilot still has control over the mixture of fuel going to the cylinders by use of the mixture lever. In turbocharged engines, the fuel control unit has an added challenge of maintaining proper fuel volume for the increased air pressure created by the turbocharger.

Engine Cooling

The primary method of cooling most piston aircraft engines is by directing ambient air over hot spots in the engine. This is called air-cooling and is the most common method of cooling a piston-powered aircraft engine.

Air-cooling is external in nature and is a direct relation to the aircraft airspeed and ambient air temperature. As a result, at times of warm air temperatures and low airspeed—such as on takeoff or initial climb on a hot day—there will be very little cooling airflow for the engine. For this reason, pilots must ensure that alternate means of cooling are used if necessary. Enriching fuel air mixture, opening cowl flaps, or increasing climb airspeed may help the pilot maintain cooler engine temperatures (Figure 2-11).

Yet pilots also need to ensure the engines do not cool too quickly as this could result in damage to the cylinders. This is a concern for pilots operating aircraft capable of reaching high altitudes or when operating during colder winter months.

In short, as the pilot of a multi-engine aircraft it is always important for you to be cognizant of the engine temperatures and maintain appropriate operating *cylinder head temperatures* (CHT) throughout all phases of flight and at all air temperatures. Always be aware of the CHT limitations for the aircraft you are operating, and adjust mixture, cowl flap position, or airspeed to remain within these limitations.

Figure 2-11. Typical cowl flap as seen on the Piper Seminole.

Measuring Engine Heat

When measuring the heat of the engine, three common locations are measured: the cylinders, the exhaust, and the turbine inlet (in engines that utilize turbocharging).

Cylinder Head Temperature (CHT)

Cylinder head temperature is a measurement of the temperature at the top of the cylinder. CHT is accurate, but the registered change is slow as it is essentially measuring the temperature of the engine's metals, which change at different rates. This is a good indicator of total engine temperature and is most often used to prevent shock cooling or overheating of the engine.

Exhaust Gas Temperature (EGT)

Exhaust gas temperature is a measurement of the air leaving the combustion chamber and is measured downstream in the exhaust manifold before the air leaves through the exhaust stack. This temperature is most commonly used for leaning, as exhaust air temperature varies most with the fuel-to-air mixture in the cylinder. As the mixture is leaned, the EGT will increase until it reaches a peak, and further leaning beyond this point will lead to a rapid decrease in temperature and may cause the engine to quit.

Figures 2-12, 2-13, and 2-14 show common ways in which EGT and CHT are displayed in analog and digital format.

Shock Cooling

Another concern relating to engine cooling is the possibility of cooling the engine too quickly, which is aptly called *shock cooling*. Shock cooling is more of a concern in larger piston engines but is an issue all piston engine pilots should be aware of.

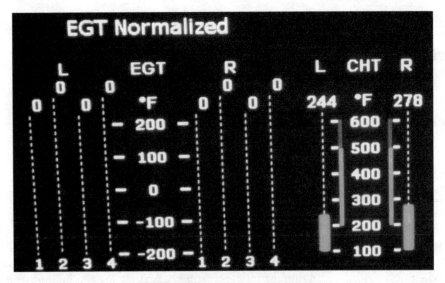

Figure 2-12. Digital engine gauges.

Figure 2-13. Cylinder head temperature.

Figure 2-14. EGT gauge.

When a hot piston engine is cooled very quickly, the potential exists for some of the metal engine components—primarily the cylinders—to crack or to separate from the engine block. With particularly large piston engines, pilots should never reduce power to idle for long periods of time, such as during decent. Powered descents will require additional distance to descend and must be planned for in advance (no more "chop and drop"). Some pilots of large piston engines recommend reducing power at a rate of 1 inch of manifold pressure per minute while descending. This technique is not necessary in small piston-powered aircraft such as the Seminole.

Lubrication

Oil system functions:
- *engine lubrication*
- *engine cooling by reducing friction*
- *removes heat from cylinders*
- *provides seal between cylinder walls and pistons*
- *carries away contaminants*

Oil is a very important component of all combustion engines. Oil prevents the metal components of the engine from grinding together, resulting in a longer useful lifespan for engine parts before they need to be replaced. Oil also dissipates heat, internally cleans the engine of dirt and metal particles, protects against corrosion, and seals gaps between co-joined engine components.

Types of Oil

There are three common types of oil in use today: straight mineral, ashless dispersant (AD), and synthetic.

Straight *mineral oil* is purely petroleum-based oil with no additives. Straight mineral oil typically is used only during initial engine break-in to help seat piston rings to the cylinder wall. A concern about continuous, long-term use of straight mineral oil is that it oxidizes when heated to high temperatures. This oxidation leads to carbon build-up and eventually a buildup of sludge, yielding higher oil consumption and possibly causing damage to engine components. To counter these concerns, oil manufacturers offer another type of oil called ashless dispersant (AD).

Ashless dispersant oil is typically used after engine break-in is complete and will reduce the oxidization and sludge build-up found in straight mineral oil. Ashless dispersant oil is actually mineral oil with an additive, and it has much better lubricating properties than straight mineral oil. The term "ashless dispersant" means that ash deposits resulting from combustion using straight mineral oil are reduced, and any ash that is present will be dispersed in the oil and returned to the oil filter and sump where it will not contaminate the engine or damage engine components.

Synthetic oil is a combination of chemical compounds that are artificially made in a laboratory. Rather than using pure petroleum, synthetic oil is made up with chemically modified components to produce a lubricant that is more resilient to extreme temperature fluctuations. Synthetic oil also tends to last longer, and makes for easier starting when the engine is cold. The main draw-back to synthetic oil is that it is more expensive than pure petroleum based oil.

In general, you will find that most multi-engine aircraft will use straight mineral oil for the break-in period or after an engine overhaul, and then switch to ashless dispersant oil. When switching from one type of oil to another, it is vital that you remove all of the previous oil before adding new oil. Never mix oil types, as this will cause unknown chemical reactions and certain engine damage. Turbocharged engines require ashless dispersant oil to be used all the time, even during engine break-in period.

Maintenance

Regular oil changes are very important for engine longevity. When oil is used for an extended time, the additives within the oil will weaken and cause deposit buildup and possible sludge buildup within the engine. Prolonged use of this depleted oil could result in engine damage. The recommended frequency of oil changes varies with the type of oil and type of filter being used, but generally the oil should be changed after 50 flight hours or four months, whichever comes first.

The oil filter is another critical component in the oil system. The oil filter removes the metal or any other contaminants from the oil system, effectively "cleaning" the engine of contaminants that result from use. The oil filter will become clogged if not replaced regularly, and thus it's recommended that it be replaced at the same time the oil is changed.

Oil Grades and Viscosity

Oil viscosity is a measurement of how thick or resistant it is to flowing. High viscosity oil is very resistant to flowing, and low viscosity oil flows easily. Cold oil has higher viscosity than warm oil. For most aircraft, the engines are exposed to all temperature extremes from very hot to very cold and the oil must be able to provide proper lubrication without damaging the engine under these extremes. In order to meet the requirements of such large temperature ranges, oil companies have added a polymer to create an oil that has multiple—usually two—viscosities. This is referred to as multi-grade oil.

Oil Storage & Delivery

There are two types of oil systems used on modern aircraft: dry-sump and wet-sump.

A dry-sump oil system—common on radial engines but not so common on horizontally-opposed engines used in modern aircraft—has a separate tank to store oil outside of the engine crankcase. The oil is delivered via oil lines to the engine where it is used and recycled back to the tank or sump.

The wet-sump oil system stores the oil directly below or behind the engine case and is considered to be integral with the engine crank case. The oil is still delivered using a pump when needed. The propeller governor also receives engine oil and will send unused oil back to the sump using return—or scavenge—oil lines.

Oil Cooler

During operation in warm temperatures, oil temperatures can get hot, resulting in lower oil viscosity or beginning to break down the additives within the oil. To prevent overheating of the oil, engine manufacturers have an *oil cooler* installed in most engines. The oil cooler is essentially a radiator that circulates the oil through a coil that is cooled using ambient airflow. In addition, in aircraft that reach high altitudes where very cold temperatures occur, oil lines can be coiled around fuel lines to transfer heat from the oil to the fuel to prevent freezing. This has the added benefit of cooling the oil.

When operating piston aircraft in cold temperatures, it is important to ensure that oil does not get too cold. For this reason, some aircraft have oil cooler winterization plates. These plates block airflow over the oil cooler to help keep the oil temperature up during operations in cold weather.

Precautions

It is imperative to know what type of oil is being used in your particular aircraft, as mixing different oil types will cause permanent engine damage. Also, it is good practice to carry a few quarts of oil in the aircraft both as a precaution and as a reminder of the oil used in your aircraft. Be sure to keep a record of when oil is added to each engine, so you can track the oil consumption of each engine. Excessive oil consumption is an indicator of possible engine or engine component problems.

Ignition

In order for combustion to occur, there must be a spark. The spark is created by a spark plug. The energy required to create the spark comes from a *magneto*. A magneto is a magnet that turns magnetic flux into electricity when it is rotated. The benefit of the magneto is that it can produce electricity independently of the aircraft electrical system. As long as the magneto is turning, sufficient electricity will be produced to cause a spark at the spark plug.

Most aircraft engines have two spark plugs in each cylinder and each spark plug is powered by a separate magneto. This is done for redundancy in case of a magneto failure, and also because it helps to create more even and efficient combustion. This means that multi-engine aircraft have four magneto switches: one for each magneto on each engine. No longer do you use a key to start the engine or control the magnetos.

It is very important that you ensure all magneto switches are on prior to start and more importantly, all magneto switches are off after your flight is complete. It is easy to forget to turn the magneto switches off; if you do forget, it means one or both of the engines are still "live." In this situation, if someone happens to turn the propeller, the engine possibly could turn over fast enough to hit the unlucky person and cause serious injury. So this step is crucial enough that despite the redundancy, always ensure the magnetos are off after every flight.

In the pre-takeoff run-up procedure, most piston aircraft require a check of the magnetos to ensure that all spark plugs are firing and both sets of magnetos are operational. It is common to check the magnetos simultaneously in order to save time: turn OFF the left magneto on both engines, notice the RPM drop, turn them both back ON, and then test the right magneto on both engines. This procedure will help in determining if one set of spark plugs is fouled (covered in engine sludge or unburned fuel) by comparing the RPM drop of both engines together. In the case of a fouled spark plug, the RPM will drop in excess of 150 RPM and the engine will run very rough. A fouled plug can be cleaned by leaning the mixture and "burning off" the sludge from the spark plug.

One way to prevent the fouling of spark plugs is to lean the mixture for taxi. Especially in fuel-injected piston engines, the idle fuel mixture is set rich to improve starting, and during low power settings can cause spark plug fouling. It is safe to lean the mixture aggressively during taxi as the power setting is low and heat will be insufficient to cause damage. If you lean for taxi, be certain to remember to set the mixture to rich before takeoff.

Exhaust

Aircraft engine exhaust systems are very important for several reasons: exhaust fumes are toxic, hot, and need to be removed from the engine quickly so that the combustion process can continue unhindered. Also, turbochargers extract power from the moving exhaust gases. Pilots must be aware of the condition of the exhaust ducting and be observant of cracks or leaks that could cause fires or carbon monoxide poisoning. Check the exhaust system thoroughly for cracks, and take note of any unusual black streaks on painted parts of the aircraft. A new exhaust leak may manifest itself as black soot markings on an area of the engine cowling that is not normally affected by the exhaust.

Most multi-engine aircraft do not use the same exhaust manifold heating systems used in single-engine aircraft as this air needs to be ducted from the engine nacelles to the cabin and often loses valuable heat in the process. For this reason, most multi-engine aircraft use separate cabin heaters. Chapter 7, covering environmental systems, will go over the specifics of this type of heater.

Engine Control and Gauges

The power control quadrant on multi-engine aircraft is very similar to single-engine aircraft. The throttles, propeller controls, and mixture controls are paired for each engine, and placed in the same order as single engine aircraft—throttles, propellers, and mixture moving from left to right (Figure 2-15). Carburetor heat control for each engine is placed near the power quadrant (below the throttles in the case of the Piper Seminole).

With piston-powered multi-engine aircraft, the engine instruments include exhaust gas temperature (EGT), cylinder head temperature (CHT), amp meters, oil pressure and temperature gauges, and fuel gauges for each engine. These instruments can be represented in either analog format or digital format (Figure 2-16). The interpretation of these gauges has already been discussed earlier in this chapter.

Figure 2-15. Typical power quadrant for a piston multi-engine aircraft.

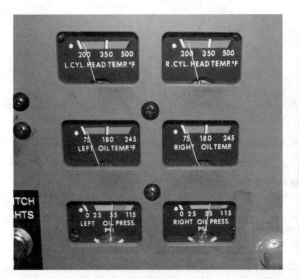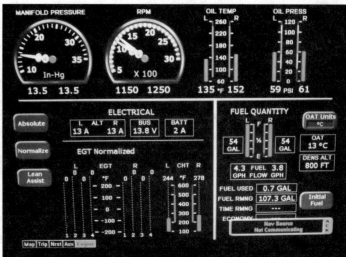

Figure 2-16. Analog (left) and digital (right) engine gauge comparison.

Best Practices for Multi-Engine Operations

Engine Start

Starting multi-engine aircraft is generally a simple process. Most aircraft manufacturers have suggested starting procedures for varying environmental and engine temperature conditions. The pilot has the choice (in most cases) of which engine to start first. Some aircraft manufacturers suggest which engine to start first based on the location of the battery (shorter distance between the battery and starter means more power available for the start) but generally it is up to the pilot to choose. During start procedures, the pilot should be carefully watching the engine start (visually out the window as well as internally on the engine instruments) in order to detect problems early. Should a problem arise during the start, the pilot should promptly follow aircraft checklist procedures.

Runup

Multi-engine aircraft need to complete a runup before each flight. The most important things to check during a runup are the magnetos, vacuum pump operation, deice system operation, pressurization system, and propeller governor. It is common to have spark plug fouling on multi-engine aircraft (especially if the pilot has not aggressively leaned the engines for taxi) and this can be recognized and remedied during runup.

Be sure to note the difference between a fouled spark plug (in which the spark plug doesn't spark due to a buildup of carbon or lead) and an overly rich fuel condition (when the air density is low and the carburetor or fuel servo delivers a fixed amount of fuel for the throttle setting). A fouled spark plug will produce a rapid drop in RPM and will usually be accompanied by engine vibration when a single magneto is selected. You can confirm the presence of a fouled plug by noting the EGT, which will increase during the single magneto operation. If a fouled spark plug occurs, engine manufacturers recommend that the pilot open the throttle slowly and smoothly to cruise RPM, and lean the mixture as far as possible (maintaining a smooth-running engine). If the engine starts to run rough, enrich the mixture slightly. Hold this condition for several seconds, then return to the proper mixture position for takeoff and recheck the magneto. If this procedure has not solved the problem, you will need maintenance intervention.

An overly rich fuel condition will produce a slow and smooth drop in RPM when a single magneto is selected. This condition can usually be remedied by performing the magneto check with the mixture leaned in accordance with the manufacturer's operating instructions. Increase power to a cruise power setting, lean the mixture until the RPM peaks, retard the throttle to the RPM specified for performing a magneto check, and then recheck the magnetos. If the problem persists, discontinue the flight and have maintenance check out the plugs and magnetos.

Takeoff

While taking off in a multi-engine aircraft there are a few considerations to keep in mind. First, if the aircraft is a conventional twin, it will have a significant left-turning tendency. Be ready to counteract this with right rudder. Also, it is a good practice to apply partial power while holding the brakes to ensure engine instruments are "in the green" before applying full takeoff power and releasing the brakes. It is far safer to check the instruments while stationary, especially when the left-turning tendency is prevalent during the early phases of a takeoff roll.

Climb

It is common to maintain full takeoff power until around 500 feet AGL. At this point, the pilot should reduce power to a normal climb power setting and begin to accelerate the aircraft to a cruise climb speed (unless best rate-of-climb is needed). Wait until reaching 1,000 feet AGL before verifying with the checklist. When reducing power in an aircraft with a constant-speed propeller, you must reduce the manifold pressure first and then decrease propeller RPM. You will notice when you reduce propeller RPM that the manifold pressure will increase slightly. The higher blade angle creates a greater workload on the engine, causing a higher air pressure in the intake manifold. A good rule of thumb is to reduce the manifold pressure to one inch below desired climb setting, then reduce propeller to climb RPM.

As the aircraft climbs, the pilot must lean the mixture to account for the decreasing air density. In normally aspirated engines, it will be necessary for the pilot to increase manifold pressure as the aircraft climbs. The manifold pressure will drop at approximately one inch for every 1,000 feet of altitude gain. In turbocharged engines, the turbocharger will maintain the selected manifold pressure as the aircraft climbs.

*This proper mixture is also referred to as the **stoichiometric mixture** — the ratio of the mixture of fuel and air that, when burned in a heat engine, leaves no uncombined oxygen nor free carbon.*

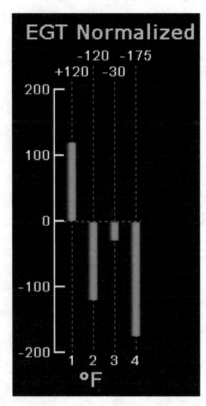

Figure 2-17. EGT normalizer.

Cruise

During cruise, the pilot must select cruise power (typically only a reduction in propeller RPM) and lean the mixture for a desired power setting or fuel burn. Regarding the systems during this time, it is crucial to monitor engine parameters (oil temperature and pressure, exhaust gas temperatures, and cylinder head temperatures) and watch for anomalies. New, digital engine instrumentation has a feature allowing the change of the instrument display to a normalized view. In this view, it is easier for the pilot to recognize changes in each parameter (Figure 2-17).

Descent

Shock cooling is the largest concern during descent and although it has already been discussed in this chapter, it's important enough that it warrants revisiting. A pilot should always be cognizant of cylinder head temperatures during descent.

There are other considerations during descent that the pilot should be aware of. As the aircraft descends, the pilot will need to make intermittent adjustments to the fuel mixture (enriching it) to compensate for the increased air density. Additionally, the pilot may have to make consistent power reductions as the aircraft descends into higher density air (approximately 1 inch of manifold pressure for each 1,000 feet of altitude).

Engine Emergencies

There are many potential emergencies relating to aircraft engines. The key to any emergency is being able to recognize potential problems early. Most common abnormal indications or emergencies will have appropriate checklist procedures published by the aircraft manufacturer, and pilots should follow these procedures. In general, if the pilot suspects severe engine damage (strong engine vibration, or noticeable fire or damage to the engine cowling), the engine should be secured using the appropriate engine securing procedure.

The most common causes of engine roughness are carburetor icing, too lean a mixture, engine-driven fuel pump failure, or magneto failure. If engine roughness is experienced, the pilot can troubleshoot by selecting carburetor heat (if equipped), enriching mixture, selecting fuel boost pumps on, or isolating magnetos to determine the cause.

Review 2
Powerplant

1. What is shock cooling and how can a pilot prevent this condition from occurring in flight? What impact does shock cooling have on the aircraft's powerplant?

2. How can a pilot control the engine temperature?

3. What is the purpose of having two magnetos on each engine?

4. How are carbureted engines different from fuel-injected engines?

5. What are the benefits of turbocharging?

6. What is the difference between turbocharging and turbo-normalizing?

7. Which of the engine gauges gives the pilot an indication of carburetor icing?

8. Should a pilot lean the aircraft while operating on the ground? Why or why not?

9. During a complete electrical failure, will the engine ignition continue to operate? Would the engine fail or continue to run? Why? How is this different in your car?

10. What are the common types of oil used in piston-powered engines? When are these oils typically used? What are the benefits/drawbacks to these types of oil?

11. Describe the float chamber and venturi on a float-type carburetor.

12. Why is applying partial carburetor heat not recommended?

13. What is the purpose of the oil cooler?

14. What are the functions of oil?

15. What is the significance of the L preceeding O in the manufacturer's engine model number?

16. Spark plug fouling is most likely to occur under what conditions?

17. What is the purpose of adjusting fuel air mixture at altitude?

18. Why does the pilot use RPM on the ground, but manifold pressure on takeoff and in flight?

19. Explain why EGT is used instead of CHT to lean the mixture.

Answers are provided in Appendix 2.

Propeller Systems

3

Chapter Focus on Propellers

Multi-engine propeller systems are more complex than single-engine aircraft for one reason: the need to feather the propeller to reduce drag and increase one-engine inoperative climb performance. The pilot of any multi-engine aircraft needs to understand how much performance is lost if the propeller is not feathered after engine failure.

In this chapter, you will learn to identify and describe the propeller system components found on multi-engine aircraft, and apply knowledge of these components to the operation and handling of these aircraft. We will discuss how to identify and apply the appropriate actions in response to a propeller overspeed emergency.

Propeller Feathering

Propellers on multi-engine aircraft have an added feature compared to those on single-engine aircraft: the ability to *feather* the propeller in the event the engine malfunctions. Feathering is when the propeller blades are rotated parallel with the relative wind. If an unpowered propeller is not brought to the feathered position it will continue to turn or windmill. This windmilling creates additional parasite drag thereby reducing performance. The purpose of feathering is to reduce this parasite drag, which will comparatively increase performance and may enable the aircraft to hold altitude or climb on one engine.

Propellers come in two types—*fixed pitch*, having blades that are not adjustable, and *controllable pitch* in which the blade-pitch is adjustable. Some adjustable-pitch propellers can only be adjusted manually on the ground with the propeller stopped; this type of adjustable-pitch propeller is not common in multi-engine aircraft. Most controllable-pitch propellers on multi-engine aircraft can be adjusted in flight by the pilot via a propeller control.

If the engine malfunctions, the drag penalty of an unfeathered propeller can be upwards of –300 fpm on smaller piston twins, and more on turboprop aircraft. Most light twin aircraft will not be able to climb or even hold altitude without the ability to feather the propeller. To put this in perspective, the single-engine climb rate for a Seminole and a Baron with one propeller in the feathered position is:

Piper Seminole +200 fpm
Beechcraft Baron +300 fpm
(Conditions: gross weight, sea level, standard atmosphere)

With an unfeathered propeller at sea level, each aircraft would, at best, be able to hold altitude. If density altitude were to increase, the aircraft likely would lose altitude (this is known as drift down). This would be comparable to a partial power failure in a single-engine airplane.

Key Terms

(in the order they appear in this chapter)

feather (a propeller)
fixed-pitch propeller
controllable pitch propeller
constant speed propeller
governor
low-pitch stop
accumulator
anti-feathering pins
propeller synchronization
propeller synchrophasing

Fixed-pitch propellers are not used in multi-engine aircraft because the pilot would be unable to feather a fixed-pitch propeller.

Propeller System Components and Features

RPM = revolutions per minute

Multi-engine aircraft with propellers have a *constant speed, controllable-pitch propeller* system. This type of system will allow the pilot to select the best propeller pitch setting for the conditions of flight. In addition, the system will maintain the pilot-selected RPM even when the propeller load changes (due to a change in airspeed or power setting). The most important benefit of this system on a multi-engine aircraft is the ability to feather the propeller.

Governor

The controllable-pitch, constant speed propeller system contains a *governor* (Figure 3-1). The governor must boost engine oil pressure in order to adjust the angle of the propeller blade. The engine oil pressure in light twins usually ranges from a minimum of 25 psi to a maximum of 115 psi. The governor's oil pump boosts pressure to around 275 psi.

The governor serves two functions:

1. Change the propeller blade angle in response to the pilot moving the propeller control levers.
2. Maintain a constant RPM setting as the air load on the propeller changes.

Controllable Pitch Function

*The compression of the **speeder spring** is controlled by the pilot via the propeller pitch control lever (propeller RPM).*

The first function of the governor is considered the controllable pitch part of the system. When the pilot moves the propeller control lever the tension on the speeder spring changes, which moves the pilot valve to allow oil to flow to or from the propeller hub. The oil pushes on the propeller piston, which changes the propeller blade angle. The propeller can be set to the desired blade angle for each different phase of flight. During takeoff, climb, and on final approach to land, the desired setting is low pitch, high RPM. During cruise flight and descent, high pitch, low RPM is used.

Generally speaking, if a pilot wants maximum power out of the engine and propeller, the propeller should be at low pitch, high RPM. If the pilot wants maximum efficiency from the propeller (during cruise speeds), the pilot should select a higher pitch, lower RPM. If the pilot wants the least drag from the propeller (during single-engine operations), the pilot should select feather, which is the highest pitch, lowest RPM (zero).

Constant Speed Function

The governor maintains constant propeller RPM despite varying air loads.

The second function of the governor is maintaining a constant engine speed, which is accomplished automatically.

When a descent is initiated in an aircraft with a fixed-pitch propeller system, the airspeed will increase, and so will the propeller RPM. During a climb, the airspeed will decrease and the RPM will decrease.

In aircraft with a constant speed propeller, flyweights are connected to the pilot valve. The flyweights spin at the same speed as the propeller. If the flyweights speed up (beyond the pilot-selected RPM) centrifugal force will push them outward, moving the pilot valve up and allowing oil to move from the governor pump to the

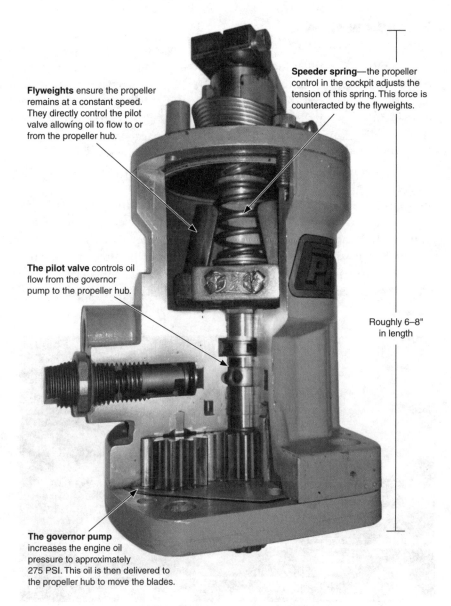

Speeder spring—the propeller control in the cockpit adjusts the tension of this spring. This force is counteracted by the flyweights.

Flyweights ensure the propeller remains at a constant speed. They directly control the pilot valve allowing oil to flow to or from the propeller hub.

The pilot valve controls oil flow from the governor pump to the propeller hub.

Roughly 6–8" in length

The governor pump increases the engine oil pressure to approximately 275 PSI. This oil is then delivered to the propeller hub to move the blades.

Figure 3-1. Propeller governor cutaway.

propeller hub; this moves the propeller blades to a higher blade angle and lower RPM. Conversely, if the flyweights slow down (below the pilot-selected RPM) centripetal force will push them inward, moving the pilot valve down and allowing oil to move from the propeller hub back to the engine oil sump.

The process described above is completely opposite in a single-engine, constant speed propeller system. In single-engine airplanes, oil increases blade angle, reducing RPM; in multi-engine airplanes oil decreases blade angle, increasing RPM. If the engine in a multi-engine airplane loses oil pressure, the pilot wants the propeller to move to the feathered position for best single-engine performance.

High Pitch/Low RPM

Nitrogen, assisted by a feathering spring and counterweights, moves the propeller toward a high pitch, low RPM position. Maintenance technicians can recharge the nitrogen by removing the spinner (Figure 3-2). Proper nitrogen pressure is based on the current ambient temperature; a chart is printed directly on the propeller dome to assist the AMT in servicing the tank. Sluggish RPM control and slow RPM recovery after throttle application indicate that the nitrogen charge in the propeller dome is low and should be serviced as soon as possible. The counterweights and feathering spring can be considered a supplement to the nitrogen charge, but are not the main moving force to high pitch/low RPM.

Therefore, there are five sources of force used to adjust the propeller blade angle; the nitrogen charge in the hub of the propeller, the counterweights, and the feathering spring all drive the propeller blades towards a higher blade angle (high pitch) and low RPM. Counteracting these forces are propeller governor-boosted engine oil, and the aerodynamic twisting force for the propellor blades, which drive the propellor blades towards a lower blade angle (low pitch) and high RPM (Figure 3-3).

flyweight: used in governors to maintain a constant RPM. Flyweights are connected directly to the pilot valve and as propeller load changes, centrifugal force moves the flyweights, allowing oil to travel to or from the propeller hub and maintaining constant RPM.

counterweight: a weight connected to the propeller hub to provide a balancing force. Generally, on multi-engine aircraft counterweights are there to help move the propeller blade to a high pitch. They are also used on control surfaces to provide balance and reduce flutter.

Figure 3-2. Nitrogen filler tube.

Forces moving the propeller toward:	
High Pitch (feather)/Low RPM	Nitrogen charge
	Counterweights
	Feathering spring
Low Pitch/High RPM	Oil pressure
	Aerodynamic twisting force

Figure 3-3. Sources of force that change propeller pitch.

Low Pitch/High RPM

Oil pressure, assisted by the aerodynamic twisting force of the propeller, moves the propeller towards a low pitch, high RPM position. Pilots who have flown a single-engine airplane with a constant speed, controllable-pitch propeller can be confused by the fact that in multi-engine aircraft, oil pressure brings the propeller to a lower pitch. The reasoning is simple, however: in a twin-engine airplane if the engine were to lose oil pressure the pilot would want the propeller to move to the feathered position—a fail-safe measure. One way to remember this is by imagining oil pressure pulling the blades away from the fail-safe feathered position (Figure 3-4).

aerodynamic twisting force—this is a force resulting from the center of pressure for the propeller blade being forward of the centerline of the propeller blade. This twists the propeller to a lower pitch and higher RPM.

Low-Pitch Stop

The *low-pitch stop* is a physical stop designed to prevent the propeller from going past a certain, preset blade angle. As airspeed drops, the governor continues decreasing blade angle to maintain selected RPM; the low-pitch stop prevents the propeller blade angle from going too low. Without a low-pitch stop, the governor would continue reducing blade angle resulting in an increase in drag, and in extreme cases this could restrict airflow to ("blanket") the horizontal stabilizer, causing a nose down pitching moment.

Once the propeller is against the low-pitch stop, the governor is no longer in control of the propeller RPM, and further RPM adjustments can only be accomplished by

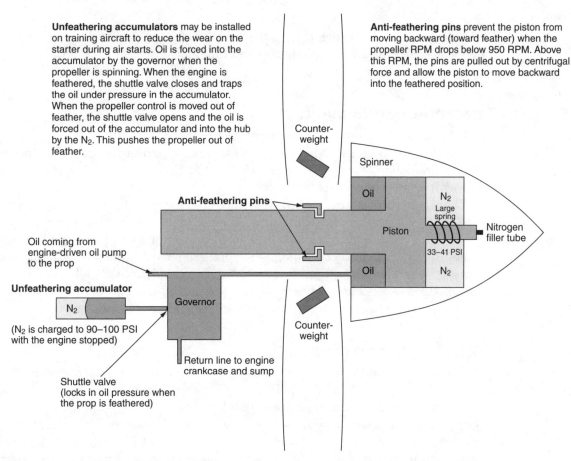

Unfeathering accumulators may be installed on training aircraft to reduce the wear on the starter during air starts. Oil is forced into the accumulator by the governor when the propeller is spinning. When the engine is feathered, the shuttle valve closes and traps the oil under pressure in the accumulator. When the propeller control is moved out of feather, the shuttle valve opens and the oil is forced out of the accumulator and into the hub by the N_2. This pushes the propeller out of feather.

Anti-feathering pins prevent the piston from moving backward (toward feather) when the propeller RPM drops below 950 RPM. Above this RPM, the pins are pulled out by centrifugal force and allow the piston to move backward into the feathered position.

Counter-weight

Spinner

Oil

N_2
Large spring

Nitrogen filler tube

Anti-feathering pins

Piston

33–41 PSI

N_2

Oil coming from engine-driven oil pump to the prop

Oil

Unfeathering accumulator

N_2

(N₂ is charged to 90–100 PSI with the engine stopped)

Governor

Counter-weight

Return line to engine crankcase and sump

Shuttle valve (locks in oil pressure when the prop is feathered)

Figure 3-4. Basic constant speed multi-engine propeller system

Figure 3-5. Unfeathering accumulator

adjusting the throttle. When taxiing the aircraft on the ground or during slow flight, the propeller is on the low-pitch stop and the pilot must reference propeller RPM when setting power.

Unfeathering Accumulators

Most light twin, training airplanes have nitrogen-charged unfeathering *accumulators* to reduce wear and tear on the starter, mostly for the purpose of practicing in-flight engine shutdowns. Figures 3-4 and 3-5 show an accumulator, both schematically and what it looks like in place.

The accumulator stores engine oil pressure from the governor. When the propeller lever is pulled to feather, the oil pressure is trapped in the accumulator by a mechanical valve. Oil pressure is then released back to the governor when the propeller control is moved out of the feather position. The nitrogen charge in the unfeathering accumulator helps force the oil pressure out of the accumulator, through the governor, and into the propeller hub. Although having an unfeathering accumulator saves wear and tear, it also causes feathering and unfeathering to take a little longer.

Anti-Feathering Pins

During engine shutdown, oil pressure drops to zero and the feathering spring forces the propeller blade to the feather position. In some aircraft, the propellers feather when the engine is shut down and oil pressure is lost. Starting an engine with a feathered propeller requires a large amount of energy, which a light twin aircraft cannot produce given the size of its battery and alternators. To prevent the propeller from feathering during engine shutdown, the Seminole as well as some other multi-engine aircraft incorporates *anti-feathering pins* (see Figure 3-4).

The pins are operated by centrifugal force. As engine speed slows, the pins fall into place at a predetermined RPM. Anytime the propeller RPM falls below 950 RPM, the pilot will be unable to feather the propeller; therefore he or she must be aware that in order to do so the propeller control lever must be moved to the feather position before the RPM goes below 950.

Prop Synchronizers and Synchrophasers

Some light twin-engine aircraft are equipped with a *propeller synchronization* system. The purpose of the synchronization system is to reduce the vibration and unpleasant noise ("wa-wa-wa-wa") made by out-of-sync propellers. The reduction or elimination of vibration and noise is accomplished by matching the RPM of the propellers.

Most synchronization systems include a *syncrophase* system, which positions the propellers at a preset phase relationship to reduce cabin noise. The phase relationship prevents blades on the left and right side from passing the cabin at the same time, reducing noise resonation (Figure 3-6).

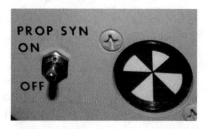

Figure 3-6. Propeller synchronizer.

Best Practices for Multi-Engine Operations

Runup

During runup, the propeller control lever should be cycled to move oil to and from the propeller hub. This is accomplished by setting a mid-level power setting (2,000 RPM in the Seminole), moving the propeller control back until the RPM drops around 300 RPM, and then bringing the propeller control back to full forward. Repeat this motion at least three times. This process will cause the propeller to sense an overspeed condition and send oil back to the engine sump. Once the propeller control is brought back to the full forward position, fresh (and warm) oil will be sent back to the propeller hub through the governor, as the propeller is now underspeed. This process is especially important during winter operations when the oil temperature at the propeller hub is cold.

When cycling the propeller, if the RPM does not drop, oil is not moving; the propeller control must be brought back a little further to engage the governor. It is equally important not to bring the propeller control too far back as this can cause damage to the propeller systems due to a high air load on the propeller blades.

The feathering function should also be checked. This is done at a lower propeller RPM (1,500 RPM in the Seminole) and is completed by moving the propeller quickly and smoothly into the feathered position. You will hear and see the blades move towards the feathered position. The propeller lever should not be left in the feathered position for more than 1–2 seconds (or an RPM drop of 500 or less) to prevent the propeller from actually feathering. The purpose of this test is to ensure that the propeller is able to move toward the feathered position; it does not need to reach a full feathered position during the test.

Although most POHs don't require it, a governor operational check can be done. To perform this check, the pilot should set a desired RPM and then increase power until the governor engages and holds the desired RPM. The throttle levers should then be moved back and forth (2–3 inches at the most) and the pilot can verify that the governor is maintaining the desired RPM.

Takeoff

During the takeoff phase, the propeller controls should be set to the full forward or low pitch and high RPM position. This will provide maximum power for takeoff and climb. The propeller control for multi-engine aircraft during the takeoff and climb phase are identical to single-engine, adjustable pitch propeller aircraft.

Cruise

In the cruise phase of flight, the propeller controls should be reduced to the recommended cruise RPM setting. This will provide the most efficient cruise performance and minimize cabin noise. When setting the propeller controls to the cruise power setting, ensure that the RPM settings are identical to prevent the audible resonance in the cabin. When the propeller RPM is set to a cruise power setting, be sure not to abruptly increase the RPM. Should an increase in RPM be necessary, move the propeller control slowly to prevent engine damage. If at all possible, adjust the propeller RPM while at low power settings.

Landing

Prior to landing, most multi-engine aircraft operating manuals suggest that the propeller controls be set to the full forward position. This is typically done in case the pilot needs to initiate a go-around, allowing maximum power to be available. Some twin Cessna operators choose to land with cruise propeller settings in order to minimize potential damage caused by abruptly increasing propeller (and engine) RPM. This technique is fine as long as the pilot is prepared to bring the propeller controls to the full forward position in the case of a go-around.

Propeller Overspeed Emergency

The only emergency typically found in the POH pertaining to the propeller is propeller overspeed. The pilot can recognize a propeller overspeed condition when propeller RPM exceeds the selected RPM or the placarded redline on the tachometer. In this situation, the pilot should immediately reduce power and airspeed to bring the RPM below redline. If this does not bring the propeller RPM below redline, the pilot can initiate a climb.

Possible causes of a propeller overspeed are a broken speeder spring, loss of nitrogen in the propeller hub, or a stuck pilot valve. In any of these cases, the propeller will be driven to the low-pitch stop by the governor-boosted oil pressure (275 PSI). At this point the propeller is acting like a fixed-pitch propeller.

Review 3
Propeller Systems

1. What is the basic difference between a single-engine propeller and a propeller on a multi-engine airplane?

2. What forces adjust propeller blade angle?

3. What forces drive the propeller to low pitch, high RPM? High pitch, low RPM?

4. What will the blade angle be if the engine loses oil pressure? How does this differ from blade angle in a single-engine aircraft in the same condition?

5. What are the functions of the propeller governor?

6. Describe how the speeder spring, flyweights, and pilot valve work.

7. Describe the function of the unfeathering accumulator.

8. Explain the purpose of the anti-feathering pins.

9. How much performance does a multi-engine airplane gain by feathering the propeller?

Answers are provided in Appendix 2.

Fuel

4

Key Terms

(in the order they appear in this chapter)

detonation
fuel venting
fuel cross-feeding
fuel transfer

Chapter Focus on Fuel Systems

Fuel is the life of an engine; without it combustion cannot occur. A wide range of fuel types are used in today's aviation engines. It is important to be aware of the different types of aviation fuel in use and the specific characteristics of each type. Also key is the how and where of fuel storage, and the delivery of fuel to the engines. Finally, an understanding of fuel planning and in-flight fuel considerations is essential when operating multi-engine aircraft, particularly on long flights or when operating with one engine failed.

This chapter will describe the components relating to fuel systems found on multi-engine aircraft, and how to apply your knowledge of fuel system components to the operating and handling of multi-engine aircraft. Identifying and applying the appropriate emergency actions for various fuel system abnormal and emergency events are also covered here.

Fuel Types

Figure 4-1 shows the various aviation fuel types: the primary and by far the most common aviation gasoline (AVGAS) is 100 LL (low lead) grade. In the U.S., grade 80/87 fuel is very uncommon—in fact it is nearly impossible to find a source for it—and thus it will not be discussed in this book (other than to mention that it is dyed red in color). Another fuel type that is hard to find is 100, although it is more common than 80/87. Numerous environmental groups have recently recommended removing the lead from 100 LL fuel. This is very much in the research and development phase, but it is highly likely that future AVGAS will be unleaded. Finally, Jet A is a kerosene-based fuel that is clear in color. Jet A is primarily used in turbine-powered aircraft; however, the new wave of diesel-powered aircraft allow the use of Jet A fuel.

Recently there has been a push in general aviation to achieve more fuel efficiency and to rely on fuel that is more environmentally friendly than 100 LL. Additionally, the environmental concerns relating to leaded fuel used in AVGAS

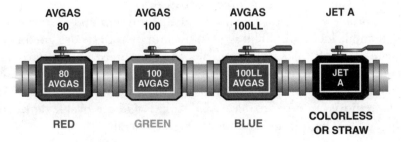

Figure 4-1. Aviation fuel grades and colors.

has supported research into using alternative fuels to power aircraft engines. One such solution being researched—and that is already in use on one particular multi-engine aircraft—is diesel fuel. Diesel fuel offers the advantages of being easily obtained in most countries, providing better fuel efficiency, and having a lower overall fuel cost at the pump than AVGAS. It is entirely possible to see future aircraft engines powered predominately by either diesel fuel, jet fuel, or other "heavy fuels."

The minimum fuel grade will be specified in the POH for the particular aircraft you are operating. The purpose of having a minimum fuel grade is to prevent *detonation,* which can cause engine damage, loss of power, or complete engine failure.

Detonation—the sudden release of heat energy from fuel in an aircraft engine caused by the fuel/air mixture reaching its critical pressure and temperature resulting in inconsistent and spontaneous combustion. This results in an unnecessary increase in cylinder pressure causing premature engine damage.

Fuel Storage

Without fuel an aircraft becomes a glider. The more fuel an aircraft can hold, the longer—and farther—it can fly. A multi-engine aircraft has an inherent disadvantage over a single-engine aircraft in this regard as it consumes more fuel in a given amount of time, which means it needs to carry more fuel. Additionally, multi-engine piston aircraft have poor fuel economy and require ample fuel storage to support longer flights. Complexity is further added by the fact that in the case of an engine failure, it may be necessary for one engine to receive fuel from a tank in the opposite wing. In short, fuel storage systems on multi-engine aircraft are complicated.

Aircraft manufacturers typically put fuel tanks in the wings, but when that doesn't provide enough storage, it is not uncommon to find fuel tanks attached to the wing tips (tip tanks), behind the engine compartment (nacelle tanks), and anywhere in between (locker tanks). In general, the closer the tanks are to the engine, the better, as this will require less pumping to get the fuel where it needs to be. If the fuel tanks are located a long way from the engines, some sort of pump will be required to deliver the fuel to the engine.

Types of Fuel Tanks

Three different types of containers can be used for fuel storage. Bladder, integral, and rigid removable tanks are the most common types in use today.

Bladder tanks are made out of a synthetic rubber material or a fabric coated in rubber. The rubber bladder tanks essentially are flexible bags that can be replaced without having to remove large sections of the aircraft skin. An additional feature of bladder tanks is that they can utilize more of the empty space under the aircraft skin without major alteration to the aircraft structure. However, a common complaint of bladder tanks is that the rubber hardens over time, eventually leading to cracks and leaks. Leaking fuel is obviously not a desirable condition, and therefore these tanks need to be inspected and replaced on a regular basis.

The rigid removable tanks are generally welded aluminum and are stronger and longer lasting than bladder tanks. The aircraft structure has to be designed in a way to accommodate the tank, meaning wing ribs and spars must be built around the tanks. The tanks do not provide any structural support. These tanks are removable to aid inspection, but this is an extensive process as the skin and part of the structure may need to be removed in order to access the tank. Rigid removable tanks are the most common tanks in light single and multi-engine aircraft.

The final fuel storage option is the integral fuel tank. Often called a "wet wing," this type of tank uses the empty spaces within the wing and aircraft structure to store fuel, in this case without the use of a bladder. In order to properly store the fuel, the structure must be well sealed to prevent leaks. In addition, due to the potential size of the tanks it is important to slow the side-to-side movement of fuel to prevent sloshing. This is done by making one-direction valves in the wing ribs that allow fuel to flow towards the fuselage but prevent fuel from flowing towards the wing tips.

Safety

From a pilot's perspective, it doesn't matter what type of fuel storage device is used—this is more of a concern for maintenance personnel working on the aircraft. The biggest concern for pilots operating aircraft with multiple fuel tanks is the proper use of fuel from the tanks, balancing fuel use between left and right fuel supply systems, and of course proper fuel management techniques to prevent in-flight fuel starvation.

A concern with fuel storage is ensuring that it allows for expansion and contracting of the air inside the fuel tank. Aircraft are capable of changing altitudes quickly, and fuel tanks need to equalize pressure rapidly to prevent tank damage; thus the need for efficient *fuel venting*. Most fuel tanks have two static fuel lines that vent the tanks externally (sometimes called "probe vents"). Some aircraft have a heated fuel vent line to prevent icing. The King Air uses a recessed NACA (see sidebar) fuel vent to prevent ice accumulation (Figure 4-2).

Another concern with respect to fuel storage is preventing the fuel from freezing in the tanks. Multi-engine aircraft can reach high altitudes, and with high altitudes comes cold temperatures. In order to prevent fuel from freezing, aircraft manufacturers allow for heat exchange from hot aircraft components such as hydraulic pumps or engine oil, to keep fuel from freezing.

NACA (National Advisory Committee for Aeronautics) was a federal agency started in 1915. NACA research and development designed multiple air intakes for automotive applications and cowlings and airfoils for aircraft applications. In the late 1950's NACA was absorbed by NASA (The National Aeronautics and Space Administration).

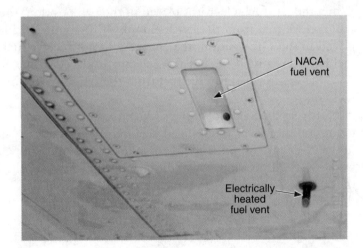

NACA fuel vent

Electrically heated fuel vent

Figure 4-2. NACA and electrically heated fuel vents on a King Air.

Delivery

Fuel needs to be at the right place (the combustion chamber) at the right time (during the intake stroke). Getting fuel from its storage location to the combustion chamber requires an intricate system of lines and pumps. In multi-engine aircraft with multiple tanks, this network of fuel lines can become complicated—especially to support the fuel tank balance, fuel transfer, and cross-feed functions that are often required in multi-engine aircraft.

Fuel *cross-feeding*, which is the delivery of fuel directly from a tank on one side of the airplane to an engine on the other side, is a feature of multi-engine aircraft that serves two purposes: (1) the pilot has access to all of the useable fuel in the aircraft regardless of which engine is running, and (2) it is a means of preventing a fuel imbalance resulting from uneven fuel feed.

Larger multi-engine aircraft often have additional *fuel transfer* capability that can move fuel from tank to tank. This differs from fuel *cross-feeding* in that during fuel transfer, fuel is being moved from one tank to another. This is done to balance the weight of the fuel across the entire aircraft, improving performance and controllability during the entire flight. On smaller multi-engine aircraft, like the Piper Seminole, which only has two fuel tanks, fuel transfer is not incorporated. The Cessna 421C has fuel transfer capability due to the increased complexity of the fuel system and the incorporation of multiple fuel tanks. It is necessary for the pilot to move (or transfer) fuel from one storage tank to another tank in order for this fuel to be fed to the engine.

In the Piper Seminole, two fuel selectors are located between the front seats. There are three positions for the fuel selectors: Off, On, and X-Feed (*cross-feed*). It makes sense to consider the fuel selectors as engine selectors—that is, the fuel selector position determines from where the engine is receiving fuel (Figure 4-3).

Figure 4-3.
Multi-engine fuel selector.

To illustrate, let's focus on the left fuel selector for discussion purposes. When the left fuel selector is placed in the On position, the left engine will receive fuel from the left fuel tank. If the same left fuel selector is placed in the Off position, the engine will not receive fuel from either fuel tank. Finally, if the left fuel selector is placed in the X-Feed position, the engine will receive fuel from the opposite (in this case, right) fuel tank.

Note that the Seminole Pilot's Operating Handbook places two limitations on the use of the X-Feed position: Do not operate both engines in the X-Feed position, and do not take off and land with a fuel selector in the X-Feed position. An additional consideration in the Seminole is the gas combustion heater, which receives fuel from the same source as the left engine. If heater operation is desired, and the left fuel selector is off, the heater will not receive fuel and therefore will not be operational. Additionally, if the left fuel selector is in the X-Feed position, the heater will received fuel from the right fuel tank.

Pumps

There are two common types of fuel pumps in use on multi-engine aircraft: electrically powered pumps and engine-driven pumps.

A general concern with any powered fuel pump is that it is cooled and lubricated by the fuel it is pressurizing. This means that if no fuel is flowing through the pump, there is no means of cooling or lubricating the pump. Continuous operation of a fuel pump running "dry" will cause damage to the pump.

The Piper Seminole has two electrically-powered boost pumps and two engine-driven fuel pumps—one of each on either side. The engine-driven fuel pumps are the primary source of pressurized fuel for the engine and the electrically-powered fuel pumps serve as a backup in case of engine-driven fuel pump failure. Additionally, the Seminole has an electric primer system to provide fuel sufficient for engine start, which requires the electrically-powered fuel pumps to be *On* in order to function.

Schematics

Figures 4-4 and 4-5 show schematics of the Piper Seminole and Cessna 421C fuel systems. Schematics are useful for determining how fuel flows within the aircraft, and can be helpful in gaining a better understanding of the fuel system.

Following are the functions of the key components of the Piper Seminole fuel system schematic shown in Figure 4-4:

- Engine-Driven Fuel Pump—delivers fuel directly to the carburetor and is powered by the engine.
- Electric Fuel Pump—an electrically powered fuel pump that serves as a backup to the engine-driven fuel pump.
- Scupper Drain—allows excess fuel to drain from the area surrounding the filler-cap.
- Fuel Vent—allows the air pressure in the fuel tank to equalize with the surrounding ambient air, preventing the tank from expanding or collapsing. It also allows excess fuel to be vented overboard.
- Fuel Flow Transmitter—measures the fuel pressure and provides a cockpit indication of fuel pressure.
- Fuel Filter—removes sediments in the fuel to prevent internal engine damage.
- Fuel Sumps—allows the pilot to drain any water or sediment from the lowest point in the fuel system. This also prevents internal engine damage or inadvertent engine failure.
- Fuel Selector—allows the pilot to select the source of fuel for a specific engine. Also allows the pilot to stop fuel flow to the engine.
- Fuel Primer—allows a small amount of fuel to be sent to the carburetor to aid in engine start. The electric fuel pumps must be on in order for the fuel primer to work in the Piper Seminole.

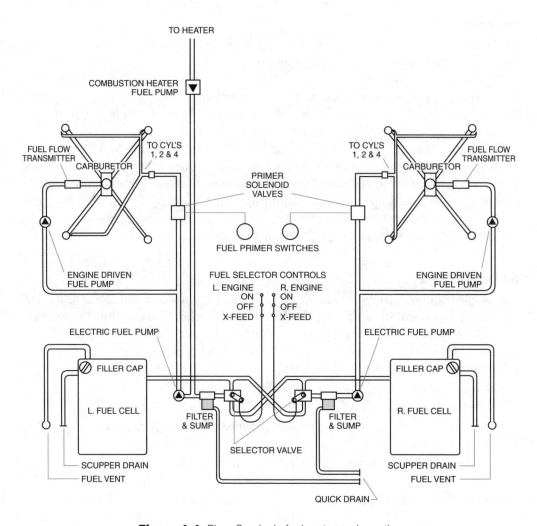

Figure 4-4. Piper Seminole fuel system schematic.

Additional fuel system components shown in the Cessna 421C fuel system schematic (Figure 4-5) include:

- Fuel Check Valve—allows fuel to travel in one direction only—the direction that is indicated in the schematic.
- Fuel Transfer Pumps—allows the pilot to move fuel from one fuel tank to another tank.
- Fuel Flow Indicator—provides the pilot with a cockpit indication of the fuel pressure for each fuel supply system.

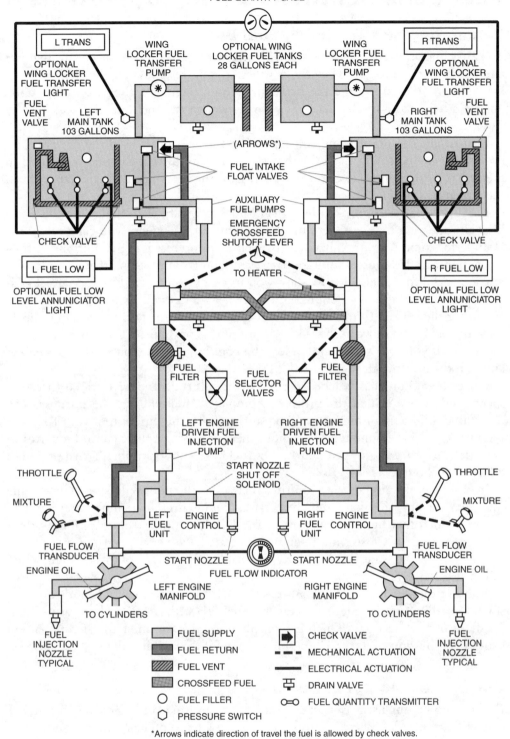

Figure 4-5. Cessna 421C fuel system schematic.

Fuel Considerations During Operations

Calculating and Managing Fuel Burn

The first operational concern with fuel is quantity: the pilot must ensure that the aircraft has enough fuel to reach the destination, plus reserves. The Federal Aviation Regulations (FARs) outline the basic fuel requirements for flight, but they don't outline a few of the hidden dangers with respect to the fuel quantity required for flight.

First of all, the regulations don't mention the fuel burn used for determining how much fuel you will need for the flight. Be careful that the fuel burn used in preflight calculations is close to (or higher than) the fuel burn that you expect from the airplane in flight.

Fuel burn changes significantly with altitude; if you are planning on climbing to a high altitude for a more efficient fuel burn, what will happen if you can't reach that altitude for some reason? What will happen if unforecast icing conditions, turbulence, or air traffic control limitations prevent you from reaching that altitude? Air traffic control may be unable to allow you to climb to cruise altitude as quickly as you would like; traffic restrictions, especially near congested airspace, are common. Whatever the reason, flying at a lower altitude than planned will have a big impact on your fuel burn, and you should be aware of this possibility. Plan ahead for these situations. If you are "stuck" down low, be cognizant of fuel burn. Reduce power and lean the mixture in these situations.

Once the aircraft has reached desired cruise altitude and accelerated to cruise speed, and you've leaned the mixture, complete a fuel check. The purpose is to determine if the remaining fuel will be sufficient for the duration of your flight. A fuel check should be conducted each hour thereafter. If air traffic control requires an early descent, once again, be cognizant of fuel burn. Low altitudes have a profound effect on fuel burn.

In multi-engine aircraft with multiple fuel tanks, the pilot will have to determine the order for burning fuel from these tanks. Some aircraft manufacturers outline recommended fuel burn procedures in the POH; if this is the case, follow their recommendations. Cessna multi-engine aircraft have very specific requirements for fuel tank usage, so it is particularly important to be aware of this procedure and follow it carefully.

Another fuel-burn issue to be aware of is that the supplemental heaters on most small to medium multi-engine aircraft use fuel. These heaters can burn as much as 3 gallons of fuel per hour, which is typically burned from one tank. If you plan on using a combustion heater in flight, plan ahead for the fuel it will use.

Use of Electric Boost Pump

Electric boost pump usage is most common for takeoff and landing only. Most aircraft checklists require the electric boost pumps be on for takeoff and landing, and off for all other phases of flight. When turning electric boost pumps off, be sure to turn off one pump at a time, and monitor engine instruments to ensure fuel flow is still positive. After landing, turn the electric boost pumps off before leaning the mixture for taxi. If this is done in the reverse order, you may notice the engines sputter when the boost pumps are turned off; this is due to the lower fuel flow during low power settings and too lean a mixture to sustain combustion. Should this occur, enrich the mixture slightly.

Emergencies

There are numerous possible emergencies relating to the fuel system, including fuel pump failure, blocked fuel filter, fuel freezing, or fuel leaks.

Fuel Pump Failure

Engine-driven fuel pumps are typically very reliable. In the event of an engine-driven fuel pump failure, the electric boost pump can provide sufficient fuel pressure to keep the engine running.

Engine-driven fuel pumps usually give warning signs before completely failing. The best indicators of an impending fuel pump failure are a significantly lower fuel flow or a change in the sound of the engine. Sometimes the change in engine sound is barely discernable, but if something sounds unusual, check the fuel flow gauges.

An electric boost pump failure is more difficult to detect in flight. On the ground, however, the electric boost pump can be easily heard before the engines are started.

Fuel Filter Blockage

A fuel filter blockage is a little more common than a total fuel pump failure. Any sort of contamination in the fuel line should get trapped by the fuel filter before it gets sent into the engine. If a significant amount of debris (or ice) collects on the fuel filter, the engine may not receive sufficient fuel to continue running. This can also be recognized by a reduction in fuel flow or a change in the sound of the engine. Therefore, sample fuel before each flight to attempt to identify any debris. The Seminole fuel drains come directly from the fuel filter, making this a very good indicator of fuel filter contamination.

Fuel Freezing

Fuel (or water in the fuel) is susceptible to freezing if the temperature becomes cold enough. Certain additives are available that lower the freezing point of the fuel. If you are operating in cold climates or at altitudes where the temperature is well below freezing, be sure to operate with fuel additives to prevent fuel freezing. The likelihood of fuel freezing in the fuel tanks is low, but when fuel flows through narrow fuel lines and through the fuel filter, the probability of this happening is much higher. If you suspect fuel freezing in flight, descend to a warmer altitude immediately, and increase fuel flow as much as possible by turning on electric fuel pumps.

Fuel system icing inhibitor (FSII)— commonly referred to as "prist," this is a fuel additive that prevents the formation of ice in the fuel vents.

Fuel Leaks

An in-flight fuel leak is a dangerous condition, especially if the leaking fuel reaches hot surfaces such as turbochargers or heat exchangers. A thorough preflight check of the aircraft is the key to recognizing fuel leaks. Pay attention to aircraft fuel levels. After each flight, have the aircraft fueled and keep track of how much fuel is in the tanks. Before the next flight, check the fuel level again and see if it has changed significantly. Fuel leaks tend to start small and get progressively worse over time. Check for puddles of fuel around the aircraft after it sits overnight. Be aware that some fuel may leak out of the fuel vents, and this is a normal occurrence.

Always check fuel quantity and fuel burn in flight. Recognizing fuel leaks early is a key to a successful outcome in this emergency situation. If you suspect a fuel leak, begin your search for suitable landing airports. Plan early—don't wait until the fuel quantity is low to begin planning for a fuel emergency.

Single-Engine Fuel Management

When operating with a single engine, it is important to properly manage the remaining fuel. For this reason, as discussed above under the topic of fuel delivery, multi-engine aircraft have the capability of cross-feeding fuel to an engine from a fuel tank on the opposite side. One limitation of cross-feeding is that it often can only be used during straight-and-level cruise. Pilots must be aware of this limitation and take appropriate fuel management actions early.

Be sure to clearly understand the difference between fuel cross-feeding and fuel transfer. Cross-feeding is delivering fuel from a tank to an opposite engine. Fuel transfer refers to moving fuel from one fuel tank to another via separate fuel lines, as is typical in airliners. Most light twin-engine aircraft have the capability to cross-feed fuel, but do not have the capability to transfer fuel. For successful emergency single-engine operations, you must know the specific fuel-delivery capabilities of the aircraft you are flying.

Review 4
Fuel

1. Describe the fuel types used in aviation engines.

2. Explain some of the research and future of AVGAS.

3. Compare and contrast the different fuel storage containers.

4. Explain the purpose and types of fuel venting.

5. Illustrate the basic fuel schematic of the multi-engine aircraft that you fly.

6. What is the difference between fuel cross-feed and fuel transfer? Which of these does the Piper Seminole include?

7. List the two types of fuel pumps found in multi-engine aircraft.

8. What limitation is common with cross-feeding fuel?

9. What is the difference between a fuel sump and a fuel vent?

10. What is the normal fuel burn of a combustion heater?

11. When should the pilot conduct in-flight fuel quantity and fuel burn calculations?

Answers are provided in Appendix 2.

Landing Gear and Hydraulics

5

Chapter Focus: Why Use Hydraulics?

Hydraulics provide a method of using liquid pressure to transmit power and multiply force. Hydraulic systems consist of actuators, pumps, lines and fluid. The fundamental principle defining hydraulics is Pascal's Theory, which states, "where there is an increase in pressure at any point in a confined fluid, there is an equal increase at every other point in the container." If this theory is correctly applied, we can get hydraulic advantage.

Another method of achieving the same results is through the use of air pressure, called *pneumatic* power. Some benefits of hydraulic power over pneumatic power are:

- more efficient and consistent power output due to the incompressibility of hydraulic fluids.
- hydraulic leaks are easier to detect than air leaks.
- hydraulic fluid operates well in a wide variety of environments, from extremely high temperatures to very low temperatures.

Some disadvantages of hydraulic power are:

- hydraulic systems are heavier than pneumatic systems.
- hydraulic fluid is highly corrosive to most materials.
- hydraulic systems require more maintenance when compared with pneumatic systems.

This chapter will cover landing gear and hydraulics system components and how to apply your knowledge of them to multi-engine operation and handling. You will also learn how to identify and apply the appropriate emergency action for each hydraulics system event, whether abnormal or emergency.

Key Terms

(in the order they appear in this chapter)

gear warning light
V_{LO}
V_{LE}
limit switch
actuator
bleed hole
low pressure control valve
high pressure control valve
thermal relief
shuttle valve
pressure switch
gear down snubber orifice
restrictor
check valve
squat switch
gear warning horn
brake rotor
brake caliper
brake cylinder

Hydraulic Systems in Multi-Engine Aircraft

Most multi-engine aircraft have at least one system powered by hydraulics—the brakes. Some aircraft (the Seminole included) also use hydraulic force to raise and lower the landing gear. In general, the larger the aircraft, the more hydraulics are needed to move components of the aircraft (due to the larger and heavier surfaces). In this chapter, the discussion of hydraulic systems will focus on landing gear and brakes.

Landing Gear

Figure 5-1.
Landing gear control quadrant.

In the Seminole landing gear system, hydraulic force is achieved by the use of an electrically powered pump. When the pilot selects a gear position (using the gear control handle) the system will provide power to an electric pump, which in turn creates the fluid pressure necessary to move the landing gear (Figure 5-1).

The pilot can confirm the position of each landing gear by looking at the landing gear lights located just above the landing gear control handle. When each gear strut is in the "down and locked" position, a micro switch closes and a green gear position light illuminates. Anytime a gear is not in a safe position (such as when it's in transit, or when one or more gear fails to move all the way down or up), the *gear warning light* will illuminate (Figure 5-2). The emergency gear extension handle is located to the left of the gear handle. This allows the pilot to extend the gear in the event of electrical or hydraulic pump failure.

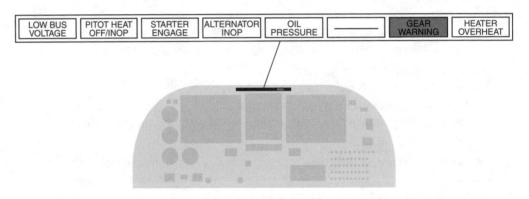

Figure 5-2. Gear warning annunciators.

Mechanical Extension of Landing Gear

Some multi-engine aircraft (the Beechcraft Baron, for example) use mechanical extension and retraction systems for the landing gear rather than hydraulics. There are some fundamental differences between aircraft with hydraulically-powered gear and mechanical gear, so you should be aware of the type of system installed in your particular aircraft.

In aircraft such as the Baron that do not use hydraulic force to raise and lower the gear, an electric motor is used to "crank" the gear up and down, similar to the system used to raise and lower flaps. Electric gear systems tend to operate much more quickly than hydraulic gear systems. But one disadvantage of the electric gear system is the method of extending the gear in the case of an electrical failure or a failure of the electric gear motor. (This method will be discussed later in this chapter under "Emergency Extension.")

Retractable Landing Gear—Speed Limitations

You should be aware of some basic speed limitations associated with retractable landing gear systems.

V_{LO} (Retract)

The gear should be retracted at or below this speed (109 KIAS in the Seminole). This speed typically is lower than the extension speed. The purpose of this limitation is to reduce load on the hydraulic pump. At higher airspeeds an increased airload is placed on the gear, and this force is transmitted directly to the pump. Retracting the gear at or below this speed will extend pump life.

Another important reason for the speed limitation relates to the hydraulic *actuators* themselves. The "upside" of the actuators has less surface area than the "downside." Less surface area translates to less hydraulic advantage. Aircraft with an all-electrical gear system, like the Baron, typically have the same retract and extend speed limitation.

Be careful not to exceed this limitation when conducting a missed approach procedure or when recovering from an emergency descent procedure.

V_{LO} (Extend)

The landing gear should not be extended when above this speed to prevent damage to the gear door. At speeds above V_{LO} (140 KIAS in the Seminole), it is possible to damage the gear doors, potentially breaking them away from the airplane.

V_{LE}

This is the maximum speed at which the aircraft can be flown with the gear in the down and locked position. This speed limitation also is to prevent damage to the gear doors.

Landing Gear Circuit Breakers

Three circuits generally protect the electrical part of the landing gear system (Figure 5-3, highlighted in yellow):

- Horn circuit breaker—protects the gear warning horn.
- Motor circuit breaker—protects the electric actuated hydraulic motor and electric motor.
- Control handle circuit breaker—controls power directly to the handle, generally used to practice gear failures.

Schematic

Figure 5-4 shows a schematic of the Piper Seminole hydraulic landing gear system with the gear extended. Key components of the system include the following:

Low Pressure Control Valve

If the down *limit switch* fails to shut off the pump during gear extension, excess hydraulic pressure will be sent back to the reservoir, preventing excess pressure from building up in the lines.

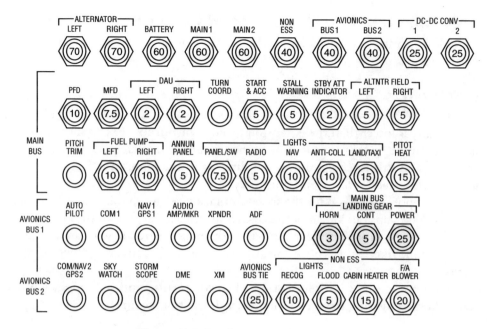

Figure 5-3. Landing gear circuit breakers.

0.020 Diameter Bleed Hole

The *bleed hole* is used by maintenance to bleed air from the system. Air is more compressible than hydraulic fluid, and if any air is trapped in the hydraulic system it will reduce the effectiveness of the system.

High Pressure Control Valve

If the pressure switch fails to shut off the pump during gear retraction, excess hydraulic pressure will be sent back to the reservoir to prevent excess pressure from building up in the lines.

Thermal Relief

The *thermal relief* valve relieves pressure above 3,000 psi due to temperature changes.

Shuttle Valve

The *shuttle valve* moves to allow hydraulic fluid to move to the actuators on both the up and the down side.

Pressure Switch

After the pressure reaches 1,800 psi, the *pressure switch* shuts off the hydraulic pump.

Gear Down Snubber Orifice

During emergency gear extension, the *gear down snubber orifice* slows the release of hydraulic pressure as it equalizes at the emergency gear valve. This slows gear extension to prevent damage to the landing gear system.

Restrictor

The *restrictor* slows the nose gear during retraction and protects it from varying fluid pressure. This prevents over-pressurizing the hydraulic line on the high pressure side

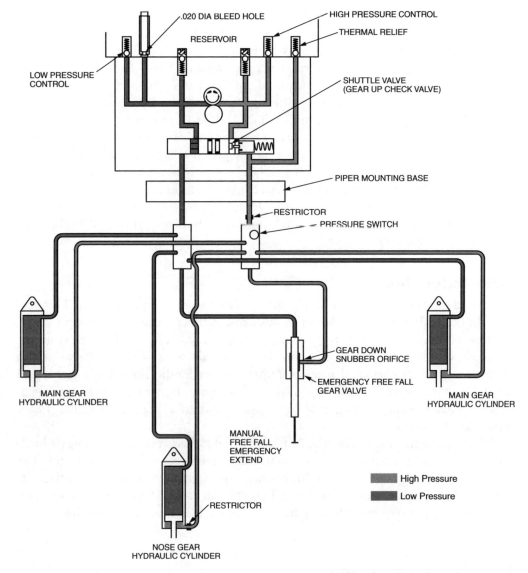

Figure 5-4. Hydraulic landing gear schematic (Piper Seminole)—gear extended.

of the nose gear actuator, preventing damage. During gear retraction, the nose gear will slow its rate of movement slightly as the nose wheel reaches the up limit. This is a result of the restrictor.

Gear Retraction

In order to retract the landing gear, the airplane must first be off the ground. Once the aircraft is airborne, the pilot can select the gear handle to the up position. The gear handle has a lever lock that prevents inadvertent gear retraction on the ground. In the Seminole, this can be overcome by pulling the gear handle out before moving it up. Some aircraft have a mechanical lever lock that automatically opens when the aircraft leaves the ground. Most gear lever systems still require the pilot to pull the gear handle out before moving it upwards.

When the gear selector is moved into the up position, the hydraulic motor begins to run and increases the pressure of the hydraulic fluid on the up side of the system.

Fluid travels from the reservoir through to a shuttle valve. The pressure from the pump pushes the shuttle and *check valve* open, allowing hydraulic fluid to travel to the up side of the hydraulic actuators, which pulls the gear up. The pump continues to run until the hydraulic pressure reaches a preset value (1,800 psi in the Seminole). Once this pressure is achieved on the up side of the system, the pressure switch shuts off the hydraulic pump. Once the pump shuts off, the gear up check valve (shuttle valve) closes, trapping high-pressure hydraulic fluid in the lines. If the hydraulic pressure drops (for example, from a leak in the hydraulic system) the pressure switch will reactivate the hydraulic pump to bring the pressure back up to desired pressure (again, 1,800 psi in the Seminole). If you hear the gear pump cycling on and off in flight, it is likely that the hydraulic system contains a leak.

It's important to understand that most hydraulic gear systems do not incorporate a gear uplock; the hydraulic pressure holds up the landing gear. If the hydraulic pressure is lost, the gear will free-fall.

Gear Extension

To extend the landing gear, move the gear selector to the down position. This will activate the hydraulic motor, which now turns in the opposite direction to create pressure on the down side of the hydraulic system. Hydraulic fluid travels from the reservoir, pushing the shuttle valve on the down side open. The shuttle valve also pushes the gear up check valve open, redirecting hydraulic fluid holding the gear up back to the reservoir. Fluid then travels to the hydraulic actuator forcing the gear down. Extending the landing gear requires less hydraulic pressure because gravity assists the gear down.

When each gear strut reaches the full "down and locked" position, it closes a down limit micro switch. Each micro switch activates a green gear-down annunciator. The hydraulic pump turns off once all three down limit switches have closed. Each landing gear strut incorporates a downlock. This is a mechanical lock that holds the gear in the down position even when hydraulic pressure is lost (after engine shut-down, for instance).

Emergency Extension

If a gear malfunction occurs in flight, the emergency gear extension procedure can be used to extend the gear. Hydraulic systems will have a valve release the pilot opens that releases pressure in the lines and allows the gear to free-fall (Figure 5-5a). There are assist springs on each landing gear to help the gear lock into place. A restrictor on the nose gear prevents the gear from slamming down and causing damage to the nose gear; this is done by reducing the sudden change in pressure. Some aircraft incorporate a hand pump (usually in the floor below the pilot's seat) so the pilot can manually pressurize the hydraulic fluid on the down side of the hydraulic system (Figure 5-5b).

Aircraft like the Beechcraft Baron have a completely electric gear system. If the electric gear motor fails, the pilot must act in place of the electric motor. There is a crank located on the floor near the pilot seat and the pilot must crank the gear down manually (Figure 5-5c). Care must be taken during this process, as the gear initially will free-fall and the crank will free-wheel. The pilot's hand should remain on the gear crank during emergency gear extension to prevent injury during this process.

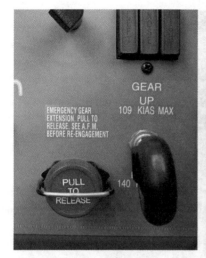  

Figure 5-5. Examples of emergency extension devices.

(a) Emergency gear extension on hydraulic systems: Pulling the handle will release the hydraulic pressure holding the gear up, allowing the gear to free-fall.

(b) Emergency gear extension pump for hydraulic gear systems: Moving the handle forward and back will provide hydraulic pressure sufficient to extend and lock the landing gear.

(c) Emergency gear crank for mechanical gear systems: Cranking the handle will extend the landing gear. The pilot should be careful not to let go of the handle as the gear will free-fall and cause the handle to spin violently.

Squat Switches

Landing gear systems incorporate micro switches to sense whether the aircraft is on the ground or in flight. These are called *squat switches* (or weight on wheels switches, Figure 5-6) and are typically used to prevent inadvertent gear retraction on the ground. When the aircraft is on the ground the squat switches are open (Figure 5.6b), creating a break in the electric circuit between the gear handle and the hydraulic pump. This means that if the gear handle is placed in the up position on the ground, the gear pump will not activate.

Once the aircraft leaves the ground, the gear strut extends and the squat switch closes, bridging the gap in the circuit. When the gear handle is placed in the up position, the landing gear pump activates and the gear retraction process begins.

Gear Annunciators

Gear lights (or annunciators) are used to advise the pilot of the position of the landing gear, and to warn the pilot if any of the gear is in an unsafe position. We've already discussed the gear down lights, but a review is worthwhile.

Each green position indicator comes on when the corresponding gear strut reaches the full "down and locked" position (and the down lock switch closes, Figure 5.6a). There is a red "gear unsafe" annunciator that turns on any time the gear is not in the selected position. Typically, this light is on during the time that it takes the gear to reach the selected position. In the case of landing gear retraction, the closure of all of the up-lock switches (Figure 5-7) will turn off the gear unsafe annunciator. If the gear unsafe light illuminates during cruise, the pilot should be aware that one or more of the landing gear struts are not retracted enough to close the up-lock switch. If, after gear extension, the pilot notices that the gear unsafe annunciator is still illuminated, this is an indication that the gear has not reached the full down and locked position. The pilot should check the three green gear indicators to see which gear has not

Figure 5-6. (a) Main gear squat switch and downlock switch. (b) Squat switch in an open condition.

Figure 5-7. Nose gear up-lock switch.

fully extended. It is good practice for the pilot to keep a hand on the gear extension handle during the extension process. Once all three green gear-down annunciators illuminate, then the pilot can remove his or her hand and continue normally.

Gear Warning Horn

The purpose of a *gear warning horn* is to alert the pilot that the gear is still in the retracted position. The difference between the gear warning horn and the stall horn is that the gear horn beeps and is not continuous. Situations that will typically activate the gear warning horn are:

1. If the gear is not down and locked and the manifold pressure on one or both engines is below a preset value or throttle lever angle (close to idle).
2. The gear selector is placed in the up position while the aircraft is on the ground.
3. The gear selector is in the up position and the flaps are moved past the approach setting (applies to some aircraft, such as the Seminole, for example).

Figure 5-8. Gear mute button.

Most light training twin-engine aircraft incorporate a gear warning horn mute switch (Figure 5-8). When pressed, the gear warning mute switch silences the horn only if the horn was activated because one or both engines is below 14 inches of manifold pressure. If the pilot activates the warning horn mute switch, the light will illuminate. It can be cancelled by extending the gear or advancing the power levers.

Day/Night Switch

Aircraft will usually provide the pilot with a way to dim the annunciator lights in the cockpit to adjust for day and night conditions. This is accomplished with a rheostat-type switch, an automatic photocell, or a day/night switch (Figure 5-9). In some aircraft the lights are dimmed when the navigation lights are turned on. This is important because the green gear-down annunciators will be dimmed with the rest of the aircraft annunciators. If the annunciators are dimmed while in bright daylight conditions, it may be difficult for the pilot to see the green annunciator lights when they are illuminated. For this reason, the pilot may falsely diagnose a gear problem.

Figure 5-9. Day/night switch.

Normal Landing Gear Operation

Transitioning from a fixed-gear airplane to a retractable-gear airplane presents some challenges to the pilot. The first is that the hydraulic or mechanical gear system adds complexity to the aircraft systems. The second challenge is the operation of the gear itself, particularly in the landing phase. There have been numerous gear-up landings due to gear malfunctions and because of pilots forgetting to put the gear down before landing.

The squat switch should prevent the gear from being inadvertently retracted on the ground, but squat switches are susceptible to sticking or failure. For this reason, never select gear up while on the ground.

On takeoff once a positive rate of climb has been established, the landing gear selector should be placed in the up position. Verify that the gear unsafe light is extinguished after the gear cycle is complete.

During normal landings the gear selector is placed in the down position abeam the landing threshold during a VFR pattern. If flying an instrument approach, the gear is extended at or just prior to the final approach fix (FAF), based on the profile. During gear extension, you should leave your hand on the selector until you receive three green lights. If one or more of the gear lights fails to illuminate, proceed to the emergency gear extension checklist. On short final, visually verify that the gear is down and locked, and announce "gear down and locked."

When cycling the gear up or down, allow the gear to reach its fully selected position before selecting a new gear position. The hydraulic pump is reversible, and if you change the direction of the pump while it is running, permanent damage to the pump could result.

Muting the Gear Warning Horn

During training flights, while maneuvering the aircraft in the practice area, it is normal to reduce the power on one or both engines below 14 inches of manifold pressure with the gear retracted. This will trigger the gear warning horn, which is undesirable. At this time you can select the gear warning mute switch to deactivate the horn. It is good operational practice to announce "no intention to land" prior to pressing the mute switch. The mute switch will illuminate when pressed; to cancel and extinguish the light, advance the power levers or extend the gear.

Landing Gear Malfunctions and Emergencies

Emergency Gear Extension

If a gear malfunction occurs in flight, follow the manufacturer's emergency gear extension checklist. The first part of the checklist is usually a basic troubleshooting procedure, and if the problem persists then the emergency gear extension procedure is executed. (See "Emergency Extension" on page 64.)

In a hydraulic gear system, if the gear has failed to lock down after following the appropriate emergency gear extension procedure, you can yaw the aircraft abruptly from side to side in an attempt to lock the gear in place. If the gear still fails to check down and lock after following this procedure, you should prepare to conduct a gear-up landing (see below).

Certain emergencies such as a complete electrical failure will complicate emergency gear extension procedures in some aircraft. In the Seminole, the free-fall valve will still operate, but the gear indicator bulbs will not be functioning. The Seminole has incorporated a mirror on the left engine nacelle for situations such as these. The pilot can see the position of the nose gear from their seat using this mirror.

Gear-Up Landings

If you are forced to conduct a gear-up landing, multiple scenarios are possible.

If the nose gear is not down and locked but the main struts are down and locked you should land on the mains and keep the nose off the ground as long as possible. At this point, it is recommended that you pull both mixture controls and shut off the engines to prevent engine damage. However, anytime you have an emergency situation your main focus should be on how to make the safest possible landing rather than on how to minimize damage to the airplane. Pulling the mixtures at this point could be enough of a distraction to cause you to lose control of the aircraft.

If one main is not down and locked but the nose gear and other main are, then you have a difficult decision to make: land gear up on the belly of the aircraft, or land on two wheels. There is no right answer to this question, but keep in mind that the aircraft will likely be easier to control directionally on its belly than on one main and the nose gear. Either way, ensure that you land at an airport with crash fire and rescue available and standing by.

If the nose gear is down and locked but the two main gears are not, the recommendation is to retract the nose gear and land the aircraft on its belly.

Off-Field Landings

Another issue with any retractable-gear airplane is determining what position the gear should be in if the pilot elects or is required to make an off-field landing. If the landing is going to be made on water, soft ground or muddy terrain, then the gear should be retracted. The gear should be extended if you will be landing on flat, hard terrain or rough terrain. Remember that these are merely recommendations; ultimately the pilot-in-command has to decide the most appropriate course of action based on the circumstances.

Pressure Switch Failure

Should the pressure switch fail in the Seminole gear system, there is no procedure in the POH to guide the pilot in addressing the problem. The pilot can recognize this problem by listening to the gear pump. If the gear pump does not shut off there is likely a problem with the pressure switch. It is best practice to pull the landing gear pump circuit breaker, select the gear handle down, and reset the gear pump circuit breaker to extend the landing gear. Leave the gear down and land at a suitable airport.

Hydraulic Leaks

Another issue the pilot may face in a hydraulic system is a leak. This can be recognized by the hydraulic pump cycling on and off as mentioned earlier in this chapter. If this occurs, the pilot should have the hydraulic system examined by a qualified technician to determine if the leak needs to be repaired. Often, the pilot is able to identify a hydraulic system leak prior to any discernable fluid leak that a technician could recognize. Additionally, the gear pump will place a large demand on the aircraft electrical system. If the gear pump is cycling in flight while the aircraft is under high electrical loads (night flight or in icing conditions) the electrical system may not have sufficient energy to power some systems. Finally, if the pilot suspects a significant leak (the gear pump does not shut off) the gear should be extended immediately while the system still has sufficient hydraulic fluid to do so.

Electrical-Mechanical Gear Systems

The emergency gear extension procedure in aircraft with electrical mechanical gear systems, such as the Beechcraft Baron, requires the pilot to crank the gear down by hand. In this case the pilot may have to exit the traffic pattern or enter a holding pattern because this procedure could take an extended amount of time. In IMC conditions, the pilot should be aware that leaning over or back to crank the gear down can cause spatial disorientation. If available, an autopilot or passenger should be used to assist the pilot with this procedure.

Brake Systems

Most light general aviation aircraft and even some turbo prop and turbo jet aircraft have a basic hydraulic brake configuration. The basic system setup for the Piper Seminole can be seen in Figure 5-10. The setup includes:

1. Brake fluid reservoir—holds the hydraulic fluid for the brake system.
2. Parking brake handle—allows the pilot to set the parking brake.
3. Brake cylinders—transmits the force the pilot puts on the toe brakes to the brake pads, which squeeze the disc and slows the tire down.
4. Brake lines—allows hydraulic fluid to travel from the reservoir to the brake cylinders and then to the brake assembly.
5. Parking brake valve—traps hydraulic pressure in the lines to hold the brake pads to the disc and prevent the main gears from rolling.
6. Brake assembly—includes the brake rotor, brake pads, brake caliper, and fluid lines. The *brake rotor* is the metal disc that is attached to the back of the wheel. This is the surface that the brake pads press against to slow the rotation of the wheel. The *brake calipers* hold the brake pads around the brake rotor and also house the brake cylinders. The brake calipers need to be set precisely to ensure the brake pads don't rub against the rotor when not brake pressure is being applied. The brake pads are made out of a material that resists wear while creating sufficient friction against the brake rotor to allow for efficient stopping.

The brakes are usually serviced by maintenance at regular intervals. In most cases, servicing the brake system involves replenishing the hydraulic reservoir, replacing the brake pads, and servicing the discs.

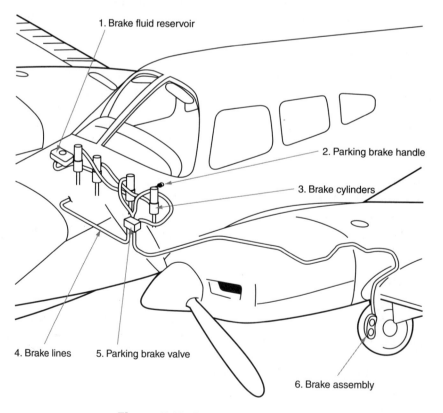

Figure 5-10. Brake system schematic.

Best Practices for Brake Operation

Preflight

The first thing you should do during preflight is to set the parking brake to prevent the aircraft from rolling. During high winds the aircraft should also be chocked (and tied down in strong winds) to ensure it does not roll when you are in front or below the wing area near the landing gear.

Brake Check

The brakes should be checked after engine start and prior to taxi. This can be done by allowing the aircraft to roll forward slightly and applying a slight amount of brake pressure. The aircraft does not need to come to a complete stop; you only need to ensure that pressure is being transmitted from the toe brakes to the main wheels. This check should be accomplished before the aircraft rolls one full length. A brake failure will be easily recognizable: the brake pedals will be "soft" or have no pressure at all. If a complete brake failure is suspected, shut both engines down immediately by placing both mixtures in the idle cutoff position.

Taxiing

The effectiveness of brakes is a function of their temperature. Hot brake pads are not as effective as cold brake pads. For this reason, you should avoid continuous brake application during taxi (dragging the brakes). Multi-engine aircraft have a tendency to taxi faster. Minimize the use of brakes during taxi out to the runway for takeoff. A cold brake will be far more effective in stopping the aircraft if you need to abort the takeoff. You can use the brakes when needed, but just avoid dragging them. During turns, use differential power along with rudder steering rather than braking.

Runup

The parking brake should be set during the engine runup. This does not alleviate the need for positional awareness during the runup. Keep an eye outside for aircraft movement during the runup, as the parking brake often can't hold the airplane stationary at high power settings. Pilots transitioning from single-engine aircraft will find that multi-engine aircraft require more brake pressure on the ground. If the ramp and taxiways are icy where the aircraft is doing the runup, consider using less power or finding an area that is free of ice.

Takeoff

Once the aircraft is cleared for takeoff (or is in position for takeoff), it is generally advisable to bring the power up partially while holding the brakes to ensure both engines are operating and producing even power. This is especially important in cold weather and high density altitudes. Keep in mind that as power is advanced on takeoff, the pilot will transition from the tachometer to the manifold pressure gauge once the propeller governor becomes active. Some pilots elect to do a "rolling takeoff." There is nothing wrong with this type of takeoff, just be aware that the performance calculations are assuming a "standing takeoff"— full power applied before brake release.

Landing

During landing, the use of brakes varies depending on the situation. It's a good practice to apply some braking right after landing, just to be sure the brakes are working and will be available to slow the airplane. Early recognition of a brake failure on landing is key to a successful outcome. Also, keep in mind that most small multi-engine aircraft do not have the anti-lock brake systems (ABS) present in most cars. This increases the chance of the brakes locking up during landing if they are used improperly. If this occurs, braking effectiveness would be reduced and the possibility of reverted rubber hydroplaning increases.

During landing, the aircraft is being slowed down with the help of two forces: drag and rolling friction. The tire itself provides a rolling coefficient of 0.2. Figure 5-11 shows various surfaces and their corresponding rolling coefficients. During high velocities right after touchdown, the brakes will be less effective than later in the landing roll when velocity has slowed. This is because more weight is transferred from the wings to the wheels as the aircraft slows.

The pilot should also ensure the parking brake is not engaged prior to landing. This scenario is more likely in aircraft with a carburetor heat knob that looks similar to or is located near the parking brake knob.

Surface	Coefficient
Dry concrete	0.7
Light rain	0.5
Heavy rain	0.3
Snow or ice	0.1–0.2

Figure 5-11. Surface rolling coefficients.

Brake Failure Emergencies

Brake failure can occur during three critical phases of aircraft operation: taxi, landing, or aborted takeoff.

During Taxi

Brake failure can occur during the taxi phase before takeoff or after landing. In either case, reduce power to idle to reduce the need for brakes. If this is not sufficient to slow the aircraft, you should pull the mixtures to idle cutoff to reduce engine thrust completely and allow the aircraft to come to a rolling stop. In certain cases, you may not be able to stop the aircraft and exiting the taxiway may be your only choice.

During Landing

You have three options if the brake failure occurs during landing. The first—and preferred—option if sufficient runway remains is to allow the aircraft to roll out and stop on its own. If insufficient runway is available, the second option is to pull the mixtures to idle cut off, shut off all electrical power, and exit the runway to the left, right, or straight ahead. The third option is to execute a go-around immediately and find a longer runway or a runway with an upslope. A go-around may not be a good option because by the time you land, apply brakes, and realize there is a failure, it's likely that insufficient runway will be available to conduct a go-around. Again, early recognition of a brake failure is the key to a successful outcome in this situation.

During Aborted Takeoff

Another scenario involves brake failure during an aborted takeoff. Aborting a takeoff can be initiated for many reasons, but brake failures at this point will likely lead to the aircraft either rolling to a stop on its own or exiting the runway

Review 5

Landing Gear and Hydraulics

1. Name and describe the different types of retractable landing gear systems.

2. Illustrate and identify the components of the landing gear system on the Piper Seminole.

3. List and explain the V-speeds associated with a retractable landing gear.

4. Describe the purpose and function of the squat switch.

5. What is the purpose of up limit and down limit switches?

6. What is the purpose of the pressure switch on a hydraulic landing gear system?

7. Describe the purpose of the gear warning horn. What conditions activate it? When can the pilot mute the horn?

8. Describe the methods of emergency gear extension.

9. Explain the function of a basic hydraulic aircraft brake system.

10. List the three critical times brake failure can occur. Explain what actions a pilot should take for each.

Answers are provided in Appendix 2.

Electrical

6

⌕ *Chapter Focus for Multi-Engine Electrical Systems*

The first glass cockpit was installed in a Boeing 767 in 1982; more recently, glass cockpits have made inroads into general aviation. As well as from the various avionics upgrades over the years, general aviation aircraft have benefited from these more powerful yet lighter-weight electrical systems. As more and more general aviation aircraft move to all-electric flight decks, pilots need to have a greater understanding of how the electrical systems power each of the components.

Therefore it is important to discuss these key electrical system components and how to apply your knowledge of them to multi-engine operation. In this chapter you will also learn, for the various abnormal or emergency situations in these systems, how to identify and then apply the appropriate emergency action for each electrical system event.

Electrical systems in general aviation can range from very basic to complex. Most multi-engine electrical systems fall somewhere in the middle. A basic review of electrical theory and terminology will be helpful in understanding the multi-engine version of these systems.

Electrical Theory and Terminology

Batteries

A *battery* is defined as a device that stores and converts chemical energy into electrical energy. Typical household batteries made by Duracell and Energizer are called primary cell batteries. These types of batteries convert chemical energy into electrical energy but do not have a secondary cell that would allow the battery to be reused. The most commonly used type of battery in airplanes is a storage battery called a *lead-acid* battery, which does contain a secondary cell. The lead-acid battery is rechargeable and used for engine-starting and as an emergency backup (Figure 6-1).

Battery capacity is a measure of how much electrical energy a battery can produce. For example, most Piper Seminoles have a 35 amp-hour battery. This means if the battery is drawing 35 amps it will last for one hour. If the battery is drawing 17.5 amps then it will last for two hours.

Battery capacity is affected by temperature, charge, and its overall condition. Cold temperatures will reduce battery performance. Older batteries that have been subjected to a lot of starting (for example, for training flights) will also have reduced performance.

Key Terms

(in the order they appear in this chapter)

battery
alternator
generator
ampere (amp)
diode
circuit breaker
bus bar (bus)
dual-fed (electrical system)
positive/negative ground
volt
alternator control unit
annunciator
tie bus
starter contactor
external power

Figure 6-1. Lead-acid battery

Alternators/Generators

Alternators and *generators* are engine–driven devices that supply electrical current to the electrical systems after one or both engines on a multi–engine aircraft have been started. They are also designed to maintain a sufficient electrical charge in the battery.

Alternators are a smaller and lighter electrical producer than generators and are generally seen on smaller multi–engine aircraft. Most of the systems components use direct current (DC); a rectifier is used to convert alternating current (AC) to DC. The other advantage alternators have over generators is that they produce consistent power over a wide range of engine RPM (Figure 6-2).

Figure 6-2. Alternator.

Amp

An *amp* is a measurement of the amount of electricity travelling through a circuit over a given amount of time (typically one hour). In aircraft, batteries are rated in amp/hours.

Diode

A *diode* is an electrical "check valve" that allows electrical energy to flow in one direction and prevents the flow of electricity in the opposite direction. A diode creates high resistance (opposition) to electrical flow in one direction and has a low resistance (high conductivity) to electrical flow in the other direction. Electricity takes the path of least resistance and will move in the direction that has high conductivity. Resistance to the flow of electricity will create heat as a by-product.

Circuit Breaker

A *circuit breaker* is used to protect and isolate electrical equipment from the electrical system. When too much current flows across the circuit, heat increases, causing expansion and the circuit breaker opens (pops). Circuit breakers can generally be reset after they cool for a specified period of time (follow the procedures in the Pilot's Operating Handbook).

Circuit breakers typically protect one component, but they can also be used to protect and isolate entire electrical buses. This is coming to be the standard in all glass cockpit airplanes.

Contactor or Relay

A contactor (also known as a relay) is an electrically powered switch. There are two types of contactors: those that require electrical power to open, and those that require electrical power to close. The benefit of a contactor over a switch is that it automatically goes to its unpowered state when power is taken away from it. This allows electrical components to be "shed" or removed from the electrical system when power is removed. Most contactors on multi-engine aircraft are the powered-closed variety, with the exception of the avionics contactor, which is typically powered-open.

Bus or Bus Bar

Bus bars receive current from the battery, alternator(s) and/or generator(s), and the current is then distributed to each of the components on the bus or sent to a different bus and its associated components.

Electrical Systems in Multi-Engine Aircraft

A typical multi-engine aircraft will have a dual-fed, negative-ground, split-bus electrical system.

Dual-fed means that more than one electrical source (usually two alternators) feeds the system.

In a *negative-ground* electrical system, the negative side of the battery is grounded to the aircraft airframe. A *positive-ground* system would work for certain electrical equipment, but devices that are sensitive to the direction of flow (i.e., diodes) would be damaged in this type of system. Also, a negative-ground system reduces metal corrosion, a factor which is particularly important for the spark plugs. A positive-ground system would cause gap widening in the spark plugs, causing late ignition.

A split-bus system is designed to have multiple buses, which are fed by the power source(s). The split-bus system allows items to be grouped and categorized as essential, non-essential, avionics-related, and in other ways. By grouping in this way, the pilot and system have the ability to isolate items and also place certain essential electrical items on multiple buses in case one bus fails.

Alternators and Battery

In the Piper Seminole, the primary source of electrical power comes from two 14-volt, 70-ampere alternators. The alternators are belt driven and are located just inside the engine cowling, right below the air intake. Alternators are air cooled, and in most cases are placed directly inside the air intake to maximize cooling. The Seminole alternator is cooled using a small stack that directs airflow from the air intake over the alternator. The magnets within the alternator do not produce much electricity on their own. For this reason, the alternator magnets are coiled with a wire, which has electric current flowing through it, called the alternator field. This amplifies the intensity of the magnets. The alternator will not produce electricity without power flowing through the alternator field. This circuit is protected by a five amp alternator field circuit breaker (Figure 6-3).

The Seminole's alternator is rated at 70 amps; however, the system can only handle 60 amps. The reason the alternator is rated higher and the system is contained to 60 amps is so that the alternator runs cooler. The 70-amp system contains more wire coil windings, which in turn reduces the operating temperature of the alternator. During single alternator operations, the Seminole POH recommends keeping electrical load below 50 amps.

Each alternator is protected by an *alternator control unit (ACU)*. The ACU regulates the voltage, protects against overvoltage, and in a dual-fed system ensures load sharing between the two alternators. During normal operations the ACU regulates bus voltage to 14 volts and maintains equal load-sharing between the two alternators. If the voltage on the tie bus exceeds 17 volts, the ACU takes the alternator offline, triggering the ALTERNATOR INOP *annunciator* light to illuminate (Figure 6-4).

Volt. A measurement of the electric potential and electromotive force.

The battery in the Seminole is a 12-volt, 35-ampere-hour battery. The alternators are 14 volts and the battery is 12 volts to allow electrical current to flow from the alternators to the battery and recharge the battery. The purpose of the battery is to provide electrical current for starting and to serve as an emergency backup in the event both alternators fail.

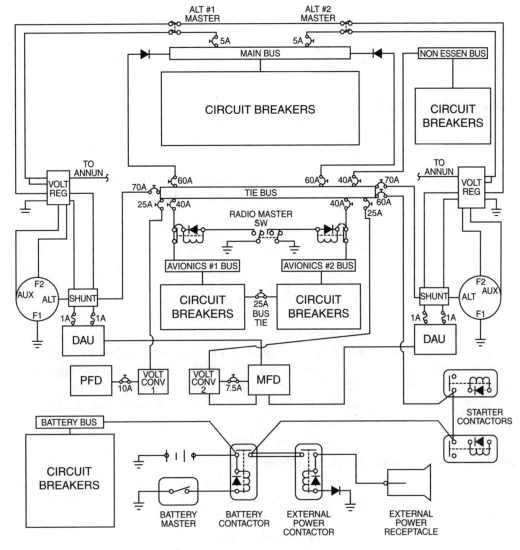

Figure 6-3. Piper Seminole electrical schematic.

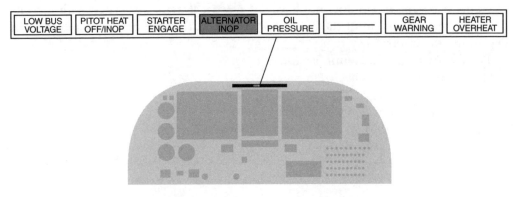

Figure 6-4. Alternator annunciator light.

The electrical switches that control the battery, alternators, pitot heat, fuel pumps, exterior lights, and avionics are generally located on the instrument, side, or overhead panels. The starters, primers, and magnetos (not part of the electrical system) are located on the left-hand side of the instrument panel near the pilot's yoke.

Circuit Breakers

Circuit breaker panels can vary widely in location. Some are found on the overhead panel, left- or right-side panel, center console, or behind the pilot seats. In certain airplanes the circuit breakers are not always consolidated, making it difficult for the pilot to locate specific circuit breakers. Be sure that you know the location of important circuit breakers, such as those for electric trim, landing gear hydraulic pumps, or flap motors.

The circuit breakers will automatically open if a device malfunctions or there is a sudden surge of current flow caused by a short. A short can easily be described using an analogy of a first-grade classroom. If one child out of twenty is misbehaving, all of the teacher's energy is focused on that one student. The same happens with a short: all of the electrical energy is sent to the short, causing an increase in the rate of flow of electricity (amps), which opens the circuit breaker. Each circuit breaker is set to open at a preset value (this value is typically written on the face of the breaker). A 5-amp breaker will open when the flow of electricity through that breaker exceeds 5 amps. The pilot can manually reset the breaker after a cooling period (usually about two minutes). If the circuit breaker trips again, the pilot should not continue to reset the circuit breaker. As a general rule, fuel circuit breakers should not be reset if they trip unless the POH states it can be done.

Buses and Power Distribution

Power distribution throughout the aircraft can sometimes be difficult to follow. One strategy that may aid in understanding the process is to break the aircraft down into electrical states and then draw out basic flow diagrams using the information provided in the POH if available. The first step is to determine which system items are powered by each bus. This information can usually be found in the POH. In some cases, the POH does not include this information and the pilot must look at the circuit breaker panel in the aircraft. A diagram of the items on the Piper Seminole buses is shown in Figure 6-5. The *tie bus* does not have any electrical items associated with it, as its purpose is to connect all of the buses. Some POHs are more helpful than others in explaining the electrical system.

The five buses on the Seminole are:

1. Hot battery bus *(grey shading)*
2. Tie bus *(white background)*
3. Avionics #1/#2 bus *(green and yellow shading)*
4. Main bus *(red shading)*
5. Non-essential bus *(blue shading)*

A hot battery bus is a bus that is always ON. Items on the hot battery bus are connected directly to the battery and are considered "hot," which means they can be turned on without turning the battery master switch on.

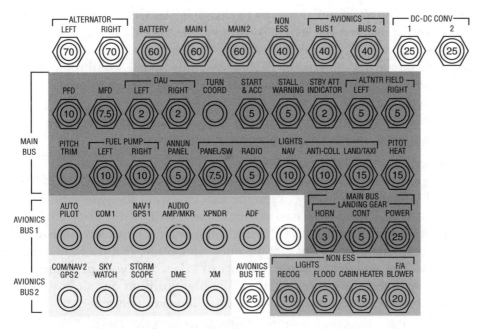

Figure 6-5. Piper Seminole—system items powered by each bus.

Electrical States

The Seminole has six electrical states (Figure 6-6):

1. No Power—all switches off, EPU not connected, hot battery bus powered.

   In this state, the hot battery bus items are the only things being powered. Items on the hot battery bus include the engine hourmeter, flight time hourmeter, and the heater hourmeter. Some multi-engine aircraft will power fuel boost pumps and auxiliary entry lighting from the hot battery bus. If this is the case, be sure that these items are not left on overnight, as the battery will be drained.

2. Battery—ON, Alternators—OFF

   In a battery power-only state, the flow of electricity passes through the *starter contactors* and then to the tie bus. The tie bus then distributes power to the PFD, MFD, avionics buses (if the avionics master switch is ON), main bus, non-essential bus, and then through the 5 amp field circuit back to the ACU. The data acquisition units are powered by the MFDs. The voltage convertors on the PFD and MFD convert DC to AC for use by the PFD and MFD.

   PFD: primary flight display

   MFD: multi-function display

   Items powered by each bus can be seen by referring to the circuit breaker panel. In this state it is likely that the avionics master switch is in the OFF position in preparation for engine start. In cold weather operations, the heater can be powered by the battery because the non-essential bus is powered. In aircraft with electric supplemental heat, be careful not to run the heater on battery power only, as electric heaters draw a lot of power; instead, plug into *external power*. The Seminole uses a gas combustion heater, and therefore isn't as susceptible to draining the battery. Caution should be used and the duration should be kept to a minimum to preserve power for engine start.

3. Battery—ON, Alternators—1 ON

   In this state the alternator takes over, powering the starter contactors, tie bus, main bus, and non-essential bus; this occurs because of its higher voltage output than the battery. The alternator also starts to charge the battery at this point. Since the alternator is powering the starter contactors, the second engine start is called a cross-alternator start. The power leaving the main bus now travels through the 5 amp field circuit and powers the ACU. Five amps are needed to run the alternator because the magnets in the alternator are not big enough to produce enough power to power itself.

In this state the battery is now being charged. This can be recognized on the battery ammeter, which will show positive amp current.

4. Battery—ON, Alternators—2 ON

Nothing changes from the previous state (Battery ON, one Alternator ON) except the ACUs balance the load between the two operating alternators. Some multi-engine aircraft have a tendency to allow uneven alternator load, while others maintain a nearly identical load sharing. Some multi-engine aircraft have a load sharing limitation, and in this case the pilot must ensure that the limitation is not exceeded. You will get to know the normal balance on your particular aircraft after a few flights. Be aware of abnormally high loads on one alternator, as this can damage electrical components or lead to alternator failure.

5. Battery—ON, Alternators—2 ON, Radio Master—ON

Operating alternators sharing load and recharging the battery.

This state is identical to the previous two states, except that the tie bus now powers avionics bus 1 and 2.

6. External Power—Connected and ON (All switches OFF)

External power in smaller multi-engine aircraft is generally designed to be HOT and close to the battery. HOT means that even when all the switches are off, when

An *ammeter* shows the total load in amperage placed on the electrical system and total load in amperage drawn from the battery in the event of an alternator failure (shown as a negative amp indication); therefore, the pilot can use it to determine the health of an alternator.

A *loadmeter* depicts the total load in amperage placed on the electrical system. When a loadmeter is at zero, the alternator is producing no current—also an indication of an alternator failure.

	Power State	Systems Powered	Explanation
1.	No power	(None)	Items connected to the hot battery bus will always receive power.
2.	Battery—On Alternators—Off	Starter contactors, Tie bus, Main, Non-essential	All buses are powered except the avionics, which are controlled by the avionics master switch.
3.	Battery—On Alternators—1 On	Starter contactors, Tie bus, Main, Non-essential	Same at state 2, however the battery is being recharged and the starter contactors are being powered by the alternator.
4.	Battery—On Alternators—2 On	Starter contactors, Tie bus, Main, Non-essential	All buses are powered. Alternator Control Unit (ACU) provides voltage regulation and load sharing between the two alternators.
5.	Battery—On Alternators—2 On Radio master—On	Starter contactors, Tie bus, Main, Non-essential. Avionics and autopilot master switches are turned on, powering the avionics and autopilot	All buses are powered. Alternator Control Unit (ACU) provides voltage regulation and load sharing between the two alternators.
6.	External power—On All switches Off	Starter contactors, Tie bus, Main, Non-essential	All buses are powered except the avionics, which are controlled by the avionics master switch.

Figure 6-6. Piper Seminole electrical states.

the external power unit (EPU) is plugged in, power is being sent to the starter contactors and most of the buses. In the case of the Seminole, the avionics bus 1 and 2 are not powered unless the avionics master switch is on. The proximity to the battery is to ensure the maximum amount of electrical energy is transferred to the battery. This is best understood by using an extension cord as an example. If I went into a home improvement store today and wanted to buy an extension cord with the same gauge of wire (thickness), the shorter cord would be able to carry more amps than the longer cord.

The external power receptacle can also be placed close to the propellers. In the Seminole, for example, it is located next to the right propeller. If one of the starters is stuck and line personnel plug in the external power receptacle, the propeller will turn. The pilot and line personnel should be aware of this possibility prior to attempting to start the engine with external power. To unplug the external power on the Seminole, the right engine should be shut down and the left should be reduced to the lowest possible RPM to reduce sparking when disconnecting the external power.

Electrical System Monitors

On a Seminole with a glass cockpit, the MFD's engine page contains the ammeters for each alternator, the bus voltage, and the current rate of charge or discharge of the batteries. There is also an alternator inoperative light and a low bus voltage light (Figure 6-7).

If an overvoltage condition occurs, the ACU will take the respective alternator offline and the red ALTERNATOR INOP light will illuminate. The system also has a voltage monitor on the tie bus.

If the system voltage drops below 12.5 volts, the red LOW BUS VOLTAGE light will illuminate. This indicates both alternators are offline and the aircraft's electrical system is receiving power from the battery only.

The annunciator lights are the same on a Seminole with a traditional cockpit, except the ALTERNATOR INOP light is yellow instead of red. The ammeters are located with the engine instrument cluster on the instrument panel.

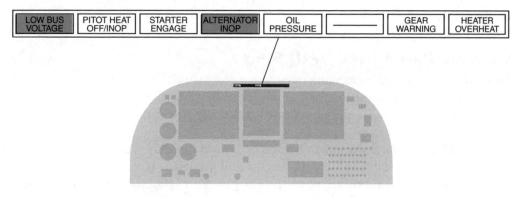

Figure 6-7. Dual alternator failure annunciators.

Normal Electrical System Operations

In today's modern, all-glass multi-engine aircraft, electrical power has replaced vacuum pumps. A benefit of this is that vacuum pumps tend to be unreliable and require frequent maintenance attention. However, one drawback to an all-electric aircraft is that in a total electrical failure, the pilot will have very few resources available to fly and navigate the airplane. It is important to understand all aspects of your aircraft's electrical system— including normal, abnormal, and emergency operations.

Normal Battery Starts

Normal starts in a light multi-engine aircraft require the use of the battery to start the left engine and the alternator to start the right engine. The basic procedures for a normal cold start can be found in section 4 of the POH under checklist and amplified procedures. Pertinent information is included in the amplified procedures section that should be reviewed prior to starting the aircraft's engines the first time. The checklist is a basic list that should be followed, but by no means covers everything that should be considered during the engine start process.

Battery health and properly priming the engine will play a large role in how smoothly the engine start process goes. The age of the battery, the amount it has been used, and the current temperature will determine the strength of the battery. In extremely cold temperatures the engine should be preheated in a hangar or by using a heating device such as a Tannis Heater. Major engine manufacturers also provide cold weather operations service bulletins that provide excellent detailed information that pilots should review. These service bulletins can be found on the manufacturer's website. Overpriming the engine can also be dangerous. Follow the procedures outlined in the POH and follow the checklist to ensure the engine is not overprimed. If overpriming is suspected, the flooded engine start checklist should be followed.

During starting, cranking should be limited to the cycle and time limitations in the POH. Most will advise a cranking limit (typically 10 seconds) followed by a specified cooling period (typically 20 seconds to a minute). This cycle can be repeated three times followed by a 10-minute cooling period. In general, if you haven't started the aircraft after these attempts, you will likely need maintenance intervention. During cold weather operations it's also possible for the starter Bendix arm to stick and prevent the starter from cranking the engine. If this occurs, maintenance should be contacted to resolve the issue.

External Power Unit (EPU) Starts

External power starts on most light, general aviation, single and multi-engine aircraft can be a dangerous proposition for the line personnel plugging in the external power. The procedure on multi-engine aircraft is relatively the same as on single-engine aircraft, except two engines must be started.

External power starts are generally used on light twins only when the battery does not have sufficient charge to turn the engine and propeller. Refer to the appropriate checklist and amplified procedure in section 4 of the POH. You should discuss the procedure with line personnel prior to starting the procedure to ensure everybody understands the process and the potential dangers.

The procedure in the Seminole requires that all switches are off prior to plugging in the external power. Once external power is connected to the aircraft it is hot, meaning the starter contactors, tie bus, main bus, and non-essential bus are powered.

In the Seminole, the battery can be used in parallel with the external power to extend cranking time. However, if the battery does not have sufficient charge then it should be left off. You can test whether or not the battery has sufficient charge by momentarily turning it on while cranking; if cranking speed increases, the battery is at a higher level than the external power source.

If the battery is depleted and the EPU is used to start one engine, you should ensure the battery is given some time to recharge prior to attempting to start the other engine. Once the alternator is brought online all of the alternator's energy will go to recharging a severely depleted battery, leaving little to no electrical power for starting. If the pilot wants to start both engines with the EPU, the battery and alternator should be left off until both engines are started. The proximity of the EPU receptacle may require the pilot to shut one engine down to allow ground personnel to safely disconnect external power.

Normal Electrical Loads

The pilot of a multi-engine aircraft should be aware of the electrical load distribution throughout the flight. To do this, the pilot should refer to the electrical ammeter (Figure 6-8) in aircraft with traditional gauges or the digital electrical system status gauges (Figure 6-9) in aircraft with digital engine representations. Watch for abnormally high loads, or conditions where one alternator is handling more electrical load than the other (one ammeter shows a significantly higher value than the other). It is beneficial for a pilot to be aware of normal load states, and be alert for significant changes to these states.

Figure 6-8. Electrical ammeter.

Figure 6-9. Digital electrical system status gauges.

The pilot of any aircraft should understand how electrical current flows into the system (see Figure 6-10 for an example of this). Larger jet aircraft manuals do a much better job of visually displaying the system on the instrument and overhead panels to make it easier for the pilot to see which alternator, generator, battery, or EPU is powering which bus. Most small, light twin-engine aircraft provide the pilot very little visual information about the flow of electrical power.

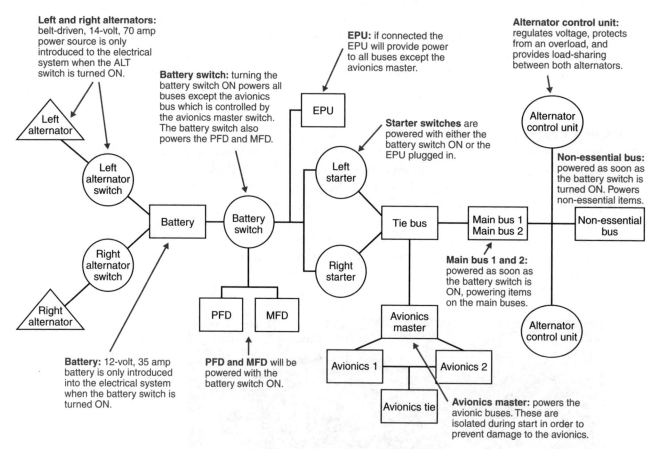

Figure 6-10. Electrical flow diagram.

Emergencies

Dual alternators offer protection in multi-engine aircraft by sharing the load under normal conditions. One alternator can power most, if not all, of the electrical system in the event of a single alternator (or engine) failure. Understanding the electric states of your aircraft and the current flow logic, along with the checklist procedure, is the first step in taking the appropriate actions in the event of an emergency situation.

Single Alternator Failure

You can recognize a single alternator failure by noting zero output on one ammeter or by the illumination of the ALTERNATOR INOP annunciator light. In this situation, you should follow the single alternator checklist. Typically, the first step suggested by the checklist is to verify the failure by reading the appropriate ammeter. The next step is to check and make sure the remaining load on the operating alternator is reduced as much as possible—below 50 amps in the Seminole. If the operating alternator is overloaded, the low bus annunciator light will illuminate or flicker to indicate the load is too high. Turn off any unneeded lights or non-essential electrical components.

Next, turn the failed alternator switch off and reset the circuit breaker. Once this is completed, the failed alternator switch should be turned back on. If it fails again, or does not turn on, it should be turned off and the flight continued on the operating alternator. By turning the alternator switch off and back on again, you are resetting the ACU. If a temporary fault or spike in electrical current activates the ACU, this reset procedure will allow the alternator to be used again. Most electrical spikes are temporary in nature; in some cases the activation of the gear system concurrently with the electric flap extension system can cause one alternator to be taken offline by the ACU. To avoid this potential issue in aircraft with electric flaps and gear systems, wait until the gear extension is complete before extending the flaps.

One alternator is capable of supplying enough electrical power to run the essential equipment for continued safe flight. Items like recirculation blowers, position lights, strobe lights, and landing lights should only be used if necessary.

Dual Alternator Failure

Dual alternator failure in any aircraft is an emergency. However, traditional aircraft have some advantages over the new technically-advanced all-glass aircraft. Traditional aircraft run the gyroscopic instruments with engine-driven vacuum pumps so they are not dependent on the operation of the electrical system for power. In the newer glass aircraft the gyroscopic instruments are replaced by a PFD and the standby attitude indicator is usually electrically driven. In most cases, the standby attitude indicator is powered by a separate battery that will continue operating for a minimum of 30 minutes after a total electrical failure. A dual alternator failure generally means the aircraft's sole source of remaining power is the battery, which means you must immediately exit IMC.

The first step is identifying a dual alternator failure. This is accomplished using the annunciator lights and ammeters. Dual alternator failure is indicated by the illumination of both the ALTERNATOR INOP and LO BUS annunciator lights. If this occurs, the procedure is generally the same as the procedure for the single alternator failure, except you are trying to reset either alternator. If only one alternator comes back online, proceed with the single alternator failure; if both fail to come back online, the only remaining power source for the aircraft is the battery.

Complete Electrical Failure

Once the primary battery or batteries are depleted, the aircraft is considered to be in a complete electrical failure. If the aircraft is equipped with a standby attitude indicator that is electrical, the standby power switch may need to be activated manually by the pilot. Follow the steps listed in the appropriate checklist for your aircraft. Realize that the electrical failure will not impact the operation of the engines; ignition is provided by the magnetos, which work independent of the aircraft electrical system. The engine-driven fuel pumps will supply adequate fuel pressure to keep the engines running.

Electrical Fire

The first challenge relating to an electrical fire is accurately identifying the source of the fire, and verifying that it is in fact an electrical fire and not a fire in the engine compartment or environmental system. Electrical fires tend to be easily identified due to the acrid smell and bluish color of the smoke. Also, an electrical fire can potentially be seen coming from under the dash or from behind the electrical components or circuit breakers.

Once you've identified the source of the fire as electrical in nature, proceed to the electrical fire emergency checklist for the particular make and model of aircraft. It may be necessary to don an oxygen mask and smoke goggles if the aircraft is so-equipped. If it becomes necessary to use a fire extinguisher in the cockpit area, be careful, as the Halon fire extinguisher will make it difficult to breathe. If oxygen is available, be sure to don an oxygen mask prior to using a fire extinguisher in a confined space.

In today's technically advanced aircraft, an electrical fire is enough of a concern that it is worth being prepared for it. It is imperative that you are familiar with the electrical fire emergency checklist and memorize the memory items associated with this checklist. Most electrical fire checklists will guide the pilot through a process of isolating electrical components in an attempt to identify the source of the fire. This process will take some time and should be done carefully while ensuring that the aircraft remains under positive control.

There are two major concerns with an electrical fire once the fire source has been located and extinguished: the potential reduction in electrically powered avionics leading to a partial panel condition, and dealing with the cockpit visibility as a result of the smoke. It may be necessary to ventilate the cockpit and cabin in order to properly see the instrument panel or to see outside the aircraft. Follow the proper ventilation procedure for your aircraft, especially if the aircraft is pressurized.

Review 6
Electrical

1. Describe the difference between a primary and secondary cell battery.

2. How is battery capacity measured?

3. Describe what a 60-amp battery rating is, in operational terms.

4. Explain the benefits of a split-bus system.

5. Summarize the effect of temperature on battery performance.

6. Describe the difference between an alternator and a generator.

7. What is the purpose of an alternator field?

8. List and explain the functions of the alternator control unit (ACU).

9. State the purpose of a diode.

10. What would cause the ALTERNATOR INOP annunciator light to illuminate?

11. What would cause the LO BUS annunciator light to illuminate?

12. Describe the function of a circuit breaker.

13. Explain the circuit breaker reset procedure in flight.

14. In a multi-engine electrical system, what does "dual-fed" refer to?

15. What does negative ground mean?

16. What is the purpose of having a 70-amp alternator for a 60-amp alternator system?

17. What information does the ammeter provide for the pilot?

18. Describe the operation of a contactor (or, relay).

19. Describe the process used to start the engine using external power.

20. What is the purpose of having a hot battery bus?

21. How can you test that the battery has sufficient charge for cranking?

22. Chart the direction of electrical flow in your specific aircraft using the Seminole examples in this chapter.

Answers are provided in Appendix 2.

Environmental

7

Chapter Focus for Environmental Systems

Multi-engine aircraft are capable of reaching high altitudes and adverse weather conditions, which creates the need for robust environmental systems and ice protection. Additionally, due to the location of the engines on the wings rather than the main fuselage, it is a challenge to direct heated or cooled environmental air into the cabin. This results in a need for more complex environmental systems on multi-engine aircraft.

Since these are more complex systems, they must be understood in regard to their operation and handing in multi-engine aircraft. You must also be able to perform the appropriate emergency actions for these systems; these key environmental system topics are covered in this chapter.

Key Terms

(in the order they appear in this chapter)

anti-ice

deice

known icing conditions

combustion heater

over-temperature limit switch

blower fan

Ice Protection

In order for an aircraft to dependably transport passengers or cargo it needs to be built to handle adverse weather conditions. Somewhere along the way, an aircraft sales department coined the phrase "all-weather airplane" to describe the versatility and adaptability of their particular aircraft model to various adverse weather conditions. This title has created an expectation among passengers, aircraft owners, operators, and even pilots that an "all-weather airplane" can handle any adverse weather condition. This is certainly not the case. It's presumptuous of pilots to say that an aircraft is capable of handling anything that Mother Nature can throw at it, and numerous accidents indicate pilots were overly reliant on the "all-weather" title given to their particular aircraft.

In short, an aircraft can be built to handle mild atmospheric disturbances, but one of the best methods of handling atmospheric disturbances is to completely avoid them—especially in the case of more significant weather phenomenon like thunderstorms, hurricanes, heavy precipitation, turbulence, or freezing rain. Yet there are a few weather conditions that an aircraft can safely operate in, with the proper aircraft equipment and the pilot's attention to the limitations given in the POH.

Freezing rain: Rain that falls through air whose temperature is lower than 0°C, which freezes upon contact with objects on the ground or in the air.

Operating in Icing Conditions

Icing is one of the most common adverse weather conditions that an aircraft can face. Before discussing individual ice protection systems it is important to briefly cover the operational hazards of operating in icing conditions. The topic of icing operational hazards, anti-icing and deicing equipment (approved use and operations) is a special emphasis area for all FAA practical tests—and rightly so as icing-related accidents continue to occur. According to the AOPA Air Safety Foundation, "even small ice accumulations—no thicker or rougher than a piece of coarse sandpaper—can reduce lift by up to 30 percent and increase drag up to 40 percent." NASA has researched aircraft structural icing in great detail and has found that close to 30 percent of the total drag associated with an ice encounter remained after all of the protected surfaces were cleared.

In short, aircraft encounters with icing conditions must be treated seriously, even in aircraft that are approved for flight in known icing conditions. Captain Robert Buck said it best with respect to icing conditions: "When ice is encountered, immediately start working to get out of it. Unless the condition is freezing rain, or freezing drizzle, it rarely requires fast action and certainly never panic action, but it does call for positive action."

Known Ice and Known Icing Conditions

"Known ice" and the phrase "*known icing conditions*" appear quite regularly when aircraft icing is discussed. So what do these terms mean? The definition of "known ice" has developed over time since FAA publications and regulations first began to refer to it. Currently, the FAA defines it as "known or observed or detected ice accretion," which means the actual presence of ice adhering to the aircraft surfaces in flight. "Known icing conditions" refers to the potential for ice to be present, in addition to the actual observed accretion of ice in flight. "Known icing conditions" encompasses both actual ice accretion and forecast or reported icing and pilots must be aware of both possibilities prior to flight into instrument meteorological conditions (IMC).

Flight in Known Icing Conditions

Pilots must determine whether or not an aircraft is approved for flight in known icing conditions. The POH for each aircraft has a list of approved types or kinds of operation. Most often found in Chapter 2 under aircraft limitations, this list will indicate whether an aircraft is approved for flight in icing conditions; if it is, there will be additional, specific limitations for flight in icing conditions. For example, the list will contain minimum flight speeds to maintain or restrictions on the use of flaps while in icing conditions.

In general, if you are operating an aircraft capable of flight in icing conditions, make sure all required components are operational before you depart. The Kinds of Equipment List (KOEL) will indicate what equipment is required for flight in known icing conditions. A preflight check of this equipment is advised (and often required by the aircraft POH) if it will be needed for the flight. Aircraft that are not approved for flight in known icing conditions must avoid icing completely.

In order to receive certification for flight in known icing conditions, an aircraft must demonstrate flight in simulated icing conditions and must "operate safely" in those conditions. Obviously, a method of preventing the formation of or removing ice from critical surfaces of the aircraft is needed.

Structural Ice Protection

There are three methods of handling ice protection: mechanical ice removal, thermal ice removal/prevention, and chemical ice removal. It is important to understand that ice protection falls under two categories depending on its time of use: *deicing* is the removal of ice after it has accumulated, and *anti-icing* is the prevention of ice formation. Some ice protection systems can act as either anti-ice or deice while others can only be used as deicing systems:

Mechanical Ice Removal

This type of ice removal pertains to the physical removal of accreted ice from a critical surface. The most common method of removing this ice is to break the ice and allow the passing airflow to clear the ice chunks away from the aircraft without damaging other aircraft surfaces. The breaking of the ice is commonly done by inflatable deicing boots located on the leading edge of critical flight surfaces. These boots are made out of rubber and are inflated by air pressure, which is often taken from a turbocharger or pneumatic pump. Additionally, a vacuum pump is used to deflate the boots and make them smooth with the leading edge of the wing (Figure 7-1).

It is recommended that pilots activate the deice boots as soon as ice accumulation is observed. In some cases pilots will find that the ice breaks off more cleanly when an accumulation of a quarter of an inch of ice builds up; in fact, some aircraft POHs require a buildup of ice before activating the deicing system. In general, it is good practice to activate early and activate often with respect to deicing boots.

Pneumatic deicing boots are far from perfect; they often fail to remove all the accumulated ice from the leading edge of the critical surfaces (Figure 7-2). Realize

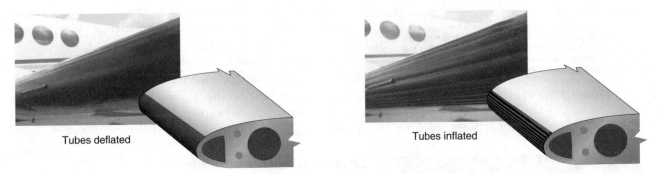

Tubes deflated   Tubes inflated

Figure 7-1. Mechanical deice boots.

"Supercooled" droplets contain water that has cooled to below the freezing point, yet is still in a liquid state. Upon contact with airplane surfaces it freezes faster and in larger ice shapes.

Photo courtesy of NASA Glenn Research Center, Cleveland OH

Figure 7-2. Some supercooled large droplet (SLD) ice formation can be missed by the deicing boots. (Photo by NASA—Lewis/FAA/NCAR-RAP)

Prop Anti-Ice Ammeter

When the system is operating, the prop ammeter indicates normal operating range. As each boot section cycles, the ammeter fluctuates.

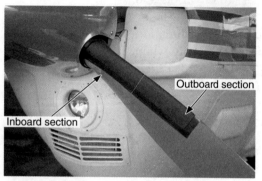

Inboard section

Outboard section

Prop Anti-Ice Boot

The boot is divided into two sections: inboard and outboard. When the anti-ice is operating, the inboard section heats on each blade, and then cycles to the outboard section. If a boot fails to heat properly on one blade, unequal ice loading may result, causing severe vibration.

Figure 7-3. Propeller deice system.

Figure 7-4. Chemical weeping wing.

that the airfoil shape is significantly changed when ice accumulates, which can result in unusual slow flight or approach and landing characteristics. Some aircraft POHs specify a minimum flight speed in icing conditions. The purpose for this minimum is twofold: to prevent ice accumulation on unprotected surfaces of the wing (on the lower surface of the wing), and to prevent aircraft upset at slower airspeeds due to disturbed airflow patterns around the airfoil.

Thermal Ice Removal/Prevention

The next method of ice protection is by using heat. Heat can be used as either a deice or anti-ice system depending on when it is activated. Heat is generally the most effective method of ice protection, but it is the most demanding on aircraft electrical systems. The most common heated surfaces include the windshield, propeller blades, pitot tubes, and fuel vents; Figure 7-3 shows an example of an anti-ice heated-boot system for propeller blades. Turbine aircraft also heat the leading edge of the critical surfaces, but this is not possible in smaller twin-engine aircraft as this method uses hot air compressed by the jet engine.

The Piper Seminole has a heated pitot tube. The pitot heat can be turned on any time ice is suspected. The POH limits the use of pitot heat on the ground to a maximum of three minutes to prevent overheating and damage to the pitot tube or its heating elements.

Chemical Anti-ice/Deice

The last type of ice removal uses a chemical—often glycol—which is sprayed or leaked onto the protected surface. Chemical ice removal is used in a few multi-engine aircraft to clear the windshield or propeller of ice. A few aircraft use chemical deicing systems on critical flight surfaces such as the wings and tail, as well (aptly named "weeping wings"—Figure 7-4).

By far the most common use of chemical deice and anti-ice is for ground application. Commercial aircraft are sprayed with chemicals to remove snow or ice from the aircraft prior to departure. Anti-ice solution can also be applied to prevent further accumulation prior to takeoff. Anti-ice solution is not typically used in smaller aircraft because the solution requires higher takeoff speeds in order for it to be removed from the aircraft on takeoff.

Cabin Environmental Systems

When it comes to managing the environment inside an aircraft, many systems work together to provide a comfortable environment for passengers and crew.

In general, the heating and cooling systems found on piston-powered multi-engine aircraft are quite basic and easy to operate (Figure 7-5). Each aircraft has its own method of providing heat and cooling and the pilot should be familiar with the specific system found on their aircraft before use. Heating and cooling systems can be electrically powered or powered by the engine. Either of these power sources will burden the aircraft systems and affect aircraft performance or electrical load. Special care should be taken during times of reduced power, single-engine, or single-alternator operations.

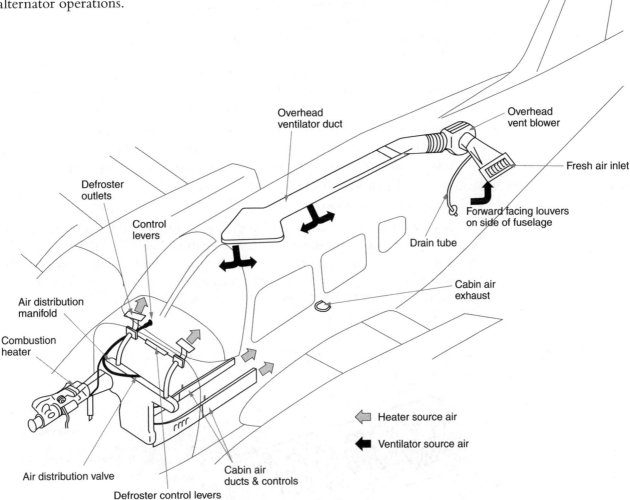

Figure 7-5. Environmental systems.

Heating Systems

The first challenge is to keep an aircraft cabin warm while the outside temperatures are cold. Even if the aircraft is being operated in areas of warmer temperatures on the surface, the temperature will drop rapidly as the aircraft climbs to higher altitudes.

All aircraft are manufactured with some method of heating the cabin. Single-engine aircraft typically extract heat from exhaust systems and direct it into the cabin. This is far more challenging in multi-engine aircraft with their engines on the wings rather than on the nose of the aircraft. Warm exhaust air will cool significantly before it reaches the cabin. In addition, when the engines are just started or are operating at low power settings, there may not be enough warm air to bring the cabin up to a comfortable temperature. For this purpose, most multi-engine aircraft—including the Piper Seminole—have a separate heating system. The most common heating system in use today on piston-powered multi-engine aircraft utilizes small combustion engines that provide a source of heat for the cabin (Figure 7-6).

In the Piper Seminole, this *combustion heater* receives fuel from the fuel supply line going to the left engine. This means that whenever the left engine is receiving its fuel, the heater is receiving its fuel. If the left fuel selector is turned off, the heater will not receive any fuel. The small combustion heater has several key components:

1. Fuel pump—The combustion heater has two integral fuel pumps to deliver fuel to the fuel nozzle. Depending on the brand of heater, it will deliver between one half to two gallons of fuel per hour to the heater while it is in operation.

2. Fuel nozzle—Inside the combustion chamber is a fuel nozzle which mixes fuel with the air in the combustion chamber.

3. Combustion air blower—A fan outside the heater unit itself draws in outside air and delivers it to the combustion chamber to be mixed with fuel and burned. The combustion air blower turns on automatically whenever the heater is started. The air is blown into the combustion chamber in a way that creates a "whirling flame" in order to evenly distribute the heat throughout the chamber.

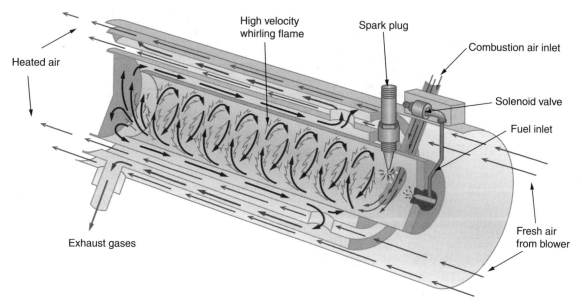

Figure 7-6. Example of a gas combustion heater (cutaway).

4. Ventilation air blower—This is another fan on the end of the heater that forces outside air over the heater core. This air will be the air that is felt inside the cabin. The ventilation air blower provides airflow to the cabin while the aircraft is on the ground. Once the aircraft is airborne and the nose wheel is fully retracted, the ventilation air blower turns off. Note that the ventilation air blower may be turned on to add airflow to the cabin while on the ground even if the heater is not running.

5. Over-temperature limit switch—In case of a problem with the heater system, there is an *over-temperature limit switch* that will stop fuel flow to the combustion chamber once the heater reaches a certain temperature—anywhere from 300–400 degrees Fahrenheit. Depending on the brand of heater, the overheat switch may require a manual reset by maintenance personnel if an overheat occurs.

6. Thermostat—The heater system has a built-in thermostat to maintain the selected temperature in the cabin. The pilot selects the desired temperature using the temperature select lever and the thermostat cycles the heater to achieve the desired cabin temperature.

7. Overheat annunciator—In the event of a heater overheat the pilot will receive a warning on the overhead annunciator.

Operating the Heating System in the Seminole

Operation of the heater system on the Piper Seminole is fairly simple. Open the fresh air intake by moving the air intake lever to the open position. This allows outside ambient air to pass over the heater and travel to the cabin, and it must be open in order for the heater to operate. Select the cabin heat switch to the cabin heat position and select the desired temperature using the temperature select lever. If the fresh air intake is not more than half open, the heater will not start as there is the potential of overheating with too little cooling airflow over the heater. If the temperature select lever is moved to the full warm position, the heater will achieve a maximum temperature of 250°F. The heater will cycle on and off to achieve the selected temperature in the cabin.

When shutting the heater down, you must consider proper cooling after shut down. The POH requires one of two methods be followed for proper cooling: shut the heater off in flight with the fresh air intake lever full open for at least 15 seconds, or on the ground place the cabin heat switch to the fan position with the air intake full open for a minimum of two minutes—or (in both cases) until the air entering the cabin through the heater outlets feels cool.

Cooling Systems

Getting fresh air into the cabin is the easiest method of cooling an aircraft cabin. For an unpressurized aircraft, this is a pretty simple task. In the Piper Seminole, an air intake near the tail will direct fresh air into overhead vents in the cabin. This fresh air intake can be closed if needed. (This fresh air intake should not be confused with the heater fresh air intake; they are completely separate systems.) A fan located in the fresh air intake duct can circulate this fresh air when the aircraft is not moving or on the ground. The switch to control the fresh air *blower fan* is near the heater switch and has two positions for operation: High Rec or Blwr Low. Once the aircraft is airborne, ram air will provide adequate air flow in the cabin without the use of the blower fan.

Some multi-engine aircraft have cooling systems to maintain comfortable cabin temperatures during hot days. The most common method of cooling small piston-powered multi-engine aircraft cabins is through the use of a vapor cycle machine, more commonly referred to as an air conditioner. Air conditioners are most commonly electrically powered (although some are belt-driven by the engine) and are a burden to the electrical system. In the Piper Seminole, the air conditioner is an optional component as it adds cost, weight and complexity to the aircraft.

Air conditioners are typically not installed on light twin-engine aircraft. Usually the pilot and passengers have the option to open the doors or windows to allow airflow. The pilot needs to ensure that all doors and windows are closed and latched properly prior to takeoff.

Emergencies

Environmental Systems

There are a few possible emergencies relating to aircraft environmental systems: heater over-temperature, carbon monoxide detection, or environmental smoke in the aircraft.

Heater Over-Temperature

In the case of a heater over-temp, the heater over-temperature annunciator will illuminate. If this occurs in flight, the pilot should turn the heater off and leave the air vent open until the annunciator is extinguished. Most newer combustion heater systems have a built-in overheat detection system that will shut the heater off automatically if a high temperature is detected.

Figure 7-7.
Electronic carbon monoxide detector.

Carbon Monoxide Detection

Most new aircraft come equipped with an electronic carbon monoxide detector (Figure 7-7). If a carbon monoxide advisory is indicated, press the reset button on the system control. Older aircraft may use a traditional carbon monoxide detector (Figure 7-8). If the indication continues, you should immediately turn off the heater, open all fresh air intakes, and land as soon as practical.

Environmental Smoke

In the event of a crack in a combustion heater's exhaust or a heater over-temperature condition, it is possible to experience smoke in the cockpit and cabin. This kind of smoke will come from the heat and defrost vents. Upon recognition of environmental smoke, the pilot should shut down the heater, close the heat and defrost vents, and open the fresh air vents. The smoke will exit the airplane through the overboard cabin air exhaust on the bottom of the aircraft.

Figure 7-8. Traditional carbon monoxide detector.

Emergencies in Icing Conditions

Emergencies encountered while in icing conditions can present severe and dire circumstances, which you must be aware of and adequately prepare for. Many accidents have occurred as a result of inadvertent flight into icing conditions or system failures while in icing conditions. Most notably, the Air France Flight 447 accident on June 1,

2009, was indicative of the potential dangers of inappropriately recognizing and responding to pitot heat system blockages due to severe icing conditions. In this Flight 447's Airbus 330, several subsequent systems failed due to inconsistent airspeed readings, but it started with this type of blockage caused by very fast ice accumulation in the pitot tube.

Pitot Heat Failure

A pitot heat failure is a concern for any aircraft encountering icing conditions. For this reason, it is best practice to check the proper function of the pitot heat systems prior to departing on an instrument flight (IFR) that has the potential of encountering icing conditions. If the pitot heat fails in flight, most aircraft will not provide the pilot any cockpit indication of the failure. You may not recognize any failure until you find yourself in an unusual attitude as a result of airspeed anomalies.

Due to the lack of cockpit indications of pitot heat failures, always be cognizant of airspeed indications and—through instrument cross check—be wary of unusual airspeed indications. If a pitot tube becomes blocked in flight, the airspeed indicator on most multi-engine aircraft (without an external pitot drain) will act like an altimeter, indicating a lower airspeed as the aircraft descends and a higher airspeed as the aircraft climbs. This can lead you into an unusual attitude. The key to properly handling a blocked pitot tube in flight is to ensure adequate instrument cross check techniques are used, and once an erroneous airspeed indication is noticed, use appropriate partial panel instrument scan techniques to exit icing conditions.

The Piper Seminole has an annunciator that illuminates any time the pitot heat is not powered, regardless of the pitot heat switch position. This provides the pilot with an indication of a pitot heat failure. This type of indication system is rare, even for aircraft approved for flight in icing conditions.

Inadvertent Icing Encounters

As a pilot, if you encounter icing conditions in an aircraft that is not equipped or approved for flight in icing conditions, you *must* exit the icing conditions immediately. Finding non-icing conditions to escape to will require a good knowledge of the surrounding weather conditions as well as the surrounding terrain and obstructions. In some cases, a descent will be the best course of action to follow and in other cases, a climb is the best course of action; this decision must be made knowing as much information as possible about the surrounding atmosphere. Care must be taken if a climb is chosen because the aircraft performance, which is already compromised due to ice accumulation, will decrease as the aircraft climbs. Additionally, any ice that has accumulated on the aircraft will not likely be able to melt as the aircraft climbs unless a significant temperature inversion exists.

Ultimately, preflight preparation is the pilot's best defense for icing encounters. Be prepared, know the weather conditions in which you'll be operating, and do not take off if your flight will encounter forecasted or suspected icing conditions.

Icing System Failure

As with any mechanical system, icing systems are potentially susceptible to failure when they are most needed—in icing conditions. As with other failures, if icing system failures occur, you should immediately leave the icing conditions and, if possible, the clouds or precipitation to reach warmer and drier air. Additionally, most system failures have appropriate checklists that must be followed. Refer to the appropriate emergency checklist relating to the icing system failure.

Common failures that occur on ice-protected aircraft include propeller deice failure, deice boot inflation failures, and engine inlet icing.

Propeller Deice Failure

The electrically-powered deice pads on most propeller-driven aircraft are susceptible to wear and potential failure. For this reason, propeller-driven aircraft with a propeller deice system installed will have a cockpit indication of the amount of amps (amperes per hour) flowing to the propeller deice pads. You can recognize a propeller deice system failure by a propeller amps indication that is below normal (outside of the green arc). If you selects propeller deice on and notice that the propeller amps indication is below normal values, or indicates zero, you should exit icing conditions immediately. Additionally, you can rapidly cycle the propeller RPM from low RPM to high RPM (within operating limitations) to try to "sling" off any accumulated ice from the propeller.

Electricity is delivered from a stationary portion to the spinning propeller blades by the use of brushes, much like a slot car or electric train set delivers power to the car or train. These brushes wear with use and need to be replaced periodically. A brush that exceeds tolerances will not allow electricity to travel to the propeller blades and will result in failure of part or all of the propeller deice pads.

Deice Boot Inflation Failure

Deice boots have significant limitations, even when they are operating correctly. If any component of the deice boot system fails, you must exit icing conditions immediately and must consult the appropriate emergency checklist.

There are multiple possible failures in the deice boot systems. In most cases, there is little in the form of cockpit indications of deice boot failures. The pilot must watch the "ice shedding" process to ensure the deice boots are working properly after each activation. If the deice boots do not inflate normally, there may be backup methods of activating the boots. Refer to emergency checklists and the aircraft POH for specific actions to follow in the case of deice boot failures.

Engine Inlet Icing

Although not directly an ice system failure, the blockage of the air inlet as a result of ice buildup is another potential concern for aircraft operating in icing conditions. Excessive ice blocking the engine air inlet could lead to a decrease in performance and ultimately an engine failure. Most multi-engine aircraft—especially those certified for flight in known icing—will have an alternate air source that the pilot can select in the case of engine inlet ice blockage. If you suspect engine inlet icing—symptoms of which include engine surging, decrease in performance while in level cruise flight, or engine failure—follow the appropriate emergency checklist and memory items relating to alternate air selection. Again, leaving icing conditions is imperative in the case of suspected engine inlet icing.

Review 7

Environmental

1. How will the pilot be notified of a heater over-temperature condition? What is the appropriate pilot response to this?

2. What effect will small amounts of ice accumulation on the wing have on lift and drag?

3. What are some symptoms of engine inlet icing?

4. Describe the difference between anti-ice and deice systems.

5. Describe the types of propeller deice systems most commonly used on multi-engine aircraft.

6. Describe the heating system in the Piper Seminole.

7. Why are air conditioners not typically installed on light multi-engine aircraft such as the Piper Seminole?

8. What should the pilot do in the case of suspected carbon monoxide poisoning?

9. What should a pilot do if he or she inadvertently encounters icing in an aircraft that is not approved for flight into known icing?

10. In your own words, define "known icing."

11. What are the three categories of airborne ice protection systems?

12. How does the pilot determine if the aircraft is certified for known icing?

13. What is a vapor cycle machine?

Answers are provided in Appendix 2.

Oxygen

8

🔍 Chapter Focus: Oxygen Delivery Systems

The use of oxygen is required at the altitudes that multi-engine aircraft can operate. Some are pressurized for comfort and convenience; these often have oxygen systems available as a backup, even though they are not legally required to have oxygen available unless they are operated under 14 CFR Part 121 or Part 135.

Pilots need to understand, then, how common oxygen delivery systems operate. The systems can be either portable or built in to the aircraft for convenience and they vary widely—from the type of mask used, to the amount of oxygen provided, and the rate of flow of the oxygen. In this chapter, multi-engine oxygen systems are explored, as well as the proper actions related to them in emergencies or abnormal conditions.

Key Terms

(in the order they appear in this chapter)

continuous flow oxygen system

pressure-demand oxygen system

aviator's breathing oxygen

diluter-demand oxygen system

oxygen regulator

Rate of Oxygen Flow

The main consideration with oxygen delivery systems is the rate of oxygen flow sent to the oxygen mask. The first option provides oxygen in a continuous flow to the mask through a *continuous flow oxygen system*. This type of oxygen delivery is most commonly found in passenger oxygen systems. The next option for delivery is called a demand system, which provides a flow of oxygen only when the user is inhaling and will stop the flow of oxygen when the user exhales. This type of system is the most common one used for crew oxygen delivery.

Another method for controlling rate of oxygen flow is the *pressure-demand oxygen system*. These systems are capable of providing oxygen to the user under pressure. When you are "pressure breathing" (i.e., breathing oxygen from a pressure-demand oxygen system) you feel the same sensation as if sticking your head out the window of a vehicle while traveling on a freeway. Air is forced into the lungs without effort (a passive process). The user has to force air out of the lungs (with active effort) in order to complete the breathing cycle. This is completely opposite of the normal breathing process and it can make pressure breathing feel unnatural and uncomfortable. The purpose of pressure breathing is to increase the partial pressure of the oxygen in the lungs, thereby allowing the user to operate at much higher altitudes than is achievable with normal-rate-of-flow oxygen systems. Pressure-demand systems are required when operating above 40,000 feet.

Aviator's breathing oxygen: A type of oxygen supply that meets certain standards to ensure it is safe to be taken to altitude. Storage methods vary and it can be gaseous, liquid or solid.

Amount of Oxygen Flow

Also an important consideration with oxygen delivery systems is the amount of oxygen that is sent to the pilot. Oxygen delivery systems come in two varieties with regards to the amount of flow: diluter-demand oxygen delivery systems, and pure oxygen delivery systems.

A *diluter-demand oxygen system* will mix—or dilute—the oxygen delivered to the user with ambient cabin air from directly near the oxygen mask. The purpose of a diluter oxygen delivery system is to save oxygen. The diluter system has a regulator that detects the ambient air pressure and mixes an appropriate amount of oxygen depending on that air pressure. These systems generally provide all ambient air (no oxygen) below 8,000 feet and provide pure 100% oxygen at or above 34,000 feet. In between these altitudes, the diluter system will adjust the amount of oxygen the user needs depending on ambient air pressure. All diluter systems allow the pilot the option of selecting 100% oxygen regardless of ambient air pressure.

A pure oxygen delivery system will provide 100% oxygen to the user at all times, unlike diluter-demand oxygen systems which mix ambient cabin air with oxygen. These systems are less complex than diluter-demand systems, but the oxygen supply is used at a faster rate.

Oxygen Masks

An important component of these systems is the oxygen mask itself. There are three common types of oxygen masks in use today: the nasal-cannula type, the oral-nasal mask with rebreather bag, and quick-donning oral-nasal masks.

Nasal-Cannula Masks

The nasal-cannula system is most common in portable oxygen systems (Figure 8-1). Nasal-cannula masks deliver the oxygen to the user's nostrils using plastic tubing and an ergonomic nose-piece, all held in place with straps that wrap around the head or ears. This type of oxygen mask is the most comfortable for prolonged use, but it can only be used up to 18,000 feet because the flow of oxygen is insufficient to provide adequate oxygen content in the lungs at higher altitudes.

The flow of oxygen in a nasal-cannula may be weak and it is possible that the user would not recognize a condition in which flow to the mask stopped. For this reason, a pilot using a nasal-cannula mask should regularly check the flow of oxygen to the mask to ensure oxygen is still flowing. Most oxygen systems have a flow meter somewhere in the oxygen line, which makes it easy to check the rate of flow.

Oral-Nasal Masks

Oral-nasal masks are designed to cover both the user's nose and mouth (Figure 8-2). The masks can form a tight seal around the user's face and thereby direct a more consistent flow of oxygen. Passenger oxygen delivery systems are most commonly oral-nasal masks with a built-in rebreather bag. The user must simply put the mask on over their nose and mouth and breathe normally. The bag does not need to inflate in order for oxygen to be flowing.

Again, some of these oxygen delivery systems provide a weak flow of oxygen and the user should regularly check the flow meter to ensure oxygen is flowing.

Oral-nasal masks come in many different shapes and sizes depending on their intended use. Passenger oxygen masks tend to be of very basic construction and do not provide a complete seal around the user's nose and mouth, whereas pilot oxygen masks fit very tightly and completely seal around the nose and mouth.

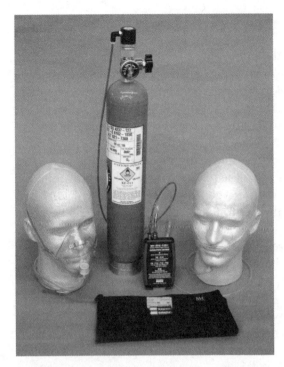

Figure 8-1. Continuous flow oxygen system with nasal-cannula (right) and oral-nasal (left) masks.

Figure 8-2.
Continuous flow mask with rebreather bag.

Quick-Donning Masks

Quick–donning oxygen masks are a type that the user can put on within five seconds or less (Figure 8-3). These types of masks are provided to the crew and generally offer a very tight seal to the user's face. It can actually be quite uncomfortable to wear these masks for a long period of time. These masks are intended to provide the user with quick access to oxygen in the case of inadvertent sudden pressurization problems.

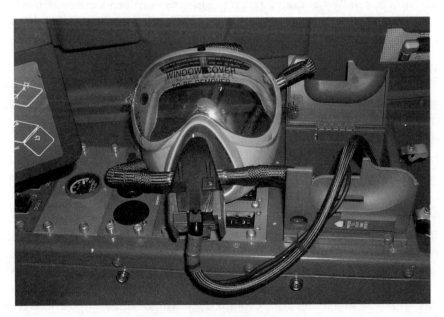

Figure 8-3. Quick-donning mask.

Tips for Use of Oxygen Systems

When oxygen use becomes necessary, the pilot should be aware of some important considerations. There are three grades of oxygen: aviation, medical, and welding oxygen, and in the U.S., medical and welding oxygen generally meet aviation requirements and can be used in aircraft. Aviator's breathing oxygen needs to be 99.9% pure to prevent freezing in the supply line. The aviator's breathing oxygen used in aircraft oxygen systems has very little moisture—less than 0.09%. This means that the prolonged use of oxygen will tend to dry out the user's mouth and nose.

Oxygen mask users must make certain that the mask forms a tight seal around the nose and mouth to ensure consistency with oxygen quantity and flow. Facial hair creates an added challenge to proper sealing of an oxygen mask and should be taken into consideration.

It's also important to realize that pure oxygen mixed with petroleum creates the possibility of fire; even petroleum-based products such as lip balm or other skin care products can be potential hazards.

Most crew oxygen masks will have a built-in microphone to allow the pilot to continue radio communications while wearing the mask. This microphone must be turned on with a switch located somewhere in the cockpit, and you must be able to locate this switch very quickly. When the use of oxygen is required, put the mask on and then establish communication.

Preflight Preparation of Oxygen Systems

Before flying an aircraft with an oxygen system, you must ensure that the system is in proper condition for use. In a few cases, pilots have attempted to use oxygen in flight and found that the system wasn't working properly. This can have catastrophic consequences, especially if the pilot is unaware that the oxygen system isn't functioning properly.

Each oxygen system will require a slightly different preflight check, so follow those recommended by the manufacturer. The preflight procedures generally share a common thread and likely will follow a checklist called the "PRICE" check: Pressure, Regulator, Indicator, Connections, Emergency, as follows below.

Pressure

The first concern with oxygen delivery systems is the quantity of oxygen. Oxygen is stored in pressurized containers and the easiest method of determining how much oxygen is in the container is by measuring its pressure. The pressure of the oxygen depends on outside air temperature, so you will have to refer to a pressure chart for the specific oxygen tank.

Regulator

Most operations choose to use 100% oxygen at all times. The reasoning for this is that when you need oxygen, you will be assured of 100% oxygen and it will not be diluted.

The next thing to check is the *oxygen regulator*. The regulator is what is responsible for sending oxygen from the container to the masks. Ensure that the oxygen masks are properly attached to the regulator and that the regulator is set to the desired position—normal or 100%. If "normal" is selected, the oxygen will be diluted.

It may also be desirable to cycle through the possible regulator positions to ensure each function works properly.

Indicator

Oxygen delivery systems usually will have a flow meter to indicate whether oxygen is available in the mask. Flow meters may be located right at the regulator or in the oxygen line leading from the regulator to the mask. If oxygen is reaching the mask from the storage tank, the flow meter will be green.

Connections

Ensure that all oxygen hose connections are secure and in the appropriate location. Leaks can be felt or heard and must be secured before flight. You can also be alerted to possible leaks in the oxygen system by an oxygen quantity that is unusually low. Try to have the oxygen tank filled at night prior to putting the aircraft in the hangar and check the quantity in the morning to locate possible leaks. Oxygen lines can get punctured or damaged in many possible areas without the pilot being aware.

Emergency

The final necessary preflight check is to ensure that the oxygen available is ready for quick use in case of an emergency. This is most commonly referring to passenger oxygen, and so should include proper preflight briefing to passengers of how and when to use the oxygen. Additionally, it is common for flight crews to check the emergency function of the crew oxygen masks. In the case of quick-donning masks, you should ensure that the mask is ready and fits properly. Put the mask on and adjust it if needed to ensure the microphone in the mask is working properly, and then restore the mask to its quick-donning location. Some pilots will also take this opportunity to clean the mask using alcohol wipes.

It is the responsibility of the PIC to ensure passengers are properly briefed on how to use oxygen. Information to cover includes the locations of masks, how to properly place the mask on your head, and how to ensure oxygen is flowing.

Regulations Relating to Oxygen

Different FAA oxygen requirements apply depending on the type of operation:

- 14 CFR §91.211 defines the oxygen requirements for aircraft operating under 14 CFR Part 91 (Figure 8-4).
- 14 CFR §135.89 defines the requirements for use of oxygen while FAR 135.157 defines the oxygen equipment requirements for aircraft operating under 14 CFR Part 135.
- 14 CFR §§121.331, 121.329, and 121.333 outline the oxygen requirements for aircraft operating under 14 CFR Part 121.

Pilots must be aware of and familiar with the oxygen regulations relating to their type of operation. Figure 8-4 shows a breakdown of oxygen requirements by altitude.

Unpressurized Aircraft Oxygen Requirements	
Cabin altitudes of 12,500 (MSL) up to and including 14,000 (MSL)	Required for crewmembers for duration of flight greater than 30 minutes.
Cabin altitudes above 14,000 (MSL) up to and including 15,000 (MSL)	Required for crewmembers for entire duration of the flight.
Cabin altitudes above 15,000 (MSL)	Required for crewmembers and all occupants.
Pressurized Aircraft Oxygen Requirements (in addition to requirements above)	
Aircraft altitudes above FL250	10-minute supply of oxygen for each occupant for use in the event of an emergency descent caused by a loss of cabin pressure.
Aircraft altitudes above FL350	One pilot at the controls must wear and use oxygen. Exception: If there are two pilots and the aircraft is equipped with quick-donning oxygen masks (can be placed on the face with one hand within 5 seconds), this requirement does not apply until operating at aircraft altitudes above FL410.
Aircraft altitudes above FL410	One pilot at the controls must wear and use oxygen for the entire duration of the flight above this altitude.

Figure 8-4. Oxygen requirements by altitude (from 14 CFR §91.211).

Use of Oxygen in Flight

If an aircraft is equipped with an oxygen delivery system, the pilot should follow the manufacturer's recommended procedures as each system varies in layout and operation. Follow FAA regulations relating to the use of oxygen in flight.

Hypoxia

If you have oxygen equipment on board and are feeling any symptoms relating to hypoxia, don the oxygen mask and descend to a lower altitude immediately. Hypoxia has an insidious onset and any symptoms should be taken seriously.

The symptoms of hypoxia are:★

- Change in visual acuity
- Feeling tired and fatigued
- Headache
- Euphoria
- Tingling in fingers and toes
- Shallower breathing

★*Symptoms will vary by individual.*

Hypoxia is a condition in which the body is deprived of adequate oxygen, resulting in degraded mental and physical performance. There are a few potential causes of hypoxia, the most common of which is breathing air at reduced barometric pressure. For example, a pilot in an unpressurized aircraft at 18,000 feet will be experiencing approximately half of the barometric pressure felt at ground level.

Emergencies

In the case of an emergency relating to the airplane's oxygen delivery systems, follow the manufacturer's recommended checklist procedure. In most cases, manufacturers will suggest an emergency descent to an altitude at which the use of oxygen is not needed (a recommended altitude is 10,000 feet). Emergency descent procedures are typically the following:

1. Reduce power to idle.
2. Select propeller controls full forward.
3. Select landing gear down.
4. Pitch the aircraft for V_{LE}.
5. Recover at safe altitude.
6. Be careful not to exceed gear retraction speeds.

Review 8
Oxygen

1. Explain diluter-demand, pressure-demand, and continuous flow oxygen systems.

2. Describe the preflight procedures relating to an oxygen system.

3. Define hypoxia.

4. How does a quick-donning mask work?

5. What regulation covers the oxygen requirements for aircraft operating under 14 CFR Part 91?

6. How does aviator's breathing oxygen differ from regular oxygen?

7. At what pressure altitude is oxygen required for crewmembers for the entire flight?

8. How is pressure breathing different from normal breathing, using the oxygen system?

9. What is the maximum altitude that a nasal-cannula oxygen mask is effective? Why is this limitation in place?

10. How can the pilots continue to communicate with ATC while using oxygen masks?

Answers are provided in Appendix 2.

Flight Instruments, Avionics, and Warning Systems

9

Chapter Focus on Modern Aircraft Avionics

In recent years, technological advancements have provided accurate sensing and monitoring capabilities to smaller general aviation aircraft that were previously limited to large transport aircraft. This has resulted in a "modernization" of aircraft cockpits, in both single and multi-engine aircraft. This chapter is geared towards familiarizing you with the modern cockpit.

The concepts discussed in this chapter are not unique to multi-engine aircraft; therefore, it follows a slightly different format from other chapters where the focus is on the differences between multi- and single-engine aircraft. Instead, here we will furnish an overview of the modern cockpit: types of engine indication and warning systems, the components in heading and attitude reference systems, cockpit displays, and some of the navigation capabilities of today's modernized aircraft.

Key Terms

(in the order they appear in this chapter)

primary flight display (PFD)

multi-function display (MFD)

horizontal situation indicator (HSI)

global positioning system (GPS)

air data computer (ADC)

attitude and heading reference system (AHRS)

Know Your Avionics Installations

Avionics packages vary greatly from one type of aircraft to the next, so be familiar with the operation of the particular avionics package on the aircraft you are flying. Use the POH, supplements, and commercial training to learn about the specific avionics setup use in the aircraft you are operating.

Digital engine indication systems are becoming more common in general aviation aircraft. These systems are capable of providing explicit details about fuel burn, cylinder head temperatures (CHT), exhaust gas temperatures (EGT), and leaning information. Engine indication systems can be found on the primary flight display (PFD) and multi-function display (MFD) or on a separate engine indication system (EIS). Most manufacturers of engine indication systems have videos and computer-based instruction software available to help you become familiar with the functions of their systems. Take the time to get comfortable with your particular system prior to your first flight.

Hardware

Glass cockpit installations generally consist of a *primary flight display* (PFD) and *multi-function display* (MFD). Most general aviation instrument panels are too small to accommodate more than one PFD and one MFD.

The PFD displays all of the traditional flight instruments in digital format. The airspeed and altimeter are tapes instead of a clock-like ("round-dial") analog instrument. The instruments are set up in a "T" pattern with the airspeed, altitude, and VSI as overlays on the attitude indicator. The heading is displayed on a *horizontal situation indicator* (HSI), which combines the heading and navigation information into one instrument. This setup reduces scanning fatigue while providing the pilot with a tremendous amount of information to increase the safety of flight (Figure 9-1).

One myth regarding glass cockpits is that "more is better." More information is a good thing, but more important than the quantity of information is having the appropriate information at the correct time. Glass cockpits can provide pilots an increased level of safety and situational awareness, but pilots still needs to understand what is being received, and how and when to use it. Figure 9-2 shows a PFD with the corresponding equivalent "traditional" instruments pointing to where the same information is contained in the glass–version display.

To understand how a glass cockpit works, the pilot needs to know what hardware is feeding flight information to the PFD and MFD screens. The PFD and MFD are merely displays; the information shown on them is coming in from various sources.

Figure 9-1. Examples of PFDs, in an Avidyne glass panel (left), and a Garmin version (right).

The PFD is an LCD screen that provides basic attitude and heading reference information along with other pertinent flight-related information. The upper portion of the PFD provides pitch, altitude, airspeed, and vertical speed information. The lower portion provides heading information and is laid out similar to a traditional horizontal situation indicator (HSI).

Figure 9-2. Primary flight display: Comparison of glass cockpit display and traditional instruments.

In some installations, the controls of the *global positioning system* (GPS) are integrated right into the PFD and MFD (e.g. Garmin G1000); in others, the GPS units are stand-alone devices that are controlled independently of the PFD and MFD. The POH and avionics supplements for your specific aircraft will contain system integration diagrams that show the interconnections between the PFD, MFD, and other avionics. In studying the integration diagrams, ask yourself if a system fails, how does it affect both the operation of the other systems and the flight itself?

Air Data Computer

The *air data computer (ADC)* is connected to the aircraft's pitot-static system and outside air temperature probe. In contrast to traditional flight instrumentation, instead of sending the static and pitot (ram air) pressure to the individual instruments, the pressure is sent to the ADC computer which calculates and displays airspeed, altitude, and vertical speed (Figure 9-3).

Attitude and Heading Reference System

The *attitude and heading reference system (AHRS)* in a glass cockpit aircraft replaces the traditional gyroscopic instruments. The AHRS uses solid-state gyros and a *magnetometer* to provide the pilot with attitude, heading, and rate information. The AHRS is made up of 3 rate sensors, one for each axis (vertical, lateral, and longitudinal). Inside each rate sensor is a solid state gyro that consists of small tuning forks which sense motion. The processing software in the AHRS combines all the outputs and displays the aircrafts attitude in relation to the horizon. The attitude indicator has been designed to be the largest instrument displayed, with pertinent data layered on the top, to the side, and below. This design reduces scanning, which decreases pilot fatigue.

The magnetometer supplies the AHRS with attitude and heading information electronically. The magnetometer has a flux valve installed in the wing, which sends heading information to the PFD. The magnetometer senses the earth magnetic field and delivers the information directly to the AHRS and displays the aircrafts current magnetic heading.

The MFD is an LCD screen that provides supplemental flight information which can include weather information, engine indication, flight plan information and even a pictorial instrument approach chart. The MFD has multiple functions, hence the name. You should take time to familiarize yourself with all of the possible screen configurations of the multi-function display.

Magnetometer. An instrument used to measure and plot the strength and direction of the Earth's magnetic field.

 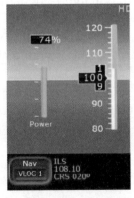 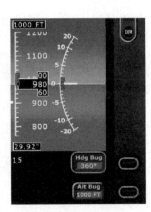 

Figure 9-3. The ADC (a) feeds static and ram air pressure information to the displays on the PFD (b, c, d).

(a) Air data computer (Teledyne).

(b) Glass cockpit PFD airspeed indicator.

(c) Glass cockpit PFD altimeter.

(d) Glass cockpit PFD VSI.

Backup Flight Instruments

The backup (or standby) airspeed indicator and altimeter work as traditional instruments in that static and dynamic pressure is sent to each individual instrument, where the information is mechanically processed and depicted (Figure 9-4). The backup attitude indicator can be powered by the electrical system or a vacuum system. The electrically driven backup attitude indicator is powered by a dedicated battery which is activated by the pilot in an emergency. Battery power will typically last 30-60 minutes.

Figure 9-4. PFD with standby/backup instruments underneath

Traditional Instrument Layout

Traditional instrument layouts in multi-engine airplanes (Figure 9-5) are very similar to their single-engine counterparts, with some differences:

- The pitot-static system is virtually the same as in single-engine aircraft, except that some multi-engine aircraft have a separate static port for the autopilot system.
- The vacuum system is similar, except that multi-engine aircraft have two engine-driven pumps and a manifold check valve.
- Most multi-engine aircraft have a horizontal situation indicator (HSI) and flight director (FD) (Figure 9-6).

Figure 9-5. Traditional flight deck layout.

Figure 9-6. Left: a standard horizontal situation indicator (HSI); right: flight director (FD).

Horizontal Situation Indicator (HSI)

The horizontal situation indicator (HSI) is a combination of slaved heading indicator and VOR/localizer. By overlaying the VOR/Localizer course on the heading indicator, the pilot is provided with much better situational awareness as to where the aircraft is in reference to the selected radial or localizer course. The HSI can be displayed in a mechanical form (Figure 9-7). The digital representation of the HSI is called an electronic HSI (EHSI) (Figure 9-8). Another benefit of the EHSI is the ability to change the view from 360 degrees to arc view, or other varying ranges of view.

One of the distinct benefits of an HSI is that it removes the possibility of reverse sensing. Reverse sensing occurs when the heading and the OBS setting are greater than 90 degrees from each other. It is possible, however, to have reverse sensing on an HSI when tuned to a localizer. To avoid this, be sure to set the head of the needle to the inbound course for the localizer.

An EHSI allows the possibility of overlaying a bearing pointer on the heading indication (*see* Figure 9-8). A bearing pointer is simply a needle that always points to a station or fix. When a bearing pointer is placed over heading information the pilot will have very valuable positional information. Bearing pointers will not work with a localizer frequency.

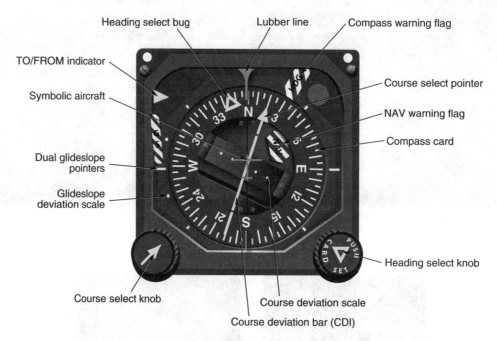

Figure 9-7. Mechanical HSI.

Figure 9-8. Electronic HSI.

Avionics Operations

Due to the specific, detailed, and complex nature of avionics packages in multi-engine airplanes, pilots must consult the POH and avionics supplements for detailed descriptions and operational insight. A multitude of avionics simulators can be used to learn knobology (the functions of buttons and switches) and even simulate flights. Using this type of software will reduce the amount of time spent heads-down in flight, thus increasing safety.

System Failures and Warnings

Air Data Computer Failure

If the ADC has a hard failure (i.e., the unit itself fails) three large red "X" marks are placed over the airspeed, altimeter, and vertical speed instruments (Figure 9-9).

Realize that a "red X"-indicated ADC failure is a *hardware* failure (of the computer itself, like when an iPhone won't turn on or your TV quits). The red X is not an indication that the pitot tube is icing over, or the static port becoming blocked; if those situations occur, different instrument indications will be affected. Both traditional and glass cockpit airplanes are susceptible to blocked pitot tubes and static ports but ADC hard-failure is within the unit itself.

In the event the ADC fails, the backup airspeed indicator and altimeter should be used (*see* Figure 9-4).

Figure 9-9. Failure of the air data computer (ADC).

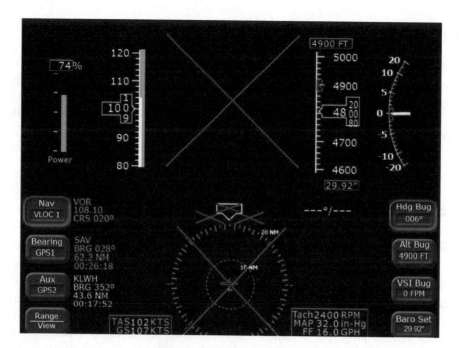

Figure 9-10. AHRS failure.

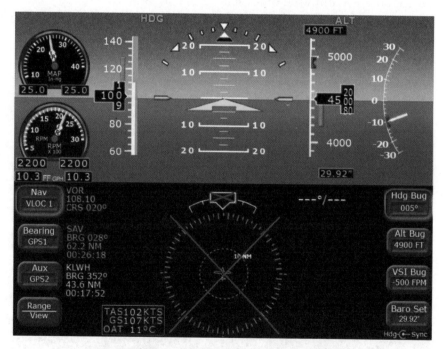

Figure 9-11. Flux gate failure (magnetometer).

Attitude and Heading Reference System Failure

A backup attitude indicator is installed to use in case the AHRS fails. Backup attitude indicators are either vacuum or electrically driven. If electrically driven, they are usually installed with a sole-source backup battery that powers the attitude indicator even if the aircraft's primary battery is depleted.

If the AHRS fails, red "X" marks are placed over the attitude and heading indicators (Figure 9-10). If only the magnetometer fails, a red X will be displayed over the heading information, but attitude information will remain (Figure 9-11).

During an AHRS failure, the pilot should immediately use the backup attitude indicator for pitch and bank information. Lateral navigation is more difficult; typically radar vectors from ATC will be the pilot's best option, along with backup GPS navigation sources.

Traditional Pitot/Static System Failures

Traditional pitot static system failures vary based on three possible conditions: (1) if the pitot-tube is blocked, (2) if the drain hole is blocked, and (3) if the static port is blocked. Any one of the three conditions can be present individually or occur at the same time. Awareness of these conditions requires familiarity with the particular aircraft's pitot-static system. The chart below describes conditions the pilot may encounter, the instrument(s) affected, the indication(s), and the action the pilot should take.

Condition	Instrument Affected	Instrument Indication	Pilot Action
1. Pitot tube blocked, drain hole open*	Airspeed	Reads "0"	Turn on pitot heat, use standby airspeed indicator
2. Pitot tube blocked, drain hole blocked	Airspeed	Acts like an altimeter	Turn on pitot-heat, use standby airspeed indicator
3. Static port blocked	Airspeed, altitude, vertical speed	Airspeed—inaccurate Altitude—frozen Vertical speed—no change	Open alternate static source, use standby airspeed and altimeter if this does not correct condition

* Some pitot-tubes are not designed with a drain hole that is accessible to the pilot (in the Beechcraft Baron, for example). In this case, the maintenance technician services this during inspection of the pitot-static system.

Review 9

Flight Instruments, Avionics, and Warning Systems

1. What does AHRS stand for?

2. What instruments are part of the AHRS?

3. What does ADC stand for?

4. What instruments are part of the ADC?

5. How are ADC and AHRS failures communicated to the pilot?

6. What is the appropriate response to an AHRS or ADC failure?

7. How are backup instruments typically powered?

8. How does an AHRS system sense heading information?

9. How can a pilot become comfortable with the operation of the avionics installed on the airplane he or she is flying?

10. What is one benefit of an HSI over a traditional VOR installation?

Answers are provided in Appendix 2.

Section II

Aerodynamics

A multi-engine aircraft adheres to all the same basic aerodynamic principles of lift, weight, thrust and drag as a single-engine aircraft. The greatest aerodynamic differences between single- and multi-engine aircraft have to do with the distribution of weight in relationship to the aircraft centerline and the ratio of excess thrust to weight.

The chapters in this section cover relevant subjects to increase your understanding of multi-engine aerodynamics, V-speeds and their definitions, properties specific to multi-engine aircraft, single-engine aerodynamics, and aircraft certification as it relates to single-engine operations in a multi-engine aircraft.

10 Multi-Engine Aerodynamics and V-Speeds

11 Flight Characteristics of Single-Engine Operation

12 Single-Engine Aerodynamics and Operations

Multi-Engine Aerodynamics and V-Speeds

10

🔍 *Chapter Focus: Applying Aerodynamics to Multi-Engines*

It is essential to have a grasp of fundamental aerodynamics when transitioning to a multi-engine aircraft. This chapter will review basic aerodynamic principles and introduce related topics specific to multi-engine aircraft.

You will learn to readily describe the four forces of flight as they relate to multi-engine aircraft. Also, you'll be able to list and define V-speeds, explain induced airflow and its importance in a multi-engine aircraft, and identify the difference between a conventional and counter-rotating multi-engine aircraft.

Key Terms

(in the order they appear in this chapter)

lift
induced airflow
weight
thrust
thrust vectors
drag
conventional twin
counter-rotating twin
performance speeds

Aerodynamics of Multi-Engine Aircraft

You are already familiar with the aerodynamic principles of lift, weight, thrust and drag (Figure 10-1), and as already stated, multi-engine aircraft in flight adhere to these same principles. However, you must now think about these factors along with the increased number of variables that influence each aerodynamic force in a multi-engine airplane.

Lift

Lift as produced by the wings of the aircraft follows the principles of fluid dynamics established by Daniel Bernoulli and the physical laws discovered by Isaac Newton. Pilots must now consider how the wing is different in a single-engine compared to a multi-engine aircraft.

Bernoulli's principle states that as velocity of a moving fluid (liquid or gas) increases, the pressure within the fluid decreases.

Newton's Third Law of Motion: For every action, there is an equal and opposite reaction (of an equal amount, in an opposite direction).

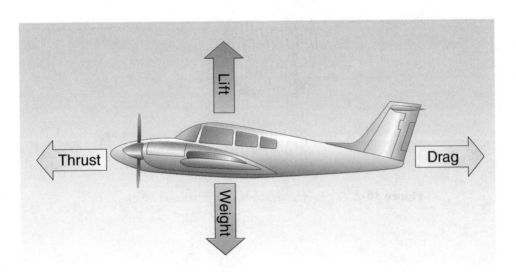

Figure 10-1. The four forces of flight.

In a single-engine aircraft, the entirety of the wing can be used to produce lift. In a typical multi-engine aircraft, however, each wing must also support an engine. If you take a bird's-eye view of a single-engine wing and a multi-engine wing, you will notice a significant difference. Aerodynamically, on the single-engine, the entirety of the wing is designed to produce lift, whereas the multi-engine wing must not only produce lift but also incorporate an engine nacelle and support the additional weight. As a result, when comparing a single-engine aircraft and multi-engine aircraft with similar fuselages, the multi-engine aircraft will have a larger wing span.

Induced Airflow

Another consideration relating to lift in multi-engine versus single-engine aircraft is the importance of *induced airflow*. In a single-engine aircraft with the engine mounted on the front of the plane, the accelerated air from the propeller or prop wash is primarily directed over the fuselage and then over the elevator or stabilator (Figure 10-2). On the multi-engine aircraft the propwash will flow directly over the wings, having a direct effect on the lift produced by the wings (Figures 10-3 and 10-4). The effect of the propwash on the elevator or stabilator is contingent on the empennage configuration and the direction of propeller rotation.

Induced airflow is also affected by changes in power settings. As power settings are changed, the amount of induced airflow over the wings and the resulting lift produced will also be changed. If power is increased, induced airflow increases and thus lift increases. If power is decreased, induced airflow decreases and thus lift decreases.

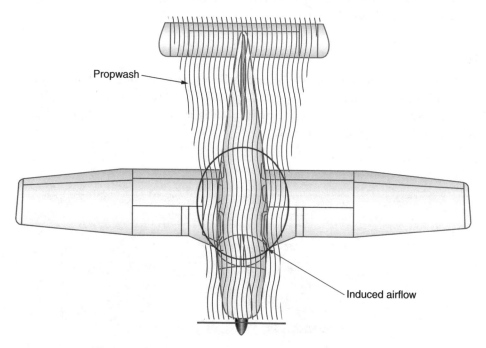

Figure 10-2. Single-engine propwash and induced airflow.

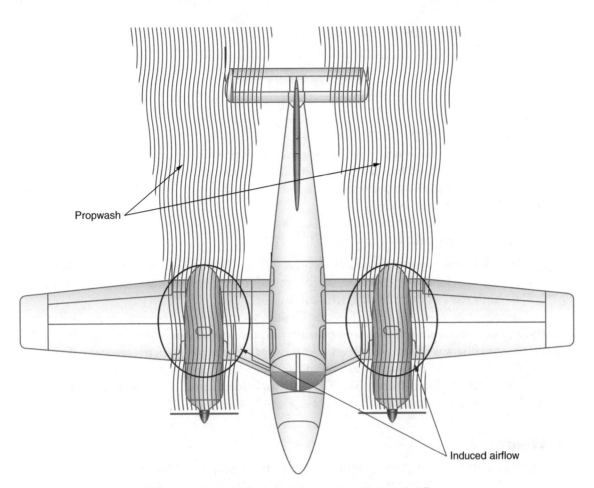

Propwash

Induced airflow

Figure 10-3. Multi-engine propwash and induced airflow.

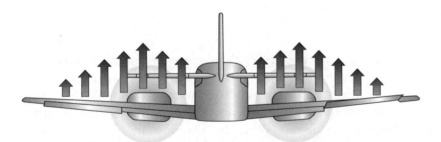

Figure 10-4. Induced airflow lift vectors.

To further analyze the phenomenon of induced airflow, examine the lift equation:

$$L = C_L \times \tfrac{1}{2}\rho V^2 \times S$$

L = Lift (pounds)

C_L = Coefficient of lift

(This dimensionless number is the ratio of lift pressure to dynamic pressure and area. It is specific to a particular airfoil shape and, above the stall, it is proportional to angle of attack.)

V = Velocity (feet per second)

ρ = Air density (slugs per cubic foot)

S = Wing surface area (square feet)

This relationship between power settings (V) and lift will require special consideration during flare and roundout, as abrupt reductions in the power settings could lead to high rates of descent and firm landings.

The effect of induced airflow is not limited to the wings of the aircraft. When flying a conventional-tail multi-engine aircraft, the accelerated slipstream produced by the propellers will also flow over the elevator, impacting the effectiveness of the elevator. In a multi-engine aircraft with a T-tail, the overall impact of the induced airflow is minimal and the elevator or stabilator effectiveness depends more directly on the speed of the aircraft.

Weight

Compared to a similar single-engine aircraft, a multi-engine will weigh more, due in part to the additional engine and corresponding ancillary equipment. This fact will have an effect on performance of the aircraft on a number of different levels, but most notably increased takeoff and landing distance compared to a single-engine aircraft.

Thrust

Thrust is the force that opposes drag. Thrust in excess of drag allows an aircraft to climb. A multi-engine aircraft has a significant increase in two-engine climb capability even with the increased weight associated with its additional engine.

Thrust and the resulting performance are two topics that play a major part in understanding a multi-engine aircraft. When both engines are operating as intended, the thrust vectors operate as they would on a single-engine aircraft. But complexity comes into play when an engine fails. The thrust vector changes location and lessens. In this situation, there are not perfectly opposing forces, but are a combination of forces that must all work together to keep the aircraft aloft or produce the least amount of sink.

If you are operating a twin aircraft that has lost an engine, you have lost 50 percent of your aircraft's thrust and approximately 80 percent of its performance. If this statement initially seems confusing, further reading will help to clarify it.

thrust vector: the resultant forward aerodynamic force produced by a propeller blade as it forces a mass of air rearward.

Thrust Vectors

When considering the *thrust vectors* for a multi-engine aircraft, the thrust comes from both engines and a total thrust must be determined and depicted to show the opposition to drag. In level flight in a counter-rotating aircraft when both engines are producing the same amount of thrust, the total thrust will be felt straight ahead much like in a single-engine aircraft. In a conventional aircraft, you might encounter some minor left-turning tendencies from the propeller factor, but for the most part the total thrust vector will be directed straight ahead (Figure 10-5).

counter-rotating aircraft: see pages 129–130.

However, in the event of a full or partial power loss, the four forces will be impacted. The resulting drag from the engine that lost power will result in a yaw and roll of the aircraft towards the failed engine.

propeller factor or P-factor: see page 134.

Drag

Drag is the force that opposes thrust. When flying a twin-engine aircraft, decreasing drag is a priority. Whether it is through retraction of the landing gear, closing of cowl flaps, or reduction in propeller RPM, a twin-engine pilot will attempt to minimize this drag and in turn maximize aircraft cruise speed and overall performance. Knowledge of drag and techniques to reduce it are important elements in becoming a proficient multi-engine pilot. Whether it is through propeller feathering or use of the zero sideslip technique (discussed in Chapter 11), reducing drag as a multi-engine pilot can be more complex, but it will play an integral role in aircraft control.

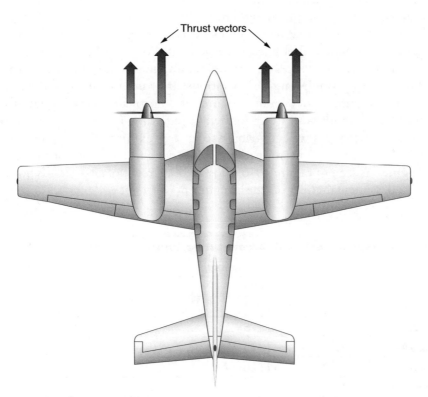

Figure 10-5. Thrust vectors in a conventionally-rotating twin.

The Four Forces and Engine Failure

When a multi-engine aircraft suffers from an engine failure, each of the four forces are impacted. The four forces will not act in direct opposition to each other, but they will operate in differing levels of asymmetry. Three of the four forces will have substantial changes.

Windmilling and feathering: see page 37 in Chapter 3.

Thrust—or more accurately horsepower—in the propeller-driven twin will be reduced by 50 percent in the case of a complete engine failure. Though a windmilling propeller will provide a large increase in drag, a secured and feathered engine will also produce parasite drag along with an increase in induced drag from the control inputs used to maintain directional control of the aircraft.

Considering the lift equation (page 126), as an aircraft loses an engine and the pilot attempts to maintain altitude, the aircraft will naturally lose airspeed and the pilot will pitch to the airspeed for maximum performance, or V_{YSE}. Velocity is also lost through the absence of induced airflow over the wing with the inoperative engine. These reductions in velocity will be counteracted through an increase in angle of attack, in order to regain the required lift to counteract the weight.

Weight will see the least amount of change in the event of an engine failure, but you should consider the slight changes in weight due to the increased G load, from the recommended bank used to counteract a failed engine. Another consideration with regards to weight is fuel burn management. Some multi-engine aircraft will have maximum fuel imbalance limitations and it's important to maintain proper fuel management during single-engine operations. If a fuel imbalance limitation does exist for your aircraft, it may be due to aircraft controllability or limitations of the autopilot. Please consult your POH for details regarding fuel imbalance limitations.

Overall, these changes will contribute to an approximate performance loss of 80 percent. This loss is an important variable pilots need to consider prior to securing a failing engine. As seen in Figure 10-6, a loss of 50 percent of an aircraft's horsepower will have a detrimental effect on the aircraft's performance.

Performance Loss of Representative Twins with One Engine Out			
Aircraft type	*All-engine climb (fpm)*	*Single-engine climb (fpm)*	*Percent loss*
Beech Baron 58	1,694	382	80.70
Beech Duke	1,601	307	80.82
Beech Queen Air	1,275	210	83.53
Cessna 310	1,495	327	78.13
Cessna 340	1,500	250	83.33
Cessna 402B	1,610	225	86.02
Cessna 421B	1,850	305	83.51
Piper Aztec	1,490	240	83.89
Piper Navajo Chieftain	1,390	230	83.45
Piper Pressurized Navajo	1,740	240	86.21
Piper Seneca	1,860	190	89.78

(Source: "Always Leave Yourself an Out" by Richard N. Aarons)

Figure 10-6. Multi-engine performance loss examples.

Conventional and Counter-Rotating Multi-Engine Aircraft

Compared to single-engine aircraft, multi-engine aircraft are designed with multiple goals in mind for the operators:

- Increased climb performance
- Increased cruise speeds
- Increased ability to operate at higher altitudes
- Increased safety through redundancy

All of the increases and potential benefits from having a second engine can also lead to increased expenses in the form of additional engines, engine parts and maintenance. One way in which a manufacturer may attempt to minimize the additional parts and maintenance costs is by using the same engine on both wings. This configuration is called a conventional twin.

In multi-engine propeller aircraft, the engines will be mounted either counter-rotating, where the propeller blades turn toward each other, or conventionally, where the propeller blades turn in the same direction. Of course there are exceptions, and a good example is the Cessna Skymaster in which the engines are mounted in the front and aft of the aircraft.

Conventionally Rotating Twin

In a *conventional twin* aircraft, both propellers will turn to the right (clockwise) from the pilot's perspective (Figure 10-7). This engine mounting defines a number of specific characteristics of a conventional twin, including left-turning tendencies, a critical engine, and single-engine controllability (all of which are covered in detail in Chapter 11).

Installing the same engine on both sides of the aircraft can have significant financial benefits. As an individual or a commercial operator, maintenance and parts can be a large expense for an aircraft. Maintenance with the conventional twin will be the same for both engines. This will reduce the complexity of the procedures and minimize aircraft downtime. In addition, since both engines use the same the parts, parts inventory for those engines will be reduced compared to the counter-rotating type of twin.

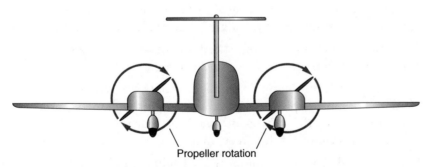

Propeller rotation

Figure 10-7. Propeller rotation in a conventional twin.

Counter-Rotating Twin

In a *counter-rotating twin*, the propellers will turn toward each other from the perspective of the pilot (Figure 10-8). The left engine will turn clockwise and right engine will turn counterclockwise. Compared to the conventional twin, many of the results or characteristics are opposite in the counter-rotating twin. In normal two-engine operations, the counter-rotating twin will not have left-turning tendencies, it will not have a critical engine as defined by the FAA, and single-engine controllability will be the same regardless of which engine has lost power.

A significant drawback of counter-rotating twins is seen in their operating expenses and maintenance costs. The engines are different and thus may have different parts and maintenance procedures, both of which will incur higher costs for the owner or operator.

The FAA defines a **critical engine** *as the engine whose failure has the most adverse effect on directional control.*

See also Figure 11-8, showing equal "rudder arms" on a counter-rotating twin.

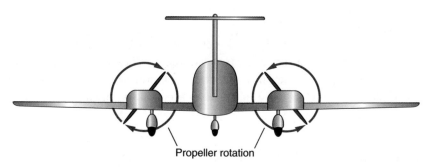

Propeller rotation

Figure 10-8. Propeller rotation in a counter-rotating twin.

Performance Speeds

Performance speeds, or V-speeds as they are commonly known to pilots, are indicated airspeeds that a pilot uses every flight. When flying a multi-engine aircraft, you will use many familiar speeds that are also used in a single-engine aircraft, but you must familiarize yourself with new V-speeds specific to operating multi-engine aircraft.

V_A Design maneuvering speed. The maximum speed at which full, abrupt control movement can be used without overstressing the airframe.

V_{FE} Maximum speed with the flaps extended. The upper limit of the white arc.

V_{NE} Never-exceed speed. Operating above this speed is prohibited since it may result in damage or structural failure. The red line on the airspeed indicator.

V_{NO} Maximum structural cruising speed. Do not exceed this speed except in smooth air. The upper limit of the green arc.

V_{S1} Stalling speed or minimum steady flight speed obtained in a specified configuration. For most airplanes, this is the power-off stall speed at the maximum takeoff weight in the clean configuration (gear up, if retractable, and flaps up). The lower limit of the green arc.

V_{S0} Stalling speed or the minimum steady flight speed in the landing configuration. In small airplanes, this is the power-off stall speed at the maximum landing weight in the landing configuration (gear and flaps down). The lower limit of the white arc.

V_X Best angle-of-climb speed. The airspeed at which an airplane gains the greatest amount of altitude in a given distance. It is used during a short-field takeoff to clear an obstacle.

V_Y Best rate-of-climb speed. This airspeed provides the most altitude gain in a given period of time.

V_{LOF} Lift off speed. The speed at which the airplane leaves the surface.

V_{LE} Landing gear extended speed. The maximum speed at which an airplane can be safely flown with the landing gear extended.

V_{LO} Landing gear operating speed. The maximum speed for extending or retracting the landing gear if using an airplane equipped with retractable landing gear.

V_R Rotation speed. The speed that the pilot begins rotating the aircraft prior to lift-off.

V-Speeds for Multi-Engine Aircraft

V_{MC} Minimum control airspeed with the critical engine inoperative. This is the minimum flight speed at which a light, twin-engine airplane can be satisfactorily controlled when an engine suddenly becomes inoperative and the remaining engine is at takeoff power.

V_{MCG} Minimum control speed on the ground. This is the minimum calibrated airspeed during the takeoff run at which, when the critical engine is suddenly inoperative, it is possible to maintain control of the airplane using the rudder control alone. This speed is not required to be published in aircraft certified under 14 CFR Part 23 and less than 6,000 pounds.

V_{YSE} Best rate-of-climb speed with one engine inoperative. This airspeed provides the most altitude gain in a given period of time in a light, twin-engine airplane following an engine failure.

V_{XSE} Best angle of climb speed with one engine inoperative. The airspeed at which an airplane gains the greatest amount of altitude in a given distance in a light, twin-engine airplane following an engine failure.

V_{SSE} Safe, intentional one-engine inoperative speed. The minimum speed to intentionally render the critical engine inoperative.

Review 10

Multi-Engine Aerodynamics and V-Speeds

1. Describe induced airflow.

2. Explain the difference between a conventional and a counter-rotating twin.

3. Describe the pros and cons of a conventional twin and a counter-rotating twin.

4. List the advantages of a multi-engine aircraft compared to a single-engine aircraft.

5. Explain how an engine failure will impact each of the four forces.

6. What is the significance of V_{MC} speed in a multi-engine aircraft?

   Answers are provided in Appendix 2.

Flight Characteristics of Single-Engine Operations

11

🔍 *Chapter Focus: Rudder Authority and the Critical Engine*

Flying a multi-engine aircraft under normal operations with both engines operating will be very similar to flying a single-engine aircraft. The greater performance characteristics of a multi-engine aircraft may require adjustments—but overall, flying is flying. This is the reason that only a small portion of your total multi-engine flight training time will be with both engines operating. This will hold true whether you are pursuing your initial multi-engine rating or a type certificate. Once you've adjusted to the speed at which operations happen, it will be time to practice abnormal and single-engine operations.

This chapter will familiarize you with the basic aspects of single-engine operations, and the performance effects when one engine is inoperative in flight. You will learn to determine the critical engine, review the law of the lever and explore how it applies to "single-engine" operations, and summarize the factors that define an engine as the "critical" one.

Key Terms

(in the order they appear in this chapter)

critical engine
rudder authority
center of gravity (CG)
weight
arm
moment
P-factor
thrust centerlines
torque
accelerated slipstream
propwash
spiraling slipstream

Rudder and Single-Engine Operations

When understanding the aerodynamic properties of a multi-engine aircraft operating on one engine, the rudder plays a very large role. You must consider how the aircraft responds to different configurations and pilot inputs.

Critical Engine

The FAA defines a *critical engine* as the engine whose failure has the most adverse effect on directional control. In a conventional multi-engine aircraft, identifying the critical engine is a simple but important step in planning.

Four different characteristics aid in determining the critical engine in a conventional multi-engine aircraft: P-factor, torque, spiraling slipstream and accelerated slipstream. How these factors are quantified deals directly with rudder authority. In our discussion in this chapter, *rudder authority* refers to the ability of the rudder to counteract yaw caused by a power loss on one engine. As defined by the FAA, determining the critical engine requires identifying the engine whose failure has the greatest effect on directional control, and the main primary flight control for directional control is the rudder. In order to have a clear understanding about how the authority of the rudder is affected by changes in the forces, we must begin with a review of the simple lever.

Simple Lever Action

In aviation, the law of the lever is introduced during the first foray into weight and balance. The formula **weight × arm = moment** is used every time you calculate an aircraft's *center of gravity* (CG). This easy formula can also aid in understanding the significance of rudder authority when you experience an engine failure.

Before getting into more detail, it's important to understand a few key terms:

Weight: For the purpose of weight and balance calculations, the weight of the aircraft is used. In determining rudder effectiveness, the force measurement of foot-pounds of pressure applied to the rudder is used. As there is no foot-pounds indicator in most aircraft, the values used will be for demonstration purposes only.

Arm: The measurement from a reference datum to a specific location on an aircraft is called the arm and is usually measured in inches. The arm used in some of our examples will be based on the distance from the CG to the rudder. Other arms will also need to be considered when determining the amount of moment needed. Depending on the scenario, arms will be measured in relationship with the thrust vector of an engine, with the rudder, or with the center of gravity.

Moment: In our examples, the moment is a force that causes rotation. When dealing with an engine failure, the required moment is used to counteract the rotation produced by the loss of power on one engine and the subsequent drag and asymmetric thrust.

The ability of the rudder to generate adequate moment under specific conditions through the law of the lever will be referred to as rudder authority. When the rudder has more authority, the available rudder deflection to control the aircraft's direction is greater; with less rudder authority the opposite is true. In multi-engine operations, the more rudder authority, the higher the chance that directional control can be maintained.

Now we can more closely examine the factors that define a critical engine and how they impact rudder authority.

P-Factor

P-factor: the left-turning tendency of an airplane at high angles of attack and high power settings. The descending blade on the right produces more thrust than the ascending blade on the left, creating asymmetrical thrust vectors. This causes the aircraft to yaw to the left; it occurs when the aircraft's longitudinal axis is in a climbing attitude in relation to the relative wind.

Propeller factor—or *P-factor* as it is more commonly known—can explain some of the left-turning tendencies felt in a single-engine aircraft. P-factor is present when the aircraft is at a positive wing angle of attack, which causes the descending propeller blade to have a higher angle of attack compared to the ascending blade. Since the propeller is an airfoil, the higher angle of attack on the descending blade will produce greater lift, or in the horizontal plane, greater thrust. This will result in asymmetric thrust and a left-turning tendency.

How the loss of a critical engine affects the performance and handling characteristics of the multi-engine aircraft can be further explained through a basic understanding of the lever.

The lever is one of the fundamental machines. Simply put, the longer the lever arm, the more easily it performs work. Looking at the engines of a multi-engine aircraft in relationship to its center line gives you an idea of the lever arms for each engine. (The center line of the aircraft is an extension of the center of gravity location—it is here, at the center of gravity, about which the aircraft yaws.) Applying an understanding of single-engine aircraft to a multi-engine aircraft, you can see how the mean thrust vector will be essentially the same for each engine (Figure 11-1). In this ideal situation, the failure of either engine would have the same yaw-and-roll effect.

But with the loss of excess thrust in an engine failure, the pilot is highly likely to adjust aircraft pitch angle higher to maintain altitude and/or to attain best single-engine rate-of-climb speed (V_{YSE}). Anytime the angle of attack is increased, the thrust vectors of each propeller blade shift the mean thrust vector toward the descending blade. This will have the effect of increasing the distance from the mean thrust vector to the aircraft centerline. With the positive wing angle of attack, the descending blade's angle of attack (because the propeller is also an airfoil) will become greater, and by comparison the ascending blade's will become smaller.

Figure 11-2 illustrates how propeller thrust vectors and mean thrust vectors change whenever there is an increased angle of attack. Applying the principle of the simple lever, we see the arm from the center of the descending blade to the aircraft center is greater from right engine and smaller from the left engine. The overall effect of this is that the aircraft turns to the left due to the shift of the mean *thrust centerlines* and the resulting force—that is, the "longer lever" or the more effective thrust arm (on the right engine). In normal two-engine operations, this left-turning tendency can be easily counteracted though simple applications of right rudder or right rudder trim.

With the larger arm on the right engine, a failure of the left engine would require more rudder force to counteract the yaw and roll produced by the right engine and its more effective rudder arm (Figure 11-3).

In the case of counter-rotating propellers, the loss of either engine would require similar rudder force to maintain directional control. This is because the arm between the mean center of thrust for either engine is the same distance from the aircraft centerline. A loss of the right engine will impart the same yawing moment as the loss of the left engine, the only difference being the direction the aircraft yaws. In contrast, a conventional multi-engine aircraft would experience a greater yawing moment if the left engine were to fail than if the right engine were to fail (Figure 11-3). This is because the arm between the mean center of thrust for the right engine and the aircraft centerline is larger than that of the left engine.

thrust centerline: imaginary line through the center of propeller hub, perpendicular to the plane of propeller rotation.

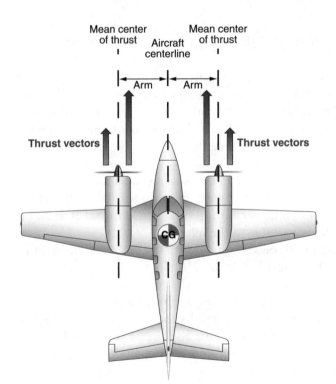

Figure 11-1. Thrust vectors, mean center of thrust, and thrust arms in straight-and-level flight.

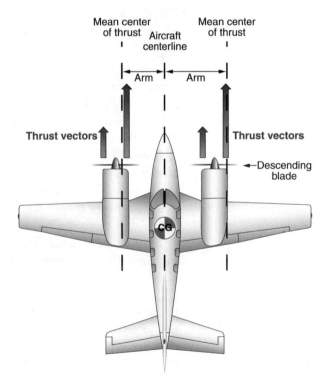

Figure 11-2. Thrust vectors, mean center of thrust shifted, and thrust arms with positive angle of attack (conventional twin).

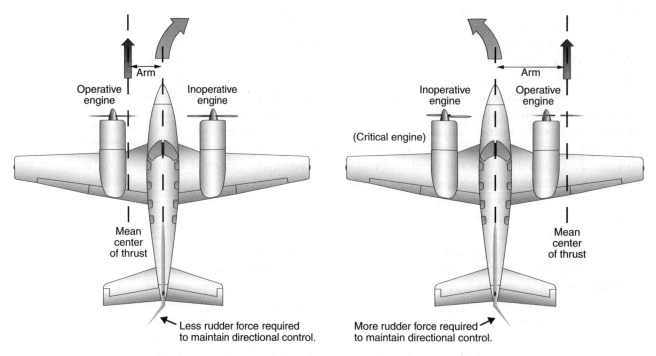

Operative engine · Inoperative engine · Arm · Mean center of thrust · Less rudder force required to maintain directional control.

Inoperative engine · (Critical engine) · Operative engine · Arm · Mean center of thrust · More rudder force required to maintain directional control.

Figure 11-3. Yawing forces created during single-engine operations.

Torque

Much like P-factor, you have experienced the effect of *torque* while flying single-engine aircraft.

Newton's third law of motion easily demonstrates the effect of torque. The law simply states that for every action there is an equal and opposite reaction. In the case of a propeller-driven aircraft, the action is the propeller turning to the right. The opposite reaction is the aircraft yawing to the left. As the propeller turns at a higher RPM, the effect of torque will be more pronounced.

Looking at the effect of torque in relation to the critical engine, there is not a simple arm difference to calculate as there was with the P-factor, but rudder authority is still the way to determine which one is the critical engine. Figure 11-4 shows the action and reaction of the forces with both engines running on a conventional twin. The action will be to the right and the reaction is to the left.

If the left engine fails, the aircraft will roll and yaw toward the failed engine, requiring a right rudder correction by the pilot. Yet with even closer scrutiny, the torque effects shown in Figure 11-4 reveal that not only does the pilot have to counter the effects of the failed engine with right rudder, but torque from the operating engine is also causing the aircraft to turn to the left (potentially more so due to the higher power setting during single-engine operations). This additional amount of rudder pressure will reduce the overall rudder authority and restrict the pilot's ability to counter any additional left-turning tendencies.

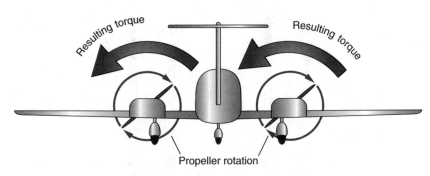

Figure 11-4. Torque resulting from propeller rotation.

On the other hand, if the right engine fails, the aircraft will roll and yaw toward the failed engine requiring a left rudder correction by the pilot. Referring once again to Figure 11-4, the aircraft will roll and yaw to the right toward the failed engine, but the torque which you had to fight during the takeoff is now assisting your efforts to counteract the effects of the failed engine. This assistance will require reduced rudder pressure and instead will increase the overall rudder authority and *enhance* your ability to counter any additional left-turning tendencies you come upon.

As a result, the loss of the left engine leads to a reduction in rudder authority as compared to a right engine failure. This fact fits nicely into the definition set forth by the FAA for a critical engine.

The critical engine is the engine whose failure has the most adverse effect on directional control.

Accelerated Slipstream

The relationships of *accelerated slipstream* and P-factor to rudder authority are very similar. As covered previously when discussing P-factor, in positive wing angles of attack, the descending blade of the propeller has a higher angle of attack. This not only will produce the increased thrust for the descending blade but will also acceler-ate more air rearward from the descending blade compared to the ascending blade (Figure 11-5). And as seen when we discussed induced airflow and the lift equation, if the air has a higher velocity, the resulting lift will be increased (Figure 11-6).

As shown in Figure 11-6, the accelerated air on the side of the descending blade of each engine depicts a higher lift vector versus the ascending blade. When the distance from the higher lift vector on the right engine (A) is compared to the distance on the left engine (B), we see a difference in the length of the arms. As a result of the larger arm length on the right engine, the relative rolling tendencies during an engine failure would be greater with a loss of the left engine than with the loss of the right engine.

Therefore in the case of a left engine failure, accelerated slipstream can amplify the aircraft's roll and yaw to the left. The pilot needs to counteract the effects of the lost engine, and remain aware of decreasing rudder authority on top of the already existing P-factor and yawing tendencies.

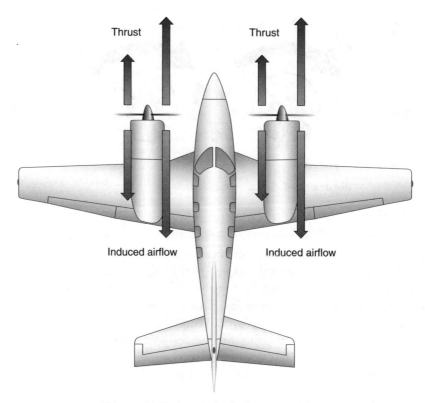

Figure 11-5. Accelerated slipstream airflow.

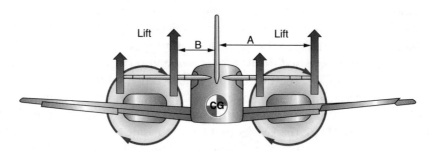

Figure 11-6. Accelerated slipstream and lift.

Spiraling Slipstream

As a propeller spins to the right, the *propwash* that is produced also spirals slightly to the right due to the rotational force of the propeller. This action on the left side of the aircraft will tend to wrap around the aircraft fuselage and ultimately impact the port side of the aircraft, imparting a slight left-turning force. With the right engine the spiraling propwash will behave in the same manner, but on that side there is no fuselage to wrap around and no subsequent impact to the rudder (Figure 11-7).

If the right engine on a conventional twin fails then the aircraft will predictably roll and yaw to the right. As the *spiraling slipstream* of the left engine impacts the rudder, it will assist in counteracting some of the yaw from the failed engine. This in turn will require less rudder pressure from the pilot and allow for increased rudder authority.

When the critical left engine fails, the slipstream now is simply windmilling into the air and not impacting the rudder at all. Because of this, a left-engine failure will require more rudder force compared to a right engine failure and will result in decreased rudder authority.

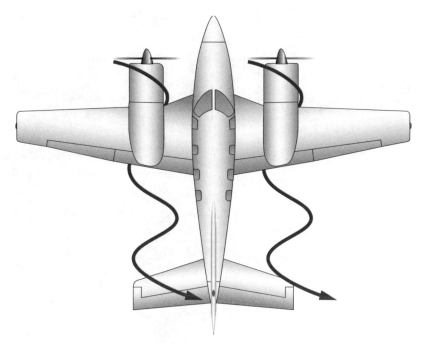

Figure 11-7. Spiraling slipstream.

Critical Engine in Counter-Rotating Aircraft

Looking at the four factors that make an engine critical, a theme arises. Each factor provides a type of unbalanced force upon the conventional type of twin aircraft, but when you put a counter-rotating aircraft into the same scenarios, none of these factors will cause one engine to be more critical than the other. The P-factor, torque, accelerated slipstream, and spiraling slipstream effects that make the left engine critical on a conventional multi-engine aircraft are no longer an issue on counter-rotating propellers. For example, the P-factor for an aircraft with counter-rotating propellers has identical rudder force requirements for the failure of either engine because the arm is the same distance from the centerline (Figure 11–8).

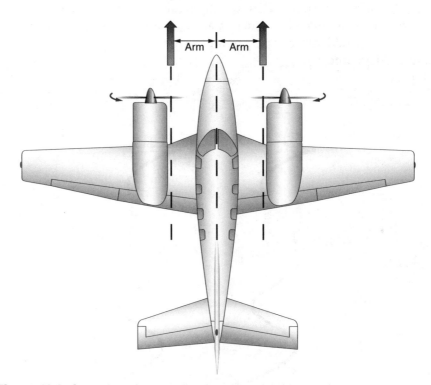

Figure 11-8. Counter-rotating propellers mean equal rudder-arm forces on each engine.

Review 11

Flight Characteristics of Single-Engine Operations

1. List the factors that determine a critical engine.

2. Summarize the law of the lever and its application to single-engine operations.

3. What is meant by rudder authority?

4. What is P-factor? Explain how it is used to determine a critical engine.

5. What is accelerated slipstream? Explain how it is used to determine a critical engine.

6. What is spiraling slipstream? Explain how it is used to determine a critical engine.

7. What is torque? Explain how it is used to determine a critical engine.

8. Does a counter-rotating aircraft have a critical engine? Why or why not?

Answers are provided in Appendix 2.

Single-Engine Aerodynamics and Operations

12

🔍 Chapter Focus for Engine-Out Operations

The discussion of rudder authority and critical engines in Chapter 11 naturally calls for further exploration of the factors affecting single-engine operations. This chapter will break down into three further categories under this subject: aircraft certification, in-flight operations, and single-engine (or, one-engine inoperative) performance.

To cover these additional factors, here you will learn about zero sideslip and techniques used to fly a multi-engine airplane with an inoperative engine. You'll learn how to discern what factors were used by the manufacturer to determine V_{MC} for your aircraft's certification (per 14 CFR Part 23). Finally, you'll identify how those aircraft certification factors affect operational V_{MC} and influence multi-engine aircraft performance.

It is important to note that when V_{MC} is determined per 14 CFR §23.149, aircraft performance is not a consideration; if a multi-engine aircraft is 6,000 pounds or less maximum weight and has a V_{S0} speed of 61 knots or less, there is no requirement for a positive single-engine rate of climb. In aircraft that do not meet these criteria, a number of additional requirements may need to be followed before certification. Further information for these types of multi-engine aircraft can be found in 14 CFR Part 23, which holds key regulations concerning multi-engine operations.

Key Terms

(in the order they appear in this chapter)

windmilling
directional control
zero sideslip
V_{MC}
service ceiling
absolute ceiling
single-engine absolute ceiling
single-engine service ceiling
horizontal component of lift
normally aspirated
keel effect
feathering propeller (feathered)
tail down force
ground effect
V_{MC} demonstration

Single-Engine Operations

Operating a multi-engine aircraft on one engine is one of the most important skills you must learn to become a successful multi-engine pilot.

Engine failures can happen during any phase of flight and the pilot's response may be different depending on many factors, including:

- Aircraft performance
- Environmental conditions
- Time in which to make a decision
- Altitude

These factors are a few of the many variables that the pilot-in-command (PIC) will need to consider in the event of an engine failure. The scenarios discussed in Chapter 14 are helpful in providing perspective on the many different ways to approach decision-making when operating a multi-engine aircraft.

When there is a loss of power on one engine, a multi-engine aircraft will behave in a predictable manner. The successful multi-engine pilot will likewise learn to behave in a predictable manner to maintain directional control and configure the aircraft for optimal performance, depending on the desired maneuver and the established emergency procedures from the aircraft manufacturer.

With the failure of one engine, the aircraft will respond by yawing and rolling toward the failed engine. Being aware of how induced airflow is affected by the engine failure will aid in understanding why these effects occur.

Induced airflow for the failed engine will be replaced by a *windmilling* propeller, producing a significant amount of drag and loss of lift. This increase in drag causes the aircraft to yaw into the dead engine, and the loss of lift will result in the aircraft rolling into the dead engine.

Keep in mind that not all engine failures are easily detectable. If the engine is experiencing a subtle or gradual loss of power, which could occur in the case of carburetor icing, the loss of airspeed, yawing and rolling may be difficult to recognize. A thorough understanding of the aircraft systems will be a significant advantage for the pilot in recognizing a failing engine. A low power setting, such as during a descent, may also make it difficult to detect an engine failure. Vigilant monitoring of the aircraft gauges and good system knowledge will again be to the pilot's advantage when suspecting an engine failure.

Flying with a Failed Engine

When presented with an engine failure, the pilot first and foremost must maintain *directional control* of the aircraft. Without directional control there is nothing else to consider. The FAA recommends that upon detecting an engine failure, the pilot should apply a combination of aileron and rudder to counteract the roll and yaw from the asymmetric forces of engine-out operations. Pitch should also be adjusted to maintain that of V_{YSE} or blue line on the airspeed indicator. Once the aircraft is under control, the pilot should utilize proper techniques to maximize the aircraft performance.

Coordinated flight with *zero sideslip*, where the aircraft is flown with the smallest profile to the relative wind, is a straightforward process when both engines are operating. Flying a multi-engine aircraft with an inoperative engine prohibits the pilot from meeting all the criteria of coordinated flight, but the technique of zero sideslip can be used to reduce drag and thus maximize performance. Zero sideslip is achieved through a combination of rudder and aileron. To best understand zero sideslip and how it is accomplished, you should first examine how the aircraft responds to rudder-only and aileron-only methods of single-engine operations.

Rudder Only

Maintaining the wings level and using only rudder, with the inclinometer centered, flying with only one engine operative will result in a moderate sideslip. This sideslip will result in slightly increased drag compared to the zero sideslip, and reduced performance. The largest negative resulting from this technique is in the form of V_{MC}. Rudder authority plays a large part in affecting V_{MC} speed. If only rudder is used to maintain the aircraft in straight flight with no help from the horizontal component of lift, the rudder authority is decreased and V_{MC} will be greatly increased. Tests have shown that V_{MC} may increase up to 3 knots for every degree of bank less than 5 degrees; that's a potential increase in V_{MC} of 15 knots (Figure 12-1).

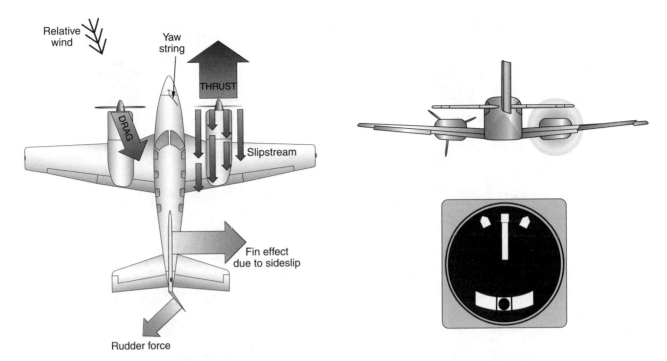

Wings level, ball centered, airplane slips toward dead engine. Results: high drag, large control surface deflections required, and rudder and fin in opposition due to sideslip.

Figure 12-1. Single-engine operations with wings level, ball centered.

Aileron Only

Bank angle and its horizontal component can be very helpful to V_{MC} speed. So helpful, in fact, that the FAA limits the maximum amount of bank during certification. On the other hand, bank and performance will have an opposite effect. Using only ailerons to maintain straight flight during single-engine operations, the pilot may need to use 8–10 degrees of bank. With no rudder input, the aircraft is in a large sideslip (remember the single-engine aircraft?). This sideslip increases the amount of frontal area of the aircraft into the relative wind, resulting in significant increases in drag, loss of lift due to blanketing, and a significant decrease in aircraft performance (Figure 12-2).

"Blanketing" (aerodynamic) refers to when the relative wind airflow is disturbed by another aircraft surface, which reduces control effectiveness of the "blanketed" flight control areas.

Zero Sideslip

Using just rudder will result in only a small detriment to performance but a significant increase in V_{MC}. Using only bank has shown to decrease the V_{MC}, but performance suffers. To get the best of both techniques—minimize V_{MC} and maximize performance—aircraft manufacturers will determine the zero sideslip for their aircraft. The combination of rudder and aileron will be determined by each aircraft manufacturer and will vary from plane to plane.

In general, the inclinometer will be positioned so it is deflected about one-half to one-third toward the operative engine. Bank will often be 2 to 3 degrees toward the operative engine. This placement of the rudder and aileron will allow the aircraft to achieve the smallest profile to the relative wind with no sideslip, and also maintain V_{MC} at a lower value compared to rudder-only operations. The result will be the optimal performance for climb or least amount of descent, with the propeller feathered and the aircraft at V_{YSE} (Figure 12-3).

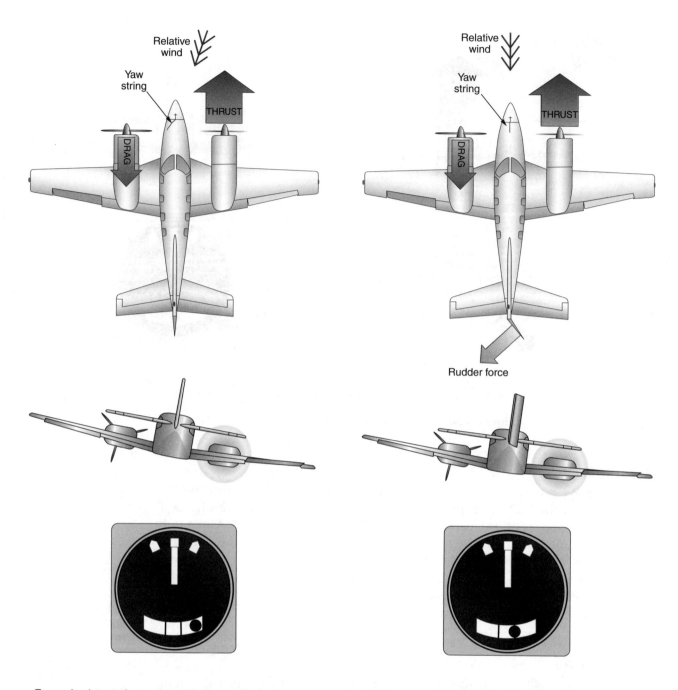

Excess bank toward operating engine, no rudder input. Result: large sideslip toward operating engine and greatly reduced climb performance.

Figure 12-2. Aileron-only method of single-engine operations.

Bank toward operating engine, no sideslip. Results: much lower drag and smaller control surface deflections.

Figure 12-3. Zero sideslip.

Remember that the aircraft V_{MC} is not determined using zero sideslip, but single-engine performance charts will often be based on the use of zero sideslip and the aircraft in the most favorable configuration.

Maximum Altitudes

When considering single-engine operations, maximum altitudes must also be understood. In addition to the *service ceiling* and *absolute ceiling*, a multi-engine aircraft will also have the single-engine service ceiling and the single-engine absolute ceiling.

The multi-engine aircraft will encounter the *single-engine absolute ceiling* when the aircraft can no longer climb with one engine inoperative. The *single-engine service ceiling* is the altitude at which the aircraft can no longer maintain a 50 foot-per-minute rate of climb with one engine inoperative. During preflight, the multi-engine pilot will determine the single-engine service ceiling factoring in the zero sideslip technique, the most favorable aircraft configuration, and V_{YSE}. This information can then be used for route planning and emergency alternatives.

absolute ceiling. *The altitude at which a climb is no longer possible.*

service ceiling. *The maximum density altitude where the best rate-of-climb airspeed will produce a 100-fpm climb at maximum weight while in a clean configuration with maximum continuous power.*

V_{MC} and Multi-Engine Certification

It is important to understand how multi-engine aircraft are certified. Part of the certification requirements define the parameters that exist when an aircraft is flown in single-engine operations at or above V_{MC}. In 14 CFR §23.149, the FAA defines V_{MC} as the calibrated airspeed at which, when the critical engine is suddenly made inoperative, it is possible to maintain control of the airplane with that engine still inoperative, and thereafter maintain straight flight at the same speed with an angle of bank of not more than 5 degrees. The method used to simulate the critical engine failure must represent the most critical mode of powerplant failure expected in service with respect to controllability. V_{MC} as set by the manufacturer is only a fixed airspeed at the exact conditions that existed during the certification process, and understanding what those factors and conditions are and how they vary is key to understanding single-engine operations.

V_{MC} is a speed determined by the manufacturer during the certification process of the aircraft following 14 CFR Part 23, which requires the manufacturer to determine the V_{MC} speed while adhering to a specific set of factors and conditions. According to 14 CFR §23.149, these factors are as follows:

1. Critical engine inoperative
2. No more than 5 degrees of bank
3. Maximum available takeoff power
4. Trimmed for takeoff
5. Flaps in the takeoff position
6. Landing gear retracted
7. Propeller controls in the recommended takeoff position
8. Most unfavorable weight (maximum takeoff weight)
9. Most unfavorable CG position
10. Out of ground effect
11. Maximum rudder force of 150 pounds to maintain control

A detailed elaboration on each of these factors follows, but also be aware that depending on your aircraft category and weight, more V-speeds may need to be calculated.

In addition to the requirement put forth by 14 CFR §23.149(a) for determining V_{MC}, for an aircraft with a maximum gross weight of 6,001 pounds or greater, the following conditions must be met in the landing configuration:

- Maximum available takeoff power initially on each engine
- Airplane trimmed for approach
- Airspeed of V_{REF}
- Approach gradient equal to the steepest used in the landing distance demonstration of 23.75 (landing distance from a height of 50 feet to a complete stop)
- Flaps in the landing position
- Landing gear extended
- All propeller controls in the position recommended for approach with all engines operating

V_{MCG}, or minimum control speed on the ground, only applies to aircraft (under Part 23) that are normal, utility or aerobatic multi-engine jets greater than 6,000 pounds or commuter category aircraft with 19 or less seats and 19,000 or less pounds.

In addition to the conditions and configurations needed for determining V_{MC}, the manufacturer must also select a speed at which the critical engine can safely be intentionally rendered inoperative, called V_{SSE}.

Flight Operation Effects on V_{MC}

V_{MC} as determined by the manufacturer is a calibrated airspeed calculated using very specific conditions. As a multi-engine pilot you will rarely, if ever, meet all the conditions set for aircraft certification. As such, V_{MC} in day-to-day multi-engine operations will be dependent on a number of factors and may be less than your V_{MC} red line, or even greater than, under some circumstances.

The diagram in Figure 12-4 shows how simple changes in altitude can affect the V_{MC} speed. It's important to also look at the other factors from the certification to see how they can be manipulated to change V_{MC}.

Using the factors established by the FAA for certification, the following section discusses how each affects the V_{MC} speed in everyday flight operations. As we look at these various factors, special attention will be given to rudder authority once again. Upon review of the FAA's definition, maintaining control of the aircraft and straight flight are given as part of the certification requirements. Aircraft control with the failure of an engine relies heavily on the rudder and its ability to counteract the additional yaw and drag that will be encountered.

The factors established by the FAA for aircraft certification will put the aircraft in the configuration that will result in the highest V_{MC} speed. Additionally, the speed generated will be sea-level calibrated airspeed.

Note: All statements about increasing or decreasing V_{MC} speed is in reference to the certification factors all remaining the same and is in relationship to the certified V_{MC} speed under the certificated

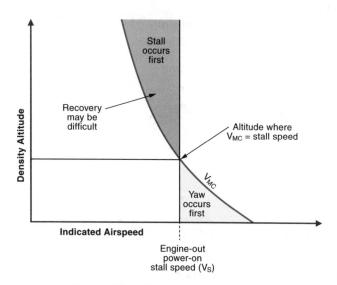

Figure 12-4. Relationship of V_{MC} to V_S.

conditions. The intention is to demonstrate that even changing just one of the factors will impact V_{MC} in the everyday flight regime.

1. Critical Engine Inoperative

The factors that make an engine critical are: torque, P-factor, spiraling slipstream and accelerated slipstream. During our discussion about these factors in Chapter 11, each one could be related back to the amount of remaining rudder authority after an engine failure—more specifically the failure of the critical engine. So the conclusion is that the critical engine will have greatest impact on rudder authority.

On the other side, the loss of the non-critical engine will not have all the negative effects of the loss of the critical engine, and V_{MC} would be decreased due to the increased authority of the rudder.

2. No More than 5 Degrees of Bank

V_{MC} is closely related to bank angle. The FAA states that for every degree of bank less than 5 degrees, V_{MC} could increase up to 3 knots. The same effect will hold true when increasing the bank angle greater than 5 degrees. V_{MC} would likely decrease, but at a substantial cost in terms of aircraft performance and overall aircraft safety.

In regards to rudder authority and bank angle, we must consider the components of lift generated in a bank. As bank is increased into the operating engine, the *horizontal component of lift* is also increased. This increase in the horizontal component of lift will in turn help to counter the coupled forces of rolling and yawing from the loss of an engine, which will reduce the workload of the rudder and increase the rudder authority (Figure 12-5). The less horizontal component of lift that is present, the less assistance is provided to the rudder and V_{MC} will increase accordingly.

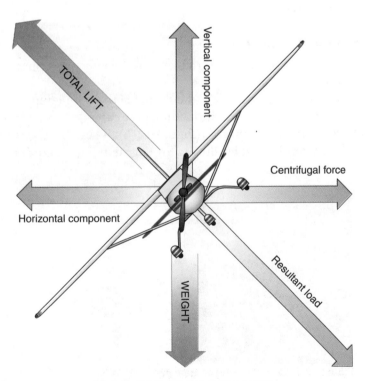

Figure 12-5. Forces during a turn.

3. Maximum Available Takeoff Power

A normally-aspirated engine is a non-turbocharged piston engine that uses ambient air for combustion.

Much of the information that was covered in Chapter 11 in the sections discussing the critical engine and induced airflow is applicable to this factor affecting V_{MC}. Considering a *normally-aspirated* engine, the maximum horsepower will be produced during takeoff due to the air density. This condition will produce the greatest amount of P-factor, torque, spiraling slipstream and accelerated slipstream.

As power is reduced on the engines through pilot input or through an increase in altitude, these critical engine effects will become less pronounced, and the amount of rudder needed to counteract the tendencies of the critical engine is less and rudder authority is increased. As a result, the V_{MC} speed will also decrease.

4. Trimmed for Takeoff

Trim has little to no effect on V_{MC} speed during flight operations.

5. Flaps in the Takeoff Position

Most piston-powered twin-engine aircraft will have a takeoff flap setting of zero degrees. How this setting ultimately affects the V_{MC} speed becomes clearer when we examine how extending flaps affects rudder authority.

The effect of flaps on V_{MC} speed is aircraft specific, but there are two theories that can be applied to the extension of flaps. The first theory is that when the flaps are extended, some of the induced airflow will be diverted over the rudder, which will make the rudder less effective and thus increase the V_{MC} speed.

The other theory is that as the flaps are extended, they extend down into the relative wind and provide a stabilizing effect similar to that of the keel a boat. This stabilizing effect would in turn lessen the yawing tendencies brought on by an engine failure and require less rudder, which increases rudder authority and results in a decrease to the V_{MC} speed.

6. Landing Gear Retracted

The effect of extended landing gear is the same as the effect described in the second theory for extension of flaps.

When the landing gear is extended, they provide the stabilizing *keel effect*. When observing the aircraft head on with the landing gear extended, you can see how they could act as little "vertical stabilizers" (Figure 12-6). These little vertical stabilizers lessen the workload on the rudder during an engine failure, and as a result would decrease V_{MC}.

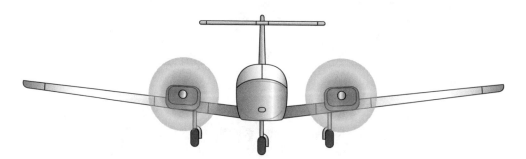

Figure 12-6. Extended landing gear acts as little "vertical stabilizers."

7. Propeller Controls in the Recommended Takeoff Position

When the critical engine is suddenly made inoperative during the determination of the V_{MC} speed for certification, the aircraft will be left with a windmilling propeller, which will produce a large amount of drag and corresponding yaw and roll into the dead engine. Counteracting this will be a large burden on the rudder and the pilot. Because of the large amount of rudder force required to counteract a failed, windmilling critical engine, the amount of rudder force is limited to that of an average pilot of 150 pounds (Number 11 on the list) for certification.

Therefore the ability to *feather* a propeller can prove to be a very useful feature for a twin-engine aircraft. As the propeller is feathered, the drag produced is substantially reduced. A windmilling propeller is said to have the same drag effect as though a flat plate were mounted to the engine instead of a propeller.

Feathering the propeller will result in a significant reduction in the amount of rudder required to maintain the aircraft in straight-and-level flight. The reduction in required rudder as a result of the feathered propeller will have the effect of reducing the V_{MC} speed. By leaving the propeller in the "recommended takeoff position," when the engine fails the propeller will likely windmill. For certification requirements, this results in the highest V_{MC} speed.

8. Most Unfavorable Weight (maximum takeoff weight)

For aircraft certified under 14 CFR Part 23, V_{MC} is determined at the most unfavorable weight. V_{MC} increases as weight is reduced. To understand this, let's look once again at the horizontal component of lift.

As the bank is increased into the operating engine, the lift will split into vertical and horizontal components with the resultant being total lift (Figure 12-5). As discussed under factor 2 (maximum 5 degrees of bank) above, the horizontal component of lift will counteract the rolling and yawing forces relieving some of the work that is done by the rudder. If the weight of the aircraft is reduced, the horizontal component of lift would also be reduced because the amount of total lift required would be decreased.

Another theory as it applies to weight is that of Newton's first law of motion. This law simply states that a body in motion tends to stay in motion and a body at rest will tend to stay at rest unless acted upon by an outside force. Once an object is moving it has inertia, and with a greater mass comes greater inertia. As inertia increases as a result of weight and acceleration, the force required to displace that object becomes greater (Newton's second law of motion). It is under this premise that an aircraft at a heavier weight will have greater inertia and hence a greater resistance to change of direction. This will in turn have a stabilizing effect on the aircraft and require less rudder to counteract the yaw and roll of the failed engine, and therefore reduce the V_{MC} speed.

9. Most Unfavorable CG Position

The CG of an aircraft is where the movement about the three axes will take place (Figure 12-7).

When an aircraft is rolled or yawed, it moves about the CG. Referring back to the Chapter 11 discussion of the rudder and its relationship to the lever action of a simple machine, a few facts emerge. As the arm is decreased the same force will produce less result, and as the arm is increased the same force will produce greater result.

When the CG is moved aft, this decreases the arm for the rudder inputs, reducing the rudder authority. As a result, more rudder deflection will be required to counteract the forces of roll and yaw toward the failed engine.

An aft center of gravity is considered the most unfavorable for a multi-engine aircraft. Figures 12-8a and 12-8b illustrate the differences in the arm from the CG to the rudder: with a forward CG the arm is longer (Figure 12-8a), making rudder inputs more effective, requiring less rudder force. The case is reversed with a rearward CG (Figure12-8b)—the arm is smaller, the rudder is less effective, requiring more rudder force to maintain straight flight.

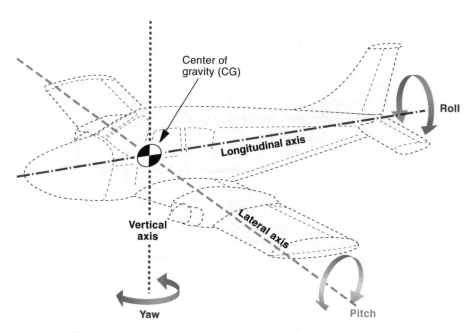

Figure 12-7. The three aircraft axes of flight with center of gravity.

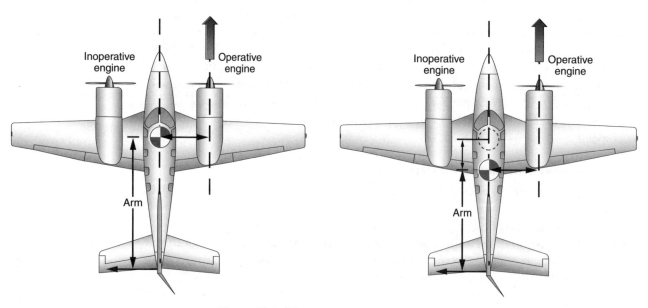

Figure 12-8. Effect of CG location on yaw.

10. Ground Effect

Similar to trim, being in ground effect has a negligible effect on V_{MC} speed.

11. Maximum Rudder Force of 150 Pounds to Maintain Control

See the explanation above under factor 7 (Propeller Controls in the Recommended Takeoff Position).

V_{MC} Factors and Your Aircraft's Performance

What can you as the pilot do to maximize your aircraft's performance during single-engine operations? The same factors reviewed above for certification of V_{MC} also are applied to maximize performance during single-engine operations.

Engine Inoperative

It is important to note that during certification and our discussion of the in-flight V_{MC} speed, the critical engine was specifically used due to its effect on rudder authority and influence on V_{MC} speed. When discussing performance and referencing performance charts, however, manufacturers do not discriminate critical or non-critical engines. With this fact in mind, it should be apparent that the loss of an engine will have a substantial negative impact on overall aircraft performance. As mentioned in Chapter 10, with the failure of an engine an aircraft will lose 50 percent of its horsepower but up to 80 percent of its performance. This can be demonstrated by calculating the climb performance with two engines operating versus one engine operating.

Figure 10-6 (page 128) shows the significant loss of climb performance during an engine failure.

No More than 5 Degrees Bank

As previously referenced, any bank less than 5 degrees may result in an increase in V_{MC} speed of about 3 knots. This maximum bank of 5 degrees for certification may have a large impact on aircraft performance.

Depending on the aircraft manufacturer and their recommended conditions for maximum performance, a bank of less than 5 degrees may be required. This specified bank and an associated inclinometer deflection results in zero sideslip. In zero sideslip, the aircraft will be in the most favorable condition as it relates to performance. For more details, see the Zero Sideslip section under "Flying with a Failed Engine" earlier in this chapter.

Maximum Available Takeoff Power

Maximum performance, within engine and propeller limitations, will be attained through maximum manifold pressure and propeller RPM. Anything less would be a decrease in the performance capabilities of the aircraft. Simply reducing the throttle and propeller to anything less than maximum will have a negative impact on aircraft performance.

Trimmed for Takeoff

Although the physical workload on a pilot flying an aircraft that is out of the recommended trim setting may be noticeable, the overall effect on performance would be negligible.

Flaps in Takeoff Position

Depending on the aircraft and the normal takeoff configuration, flaps could have a positive or negative effect.

The majority of multi-engine aircraft will use a zero-degree flap setting for takeoff. The zero-degree setting will also be the flap configuration that will give the best overall aircraft performance. So if an aircraft uses zero-degree flaps for takeoff, then a flap setting greater than zero degrees would decrease overall aircraft performance.

If an aircraft is required to use flaps for normal takeoff, the effect on performance can be either positive or negative.

Using the required flaps for takeoff, the takeoff performance should be better than if flaps were not used. This increase in aircraft performance will be short-lived because once airborne, the extended flaps will have a negative impact on climb and cruise performance.

If an aircraft is required to use flaps for takeoff, then overall performance of the aircraft will increase as the flaps are retracted. On the other hand, if flaps were greater than that required for takeoff, performance would most definitely decrease.

Landing Gear Retracted

The retraction of the landing gear eliminates a significant amount of parasitic drag, giving the aircraft a key configuration component for optimal performance. Multi-engine aircraft with retractable landing gear will have little to no streamlining to reduce parasite drag when the landing gear are lowered, so a significant decrease in performance should be expected.

Considering how performance is generally measured, the best climb performance will occur when there is the greatest difference between thrust and drag. As previously discussed, with a failed engine, performance could decrease around 80 percent in the most favorable configuration. This performance would be further reduced when drag is introduced from lowering the landing gear. An increase in drag would mean an increase in the power required to maintain the desired performance. This necessary increase in power will decrease the excess thrust available and reduce overall aircraft performance.

Propeller Controls in Recommended Takeoff Position

In the event of an engine failure, ensuring the propeller is in the feathered position is an important step in configuring the aircraft for the best single-engine performance. With the propeller in the recommend takeoff position, the propeller will not be feathered (assuming no auto-feather feature) and will windmill. A windmilling propeller can create substantial drag, causing single-engine performance to suffer. For example, with a propeller windmilling, the Piper Seminole could see a performance decrease of about 200 feet per minute.

Most Unfavorable Weight

An aircraft that weighs less than maximum takeoff weight will have better performance compared to the aircraft at maximum. As is evident from aircraft performance charts, when an aircraft is heavier, takeoff ground roll increases, climb performance decreases, and cruise speed is less.

To aid in explaining the reason why performance decreases with weight, simply look at the four forces. Lift opposes weight and thrust opposes drag. As weight increases, the amount of lift required to oppose it increases. With greater lift comes greater induced drag, and as drag increases the amount of excess thrust is decreased. As excess thrust is decreased the overall performance of the aircraft is diminished. In single-engine operations, the excess thrust margin may already be small and increases in weight can reduce it even further.

Most Unfavorable CG Position

As the CG moves aft, the amount of nose-down tendency is reduced and less tail-down force will be required to stabilize the aircraft (Figure 12-9).

Tail down force is also known as negative lift. When lift is produced downward it essentially increases the "weight" of the aircraft and the aircraft will need to produce enough lift to counteract the actual weight in addition to the downward force produced by the tail down force. When tail down force is decreased, the amount of lift required is also decreased and the induced drag will be reduced as a result. This reduction in total drag will allow a greater power-to-weight ratio and increase overall aircraft performance.

If the CG and CP diverge (become further apart) a larger tail down force would be required and the effect on lift, drag and aircraft performance would be the opposite of that described above.

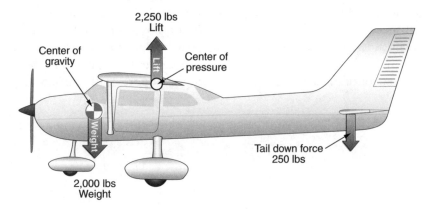

Figure 12-9. Effect of CG location on tail down force.

Ground Effect

Similar to how overall performance is affected by a reduction in tail down force, it is also affected by way of ground effect. In *ground effect*, the induced drag is reduced because of the interruption of the wingtip vortices by the ground. This interference causes a reduction in total drag, thus increasing the power-to-drag ratio and increasing performance. When the aircraft departs ground effect, the full amount of drag will be felt by the aircraft and the performance will accordingly be reduced.

Maximum Rudder Force—150 Pounds

Rudder force may play an important role in accurately determining the aircraft V_{MC} speed but the overall effect on performance will be negligible.

V_{MC} Demonstration

Understanding the behavior of a multi-engine aircraft just before, during and after a loss of directional control is best learned in a controlled, safe environment. The FAA has established a maneuver called the *V_{MC} demonstration* that is a required maneuver in a multi-engine practical test. The objective for this maneuver is for the pilot to understand V_{MC}, the factors that affect it in flight, and the proper recovery procedures. The proper technique for conducting the V_{MC} demonstration can be found in the *Airplane Flying Handbook* (FAA-H-8083-3) or the appropriate practical test standards. Earlier in this chapter, we discussed in depth the effect of the various factors on V_{MC} speed. During the V_{MC} demonstration with its FAA-recommended recovery altitude of 3,000 feet AGL, the pilot also needs to consider the aircraft's stall speed and its relationship to V_{MC} speed (*see* Figure 12-4).

The figure shows the typical certification spread between V_S and V_{MC} for multi-engine aircraft where V_{MC} is a few knots greater than V_S. In an airplane with normally aspirated engines, the V_{MC} speed will decrease with an increase in density altitude while stall speed remains constant. Depending on environmental conditions, there will be an altitude where stall speed would be reached prior to V_{MC} speed. If a multi-engine aircraft with one engine inoperative enters a single-engine stall prior to V_{MC}, the loss of control of the aircraft could be abrupt and potentially difficult to recover from.

Review 12

Single-Engine Aerodynamics and Operations

1. What is the effect of using only rudder to counteract an engine failure?

2. What is the effect of using only aileron to counteract an engine failure?

3. Describe zero sideslip.

4. List the factors used for V_{MC} certification for a light twin.

5. List the factors for V_{MC} certification, showing how each relates to V_{MC} speed and aircraft performance.

6. What is the reason for performing a V_{MC} demonstration?

7. What happens to V_{MC} speed as density altitude increases? What is the significance of understanding this phenomenon?

   Answers are provided in Appendix 2.

Section III

Multi-Engine Operations

Pilots should always be aware of the details of aircraft performance and prepare for them prior to each flight. 14 CFR §91.103 requires that certain prefight calculations be completed before commencing any flight. Although multi-engine aircraft require performance calculations very similar to those for single-engine aircraft, some additional performance values must be calculated prior to multi-engine flight. These include accelerate-stop and accelerate-go—if provided—as well as single-engine rate of climb, and single-engine service ceiling.

Before you can calculate these performance values, you need to first calculate the aircraft's takeoff and landing weights. Chapter 13 covers the details relating to multi-engine aircraft weight and balance procedures and calculations. Following that is an explanation of the performance calculations specific to multi-engine aircraft. The final chapter of the book discusses FAA regulations that apply to multi-engine aircraft and operations.

Weight and Balance

13

Chapter Focus: Calculating Weight and CG Location

On August 20, 2001, a Cessna 402B departed from Marsh Harbor in the Bahamas and crashed shortly after liftoff, killing all eight passengers and the pilot. The National Transportation Safety Board (NTSB) investigation revealed that the aircraft was over-weight and the center of gravity (CG) was outside the flight envelope. Weight and balance calculations are a critical component of preflight preparation in any type of aircraft, whether large or small. These calculations are especially critical when aircraft are operating near the maximum weight limitations.

The calculation of weight and balance is fundamentally the same for all categories, classes, and types of aircraft. Pilots must grasp the principle of aircraft weight and balance control, and especially, the effect that both the weight and CG location have on multi-engine aircraft performance. Just the improper, incomplete, or nonexistent exercising of weight and balance calculations prior to flight routinely leads to accidents and is commonly cited in NTSB reports as a contributing cause of accidents. As in the accident example above, this can have fatal consequences.

For this reason, it is important to be aware of the dangers associated with operating aircraft outside of their design weights and CG envelopes. Multi-engine aircraft have the added complication of the need to consider single-engine performance and flight characteristics, which are directly affected by weight and CG location. Therefore the proper weight-and-balance calculations and procedures are covered in this chapter, including key factors that affect weight and balance, how to complete relevant calculations, and how to identify and apply the appropriate corrective measures for abnormalities and exceedance (or, going outside limitations).

Key Terms

(in the order they appear in this chapter)

zero fuel weight

moment

arm

center of gravity (CG)

datum

basic empty weight (BEW)

payload

ramp weight/taxi weight

takeoff weight

landing weight

station

Weight and Balance Log

Figure 13-1 shows an example of a completed weight and balance log for a Piper Seminole, found in Section 6 of the POH. The information in Figure 13-1 is for a sample problem involved in the upcoming discussion in this chapter.

Zero Fuel Weight

Zero fuel weight is a measurement of the weight of the aircraft with all passengers, baggage and crewmembers—but as the name implies, it does not include the weight of the fuel. Zero fuel weight is typically a structural concern, specifically due to stress near the wing root, which is an attachment point. The structural stress is caused by flexing; the fuel in the wing provides structural strength by reducing wing flex.

Most small aircraft do not have a maximum zero fuel weight limitation; however, zero fuel weight can be used in calculations to determine how much

Weight and Balance Log—Piper Seminole

Item	Weight	Arm	Moment
Basic empty weight	2,688.8	86.16	231,669.39
Pilot and front passenger	360	80.5	28,980.00
Rear seats	0	118.1	0
Baggage compartment	25	142.8	3,570
Zero fuel weight	3,073.8		264,219.39
Fuel: 80 gallons	648	95	61,560
Ramp weight (3,816 max)	3,721.8	87.53	325,779.39
Fuel for start, taxi, and runup: 2.67 gal	-16.0	95	-1,520
Takeoff weight (3,800 max)	3,705.8	87.5	324,259.38
Fuel for flight: 35 gallons	-210	95	-19,950.00
Landing weight	3,495.8	87.05	304,309.38

Be sure that weights are within maximum compartmental limitations and ramp and takeoff weights are below maximum limits.

Figure 13-1. Sample of a completed weight and balance table.

Note: Your calculator might get slightly different numbers (by small amounts); this is due to a rounding error that occurs with large arms.

fuel can be carried when passengers and cargo must be carried. In the example shown in Figure 13-1, the Piper Seminole could take 648 pounds of fuel (or approximately 108 gallons assuming a weight of 6 pounds per gallon of AVGAS) to reach the maximum ramp weight limitation of 3,816 pounds. If the flight required in excess of 108 gallons of fuel, it would be necessary to include a fuel stop along the route.

Calculating zero fuel weight is also useful for determining the in-flight weight of the aircraft. If the zero fuel weight is known, the pilot can quickly determine the current weight of the aircraft by adding the weight of the fuel remaining in the fuel tanks to the zero fuel weight. For example, if the zero fuel weight is 3,073.8 pounds and the pilot reads the fuel quantity to be 50 gallons (300 pounds), the aircraft currently weighs 3,373.8 pounds.

In short, the zero fuel weight calculation may not be required, but it is always useful.

Moment

Moment is a measurement of force. Referencing a common physics equation, force is equal to mass multiplied by the distance of the object from a reference point. Moment is a technical term for force. With this in mind, we can see moment is "pivotal" in calculating center of gravity (and here, the pun is intended). Moment is also important to consider when determining the maximum force that a flight control can impart on an aircraft.

Moment = Weight × Arm

Arm

The term *arm* refers to the distance from the datum (an arbitrary reference point) to the center of gravity of an object. There are two important truths to remember about all matter: everything has mass (weight), and everything that has mass can be balanced at a single point (i.e., a center of gravity). Arm is the distance (in inches) from the datum to the center of gravity of each object in the aircraft. Arm can also be calculated for the aircraft in its entirety; this is the *center of gravity* of the aircraft—the single point through which the entire weight of the aircraft acts.

Using a bit of algebraic magic on the "golden," or key equation in weight and balance calculations, you'll observe that:

$$\text{Arm} = \frac{\text{Moment}}{\text{Weight}}$$

The following is also true:

$$\text{Center of gravity} = \frac{\text{Moment}}{\text{Weight}}$$

A "golden equation" is mathematically balanced and is a key calculation in a set of problems to be worked out.

Datum

We've already alluded to the meaning of *datum*; it is defined as an arbitrary reference point from which everything on an aircraft is measured. The aircraft manufacturer determines the location of the datum. Again, its purpose is only as a reference or baseline to use in determining the location of the center of gravity of the aircraft.

Weight and Balance Calculations

Now that you know the key equation, you can use it to calculate center of gravity. In order to determine the center of gravity for an aircraft, you need to gather some information.

Aircraft Basic Empty Weight and Moment

First, you need the *basic empty weight* (BEW) and moment of the aircraft. Whenever equipment is added or removed from an aircraft, the BEW and moment is updated (by maintenance). Be sure that you are referencing the most current, up-to-date BEW and moment numbers for your aircraft.

Sometimes the moment is not indicated, but rather the center of gravity is shown. Remember:

Moment = Weight × Arm (center of gravity in this case).

Weight and Location of Payload

Next you need to know the weight of your *payload* (passengers and cargo, but not fuel). This is a critical step, and one that pilots often don't take seriously enough, sometimes with fatal results. Gathering accurate passenger weights can be a touchy subject; sometimes it's more accurate and discreet to estimate. Don't forget to include the weight of carry-on baggage, winter garments, and anything else that is coming on board. The little things add up, so be sure to include everything in your weight and balance calculation. Note that items must be secured with tie-downs or cargo netting to prevent shifting during flight.

Once you have an idea of the weight of your payload, you need to determine the moment of your payload. Back to that key equation: Moment = Weight × Arm. You know the weight, so now you need to determine the arm (or distance from the datum). Luckily, you don't need a tape measure because this information is avail-

Standard empty weight consists of the airframe, engines, and all items of operating equipment that have fixed locations and are permanently installed in the airplane including fixed ballast, hydraulic fluid, unusable fuel, and full engine oil

Basic empty weight is the standard empty weight plus optional and special equipment.

Basic Empty Weight does not include crew weight, so you must include crew weight in the calculation.

Basic Operating Weight includes crew weight so you do not include crew in the weight and balance calculations.

able in Section 6 of the aircraft's Pilot's Operating Handbook (POH). Multi-engine aircraft often have various cargo compartments and seating accommodations. It may be necessary for you to "guide" certain passengers to specific seat locations in the interest of keeping the center of gravity within limits.

Weight of Fuel

Next, you need to know how much fuel is needed for the flight. Calculating required fuel is part of flight planning. Assuming you've completed the preflight planning, you will have determined the fuel required for the flight. AVGAS weighs 6 pounds per U.S. gallon.

Total Weight of Aircraft

Once you know the weight of everything on the aircraft, you can determine the total weight of the aircraft to ensure it is below the maximum weight limitations. Add up all of the weight, including the BEW. This will give you the *ramp weight* or *taxi weight*. Next, subtract fuel used for start, runup and taxi to determine the *takeoff weight*. Make sure these weights are below the maximum limitations.

Center of Gravity Location

Next, determine the location of the center of gravity. This will serve two purposes: ensure the aircraft is within the balance envelope, and indicate the controllability of the aircraft.

To determine the location of the center of gravity, refer back to the "golden," or key equation; now you are trying to calculate arm, which is equal to moment divided by weight:

$$\text{Arm} = \frac{\text{Moment}}{\text{Weight}}$$

You already know the weight, but now you need to add up all of the moments, and divide that number by the total weight of the aircraft. This will give you the location of the center of gravity measured in inches from the datum.

Landing Weight and Center of Gravity

As the aircraft uses fuel, the weight and location of the center of gravity will change. It's important to be aware of how the center of gravity changes as fuel is burned. For this reason, you must also calculate the weight and center of gravity location of the aircraft at landing.

Calculating *landing weight* and center of gravity is relatively simple: subtract fuel used for the flight from the total aircraft weight, and subtract the moment of that fuel from the total moment of the aircraft. Once again, determine the center of gravity using the key equation.

The Steps of Calculating Aircraft Weight and Center of Gravity Location:

1. Determine aircraft BEW and Moment from Section 6 of the POH.
2. Determine weight and location of the payload.
   - Estimate passenger weights—or ask passengers for their individual weights.
     - If estimating passenger weight, use the FAA standard passenger weights.
   - Determine weight of passenger baggage.
     - Have a basic scale available to weigh each bag.
3. Determine weight of the fuel.
   - Determine gallons of fuel on board and multiply by 6 (weight of 1 gallon of AVGAS).
     - (120 Gallons × 6 = 720 lbs.)
4. Add up 1, 2 and 3 to determine the total weight of the aircraft.
5. If the moment is not given, multiply weight x arm to determine the total moments.
6. Determine the CG location using the total weight, moment, and POH.

Standard weights: Values used when specific weights are not available. Examples of this are as follows—

Crew and passengers: 170 lbs each

Avgas: 6.0 lbs/U.S. gal

Turbine engine fuel: 6.7 lbs/U.S. gal

Lubricating oil: 7.5 lbs/U.S. gal

Water: 8.35 lbs/U.S. gal

Weight and Balance Example

The weight and balance log in Figure 13-2 (on the next page) shows calculations for a flight in a Piper Seminole. For the purposes of this example, the weights are:

Pilot—190 lbs.
Front passenger—170 lbs.
Baggage area—25 lbs.
Fuel used—35 gallons

Weight and Balance Worksheet Instructions

The Piper Seminole POH provides a blank weight and balance worksheet for pilots to use in order to determine aircraft weight and balance for each flight. This form includes the arm for each station that will be used for weight and balance calculation.

Basic Empty Weight and Moment

For this example, we have provided the basic empty weight and corresponding moment—2,688.8 pounds and a moment of 231,669.38 pound-inches. Place these numbers at the top of the weight and balance worksheet under the corresponding weight and moment headings.

Pilot and Passenger Weights and Moment

Next, when you have determined the weight of the passengers, enter the appropriate values into the weight and balance worksheet. Notice that the passengers are separated by the station in the aircraft—the front passenger and pilot are in the same station (the arm is the same for both front seats) and the rear passengers are in the same station (the arm is the same for both rear seats). Next, multiply the weight at each station by the arm for that particular station. In our example, we multiply the total weight of the front passengers (360 lbs.) by the arm of 80.5 inches. This provides us a moment of 28,980 pound-inches. Place this value under the corresponding moment heading. In this example we don't have any rear passengers so we can leave that particular line blank in the worksheet.

Baggage Weights and Moment

Now we need to do the same with the baggage weights. Place the weight of the baggage (25 lbs. in our example) under the weight heading on the baggage compartment line in the weight and balance worksheet. Now multiply this value by the arm provided (142.8 inches). This equals 3,570 pound-inches. Place this value under the moment on the baggage compartment line.

Fuel Weight and Moment

Finally, we need to include the weight of the fuel on board the aircraft. In our example, we are taking off with full fuel (108 gallons). Multiply 108 gallons by 6 lbs. to determine the weight of the fuel on board. This yields 648 lbs. Place this value under the weight column in the fuel line. Next, multiply the weight of the fuel (648 lbs.) by the arm provided in the weight and balance worksheet (95 inches). This yields 61,560 pound-inches; place this value under the moment heading in the fuel line.

Ramp Weight

Now add up the weights listed and place the sum (3,721.8 lbs.) in the ramp weight line and do the same for the moment column (325,779.38 pound-inches). Be sure that the ramp weight is below the maximum ramp weight of 3,816 lbs.

The standard formula for weight and balance is Weight × Arm = Moment. When you need to calculate an Arm, divide the Moment by the Weight. You'll use this when determining the arms for BEW, ramp weight, takeoff weight, and landing weight.

Item		Weight	x	Arm/Station	=	Moment
Basic empty weight	+	2,688.80	x	86.16	=	231,669.39
Pilot and front passenger		360	x	80.5	=	28,980.0
Rear seats		0	x	118.1	=	0
Baggage compartment		25	x	142.8	=	3,570
Zero fuel weight		3,073.8				264,219.38
To determine zero fuel weight (ZFW), add all the above weight values together. The ZFW moment can be determined by adding all the above moment values.						
Fuel: 108 gallons		648	x	95	=	61,560
Avgas weighs an average of 6 pounds per gallon. To determine the weight of your fuel onboard, multiply the gallons by 6.						
Ramp weight (3,816 max)		3,721.8	x	87.53	=	325,779.38
Ramp weight is the ZFW plus the fuel on board. Ramp moment is ZFW moment plus fuel moment. Ramp arm is ramp moment divided by ramp weight.						
Fuel for start, taxi, and runup: 2.67 gallons	−	-16	x	95	=	-1,520
16.0 pounds or 2.67 gallons for start, taxi and runup is the amount supplied by the aircraft manufacturer.						
Takeoff weight (3,800 max)	=	3,705.8	x	87.50	=	324,259.38
The estimated burn prior to takeoff is 16.0 pounds. This should be subracted from ramp weight to determine the takeoff weight. The takeoff moment is computed by subtracting the fuel moment from the ramp weight moment.						
Fuel for flight: 35 gallons	−	-210	x	95	=	-19,950.00
Landing weight	=	3,495.8		87.05		304,309.38
Landing weight is calculated by subtracting the estimated fuel for flight weight (gallons x 6) from the takeoff weight. The landing weight moment is determined by subtracting the fuel for flight moment from the takeoff weight moment. The landing weight arm is calculated by dividing the landing weight moment by the landing weight.						

Figure 13-2. Weight and balance log for the Piper Seminole (from POH "worksheet").

Taxi Fuel

In order to determine an accurate takeoff weight, we need to include the fuel that is used for engine start, runup and taxi to the runway. The Piper Seminole POH provides an average fuel consumed of 16 lbs. This weight and moment is also provided in the weight and balance worksheet provided in the Piper Seminole POH.

Takeoff Weight and Moment

To determine the takeoff weight of the aircraft, we simply subtract the fuel used for startup, runup, and taxi from the ramp weight. This yields a takeoff weight of 3,705.8 lbs. Place this number in the takeoff weight line under the weight column. Now do the same for the moment column. This yields 324,259.38 pound-inches. Enter this number in the takeoff weight line under the moment column in the weight and balance worksheet. Be sure the takeoff weight is below the maximum takeoff weight of 3,800 lbs.

Takeoff Center of Gravity

To determine the center of gravity simply divide the moment (324,259.38 pound-inches) by the takeoff weight (3,705.8 lbs.). This yields 87.5 inches as our center of gravity location.

Fuel Burned

In order to determine our landing weight, we need to subtract the fuel burned during flight from our takeoff weight. In our example we provided a fuel burn of 35 gallons. To determine the weight of the fuel burned, simply multiply 35 gallons by 6 (the weight of 1 gallon of fuel). This yields 210 lbs. Place this number in the fuel for flight line of the weight and balance worksheet. Again, we need to calculate the moment of the fuel burned: multiply 210 lbs. by the arm (95 inches) to yield 19,950.0 pound-inches. Place this number under the moment column in the fuel for flight line.

Landing Weight

Landing weight is calculated by subtracting the estimated fuel for flight weight of 210 lbs. from the takeoff weight of 3,705.8 lbs. This yields the landing weight of 3,495.8 lbs. Landing weight moment is determined by subtracting the fuel for flight moment of 19,950 from the takeoff weight moment of 324,259.38, yielding the landing weight moment of 304,309.38.

Finally, the landing arm, or CG needs to be calculated. This is done by dividing the landing weight moment of 304,309.38 by the landing weight of 3,495.8, yielding a CG/arm of 87.05. Using this value and the landing weight, a determination can be made as to whether the aircraft's landing weight falls within the operating envelope.

Weight and Balance Limitations

Now that you know the weight of the aircraft and the location of the center of gravity for takeoff and landing, the next step is to verify that the center of gravity is within the flight envelope for all phases of flight. To do this, reference the Center of Gravity Envelope in Section 6 of the POH (Figure 13-3).

As you can see, in this example the CG is not within the envelope. Without completing the weight and balance calculation, you would not have been aware of this problem, and could have become another accident.

You have a few options to bring the weight and CG within the envelope:
1. Move weight within the aircraft
2. Reduce total weight
3. Increase total weight

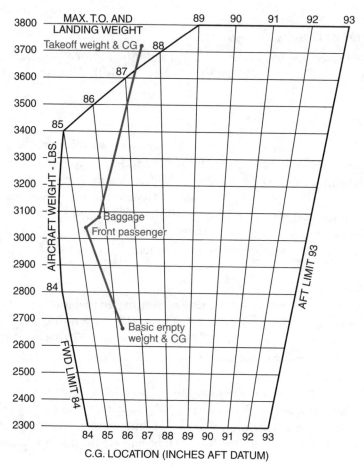

Figure 13-3. CG outside of limits.

Moving Weight

If you decide to move weight within the aircraft (in this case, by moving the front passenger to the rear seat), you can use another simple formula to determine the new CG:

$$\frac{\text{Weight to be shifted}}{\text{Total weight}} = \frac{\Delta CG}{\text{Distance weight is shifted}}$$

Obviously, the weight of the aircraft is not changing; only the moment and location of the center of gravity are changing. In order to determine the change in the center of gravity as a result of this move, the formula needs to be rearranged slightly:

$$\Delta CG = \frac{\text{Weight to be shifted} \times \text{Distance weight is shifted}}{\text{Total weight}}$$

After inserting the numbers into the equation, the result is:

$$\Delta CG = \frac{170 \times 37.6}{3,720} = 1.71$$

The weight of the passenger being moved is 170; 37.6 is the distance between the front seat arm and the rear seat arm (or the distance that the weight is moved). Total weight (3,720) is the current total weight of the aircraft. This yields an answer of 1.71, which is how far the CG has moved aft as a result of moving the passenger to the rear seat. Referencing the envelope, we can see that this brings the center of gravity within the forward limit (Figure 13-4).

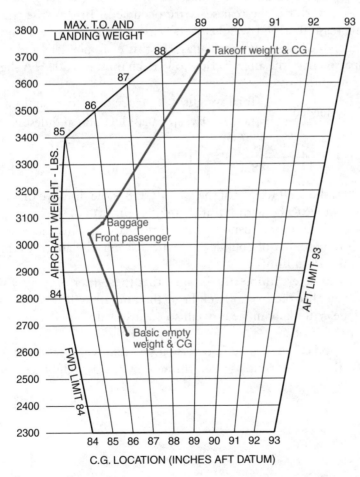

Figure 13-4. CG moved inside of limits.

Station: A location in the airplane that is identified by a number designating its distance in inches from the datum. The datum is, therefore, identified as station zero. An item located at station +50 would have an arm of 50 inches.

Sometimes, it may be beneficial to have passengers of different weights trade places, yielding a net change in the center of gravity. To determine how much weight needs to move from one *station* to another, we need to rearrange the formula once more:

$$\text{Weight shifted} = \frac{\text{Total weight} \times \Delta\text{CG}}{\text{Distance weight is shifted}}$$

$$\text{Weight shifted} = \frac{3{,}720 \times 0.8}{37.6} = 79.15$$

In this formula, the total, fully loaded weight of the aircraft is 3,720 pounds. The 0.8 represents the distance that the center of gravity must be moved in order to get back within the forward limit. The current center of gravity is 87.5 and we would like it to be 88.3 in order to be safely within the forward limit. 37.6 is the distance between the front seats and the rear seats. This equation yields an answer of 79.15 pounds, which is the amount of weight you need to move from one of the front seats to one of the rear seats.

Increasing or Decreasing Total Weight

Sometimes it's not possible to move weight within the aircraft by repositioning passengers. A passenger might be required to sit in front (for example, if he/she is your flight instructor or if the rear seats are occupied). In this case, then the next option is to increase the total weight of the aircraft. This can be accomplished by adding passengers, baggage, fuel, or ballast. In this example, let's add ballast to the baggage compartment of the aircraft. But how much must be added? A slightly different formula is used in this case:

$$\text{Ballast weight needed} = \frac{\text{Total weight} \times \text{Distance needed to shift CG}}{\text{Distance between ballast location and desired CG}}$$

$$\text{Ballast needed} = \frac{3{,}720 \times 0.8}{142.8 - 88.3} = 54.61$$

Again, 3,720 is the total weight of the aircraft, 0.8 is the distance that the center of gravity needs to move to be within limits, 142.8 is the arm of the baggage compartment, and 88.3 is the desired center of gravity location. This yields an answer of 54.61, which is the number of pounds of ballast that must be added to the aircraft in order to move it within limits.

Be careful when determining the distance that the center of gravity must move: you must consider that the overall weight of the aircraft will increase. This means that the envelope will likely move as well, so ensure that you take this into account when using this method.

The same method could be used in reverse if you remove weight from the aircraft. You would use the same formula to determine how much weight to remove.

Review 13

Weight and Balance

For the following questions, determine the takeoff weight, center of gravity location, and whether or not the preceding values are within limitations (see Figures 13-5 through 13-8). If any of the values are not within limitations, use adequate aeronautical decision making (ADM) to bring the aircraft within limitations.

1. Aircraft: PA44-180 Piper Seminole
Aircraft BEW .... 2,682.78 lbs
Moment .... 230,695.71 in/lbs
Pilot .... 220 lbs
Passenger 1 .... 200 lbs
Passenger 2 .... 150 lbs
Baggage .... 50 lbs
Takeoff fuel .... 85 gal

Takeoff weight _____
Center of gravity _____
Are these within limitations? _____

_____

2. Aircraft: PA44-180 Piper Seminole
Aircraft BEW .... 2,682.63 lbs
Moment .... 230,398.03 in/lbs
Pilot .... 150 lbs
Baggage .... 250 lbs
Fuel .... 108 gal

Takeoff weight _____
Center of gravity _____
Are these within limitations? _____

_____

3. Aircraft: Cessna 421C
Aircraft BEW .... 5,213.56 lbs
Moment .... 796,126.72 in/lbs
Pilot .... 190 lbs
Passenger seat 1 .... 215 lbs
Passenger seat 2 .... 170 lbs
Passenger seat 3 .... 170 lbs
Nose baggage .... 50 lbs
Baggage A .... 10 lbs
Baggage B .... 10 lbs
Wing lockers .... 15 lbs
Fuel (Main tanks) .... 100 gal
Fuel (Aux tanks) .... 76 gal
Fuel (Lockers) .... 52 gal
Fuel burn during start/taxi .... 8.33 gal
(main tanks)

Takeoff weight _____
Center of gravity _____
Are these within limitations? _____

_____

Answers are provided in Appendix 2.

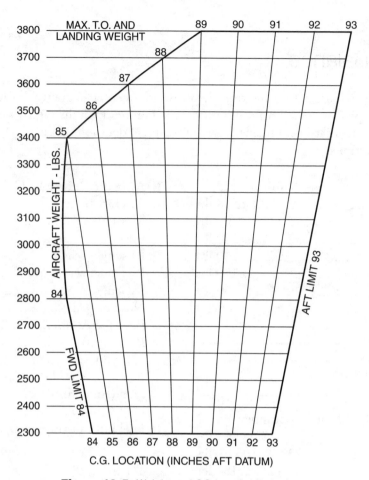

Figure 13-5. Weight and CG location limitations.

Item	Weight (lbs)	Arm aft (inches)	Moment (in/lbs)
Basic empty weight			
Pilot		80.50	
Front passenger			
Passenger 1		118.10	
Passenger 2			
Baggage area (200 lbs. max.)		142.80	
Fuel (108 gallons max)		95.00	
Ramp weight			
Fuel for runup (2.67 gallons)	-16.0	95.00	-1,520.00
Takeoff weight (3,800 lbs. max.)			
Fuel use for trip		95.00	
Landing weight			

Figure 13-6. Weight and balance table for PA44-180
(for calculations in Review 13 questions 1. and 2.)

Item	Weight	Arm	Moment/100
Basic empty weight	5,213.56	152.70	7,961.27
Pilot		137.00	
Seat 1		137.00	
Seat 2		162.00	
Seat 3		162.00	
Seat 4		190.00	
Seat 5		190.00	
Seat 6		218.00	
Nose		71.00	
Wing lockers		186.00	
Baggage A		266.00	
Baggage B		282.00	
Zero fuel weight			
Fuel (main tanks)		152.00	
Fuel (aux tanks)		164.00	
Fuel (lockers)		164.00	
Ramp weight			
Taxi fuel	-50		-83.00
Takeoff weight			
Fuel burn		152.00	
Locker fuel burn		164.00	
Landing weight	0		0.00

Figure 13-7. Weight and balance table for Cessna 421C (for calculations in Review question 3.)

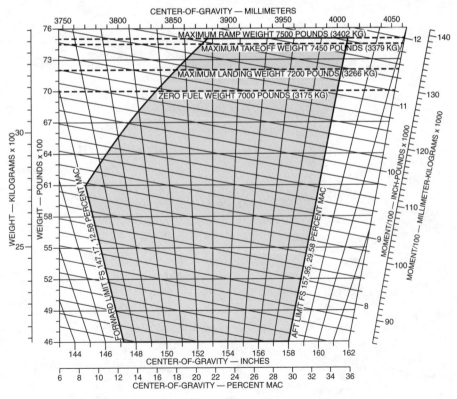

Figure 13-8. CG limits envelope graph for Cessna 421C.

Performance Calculations

14

🔍 Chapter Focus for Calculations and Scenarios

After determining the takeoff and landing weight of the aircraft, the location of the center of gravity, how the center of gravity moves in flight, and ensuring the calculations are within limits, the next step is to calculate the performance of the aircraft. Calculating aircraft performance (specifically takeoff and landing distance) is a regulatory requirement per 14 CFR §91.103. However, it is good practice to be aware of more than just takeoff and landing distance, especially in multi-engine aircraft.

At a minimum, you should calculate all of the following before a flight in a multi-engine aircraft: takeoff distance, accelerate-stop distance, accelerate-go distance (if one is published for your particular aircraft), single-engine rate of climb, single-engine service ceiling, and landing distance. If the flight is a cross-country, also be aware of planned true airspeed (TAS) and planned fuel burn at cruise. The scenario-based examples in the last section will help bring these important calculation exercises into real-world multi-engine operation situations.

Key Terms

(in the order they appear in this chapter)

takeoff distance (TOD)

landing distance

takeoff ground roll distance

accelerate-stop distance (ASD)

accelerate-go distance

landing ground roll distance

single-engine service ceiling

single-engine rate of climb

Takeoff and Landing Distance

For quick reference to performance information in flight, it is common for pilots to fill out a Takeoff and Landing Distance (TOLD) card. All pertinent performance information should be included on a TOLD card, and space is often provided for copying IFR clearances, ATIS, and other pertinent information. The TOLD card is a quick and easy reference to use during takeoff and approach briefings (Figure 14-1).

Aircraft:	DATE:	**TOLD CARD**

Pressure Altitude Departure _____

Takeoff Distance _____ V_R _____

Accelerate Stop _____

Accelerate Go _____ V_{REF} _____

OEI Climb _____

OEI Service Ceiling _____   Zero Fuel WGT _____

Pressure Altitude Destination _____   Takeoff WGT _____

Landing Distance _____   Landing WGT _____

DEP ATIS: _____

DEST ATIS: _____

CLNC: _____

Figure 14-1. Example TOLD card.

Factors That Affect Performance

Much as is the case with a single-engine aircraft, there are many factors that affect aircraft performance. Refer to Table 14-1 for a summary of these factors.

First of all, the heavier the aircraft, the longer the *takeoff distance (TOD)*, the lower the climb performance, and the longer the *landing distance*. The inverse is true for a lighter aircraft. Runway slope only affects the ground roll performance numbers. For a runway with an upslope, the takeoff distance will be greater and the landing distance will be shorter. With respect to wind, a tailwind will increase takeoff, landing and accelerate-stop distance. The inverse is true for a headwind component.

The runway surface conditions only affect the ground roll numbers. If the runway surface is slippery, braking performance will be degraded and landing distance and accelerate distance will increase.

Density altitude (which includes air temperature and humidity) also has an impact on aircraft performance. The higher the density altitude, the longer the takeoff, accelerate-stop, and landing distance. The in-flight performance will also decrease resulting in a lower rate of climb.

The aircraft center of gravity only has an effect on flight performance. The farther forward the center of gravity, the lower the performance resulting in a slight decrease in the rate of climb.

Calculations

In order to properly calculate aircraft performance, you need to gather additional information: outside air temperature, altimeter setting, wind, runway length, and runway environment, in addition to the aircraft weight. Once you are armed with this information, you can reference the performance charts found in Section 5 of the POH. For this example, we'll use the Piper Seminole performance charts.

Information for Performance Calculations:
    Aircraft Type: Piper Seminole (PA44-180)
    Takeoff Weight: 3,550 lbs.
    Landing Weight: 3,450 lbs.
    Route of Flight: KCEC to KMFR
    Altitude for Flight: 9,000 feet
    KCEC, Crescent City, CA
        Airport Elevation: 61 ft.
        Runway: 17/35: 5,001 ft.
    KMFR, Medford, OR
        Airport Elevation: 1335 ft.
        Runway 32/14: 8,800 ft.

METAR Weather Reports:
KCEC 292021Z AUTO 17015KT 1 3/4SM +RA BR FEW018 BKN032 OVC050 13/12 A2968 RMK AO2

KMFR 061853Z 28018KT 10SM OVC041 08/01 A3027 RMK AO2 SLP252

Factor		Takeoff Performance	Flight Performance	Landing Performance
Weight	Heavy	Increases takeoff distance	Decreases rate of climb Decreases cruise speed	Increases distance
	Light	Decreases takeoff distance	Increases rate of climb Increases cruise	Decreases distance
Runway Slope	Up	Increases takeoff distance	Not applicable	Decreases distance
	Down	Decreases takeoff distance		Increases distance
Wind	Tailwind	Increases takeoff distance Increases accelerate-stop distance.	Decreases rate of climb	Increases distance
	Headwind	Decreases takeoff distance Decreases accelerate-stop distance	Increases rate of climb	Decreases distance
Runway Surface Condition	Wet	Increases accelerate-stop distance	Not applicable	Increases landing ground roll
Density Altitude	High	Increases takeoff distance Increases accelerate-stop distance	Decreases rate of climb	Increases distance
	Low	Decreases takeoff distance Decreases accelerate-stop distance	Increases rate of climb	Decreases distance
Center of Gravity	Aft		Increases rate of climb	
	Forward		Decreases rate of climb	
Air Temperature	High	Increases takeoff distance Increases accelerate-stop distance	Decreases rate of climb Decreases cruise	Increases distance
	Low	Decreases takeoff distance Decreases accelerate-stop distance	Increases rate of climb Increases cruise	Decreases distance
Humidity	High	Increases takeoff distance	Decreases rate of climb Decreases cruise	Increases distance
	Low	Decreases takeoff distance	Increases rate of climb Increases cruise	Decreases distance

Table 14-1. Effect of Various Factors on Aircraft Performance

Winds and Temperature Aloft Forecast (FB):
DATA BASED ON 061200Z
VALID 061800Z FOR USE 1700–2100Z. TEMPS NEG ABV 24000
FT30006000 900012000 18000 2400030000340039000
BIH99003505+02 3107-04 3020-17 3025-30 342245 342654 283060
BLH 3307 9900+11 2614+05 2623+00 2539-13 2650-26 256642 247752 259157
FAT 3307 3314+07 3213+02 3212-02 3022-17 3125-30 352745 353054 302760
FOT 3621 3319+08 3230+01 3134-06 3144-18 3145-29 315344 315354 315565
ONT 9900 3507+10 3210+04 3116-01 2725-15 2741-28 255544 256652 266356
RBL 3513 3614+06 3421+01 3325-05 3031-18 3039-30 314745 315254 315165

Let's go through the steps of calculating the performance numbers for this flight given the weather information above.

Step 1. Pressure Altitude

Pressure altitude is the height above the standard datum plane, 29.92 in. Hg (Figure 14-2). To calculate pressure altitude, use the following formula:

(29.92 − current altimeter) × 1,000 = (+/− this number from field elevation to calculate pressure altitude)

Inserting the values from our example:

(29.92 − 29.68) × 1,000 = 240

Add 240 to KCEC field elevation:

240 + 61 = 301 ft.

Pressure altitude = 301 ft.

The pressure altitude is important for calculating aircraft performance, and some aircraft have a limitation on the maximum or minimum pressure altitude for departure.

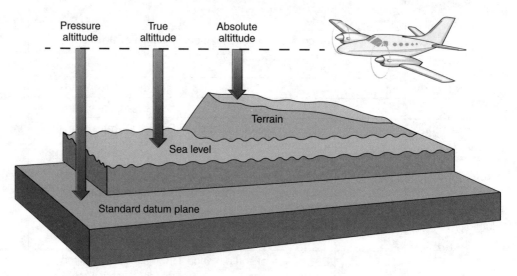

Figure 14-2. Pressure altitude.

Step 2. Takeoff Distance

Takeoff distance can be calculated one of two ways: either as the total ground roll (from brake release until all wheels leave the ground), or the total distance from brake release until the airplane reaches 50 feet above the ground. In this example, we will calculate both ground roll and takeoff distance over an obstacle.

Takeoff Ground Roll

Referencing Figure 14-3, there are 6 steps to determine the *takeoff ground roll distance*.
1. Begin the chart at 13 degrees Celsius found on the KCEC METAR report and draw a vertical line up to the previously calculated pressure altitude of 301 feet.
2. Beginning from the point in step one, draw a horizontal line to the right until it intersects the vertical reference line.

TAKEOFF GROUND ROLL - SHORT FIELD EFFORT

ASSOCIATED CONDITIONS:
Wing Flaps: 0°
Cowl Flaps: OPEN
Power: 2700 RPM & FULL THROTTLE
BEFORE BRAKE RELEASE
Runway: PAVED, LEVEL & DRY

WEIGHT POUNDS	ROTATE SPEED KIAS (3800 LBS.)
3800	70
3400	66
3000	62
2600	57

CAUTION
BEST ONE ENGINE INOPER-ATIVE RATE OF CLIMB IS LESS THAN 50 FPM IF T.O. WT. IS IN THE SHADED AREA.

EXAMPLE:
O.A.T.: 8°C
Airport Pressure Altitude: 1250 FT
Weight: 3430 LBS
Wind Component: 6 KT HEADWIND
Takeoff Ground Roll: 860 FT

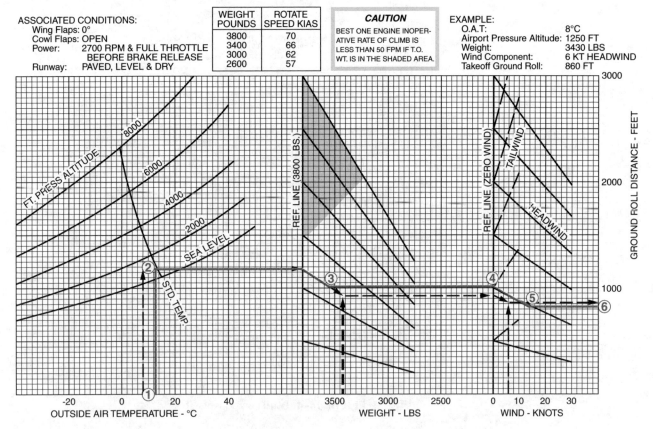

Figure 14-3. Takeoff ground roll.

3. From the intersection of the horizontal line from step two and the reference, draw a line parallel to the angled chart lines down to the right until reaching the takeoff weight (3,550 lbs.) and make a mark.

4. From the mark in step three draw another horizontal line to the next reference line and make a mark.

Prior to the next step, the headwind or tailwind for the takeoff runway must be determined using a headwind/crosswind chart and the observed winds.

First corrections will need to be made for the differences between magnetic and true north. Runways are aligned in relationship to magnetic north but weather reports or forecasts in the textual format are reported in true north. To compensate for this difference we must adjust the METAR winds to magnetic for maximum accuracy. As KCEC has a magnetic variation of 16E, 16 degrees will need to be subtracted from the METAR winds to change them to magnetic direction.

The reported winds in the METAR are 170 degrees at 15 knots. Subtracting the variation the magnetic winds will be 154 degrees at 15 knots.

Now that the magnetic wind direction is known, it can be used in the crosswind chart shown in Figure 14-4, following the steps shown with the chart on the next page.

WIND COMPONENTS

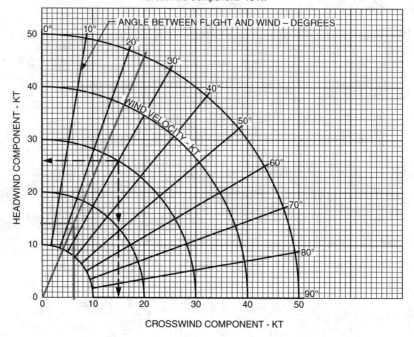

Example:
Wind velocity: 30 KT
Angle between flight path and wind: 30°
Headwind: 26 KT
Crosswind Component: 15 KT

Figure 14-4. Wind components chart.

a. Determine the angular difference between the runway and the wind direction. Runway is 177 degrees minus wind direction of 154 degrees, resulting in the angular difference of 23 degrees.

b. On the crosswind chart the straight lines radiating from the 0 on the vertical axis are numbered from 0 to 90 degrees; this is the angular difference between the runway and magnetic winds.

c. Between the 20- and 30-degree lines on the vertical axis, estimate where 23 degrees falls and draw a straight line that radiates outward and upward paralleling the existing lines.

d. The arcing lines on the chart ranging from 0 to 50 knots represent the wind speed. Using the known wind speed of 15 knots at KCEC, follow the arced line until it intersects the straight line that was previously drawn and make a mark.

e. Starting at the mark from step d, draw a horizontal line to the left until reaching the edge of the chart. The number that is intersected represents the headwind component. In this example, the headwind is determined to be 14 knots.

f. Starting again at the mark from step four, draw a vertical line downward until reaching the bottom of the chart; the number that is intersected is the crosswind component (in this example, 6 knots).

5. Starting at the mark from step four, draw a line parallel the wind lines (upward for tailwind and downward for headwind) to the known headwind/tailwind component (14 knots) and make a mark.
6. The final step is to draw a horizontal line to the edge of the chart, which will correspond to the takeoff distance.

Takeoff ground roll = 825 ft.

Takeoff Distance Over 50-foot Obstacle

Referencing Figure 14-5, use these 6 steps to determine the takeoff distance.

1. Begin the chart at 13 degrees Celsius found on the KCEC METAR report and draw a vertical line up to the previously calculated pressure altitude of 301 feet.
2. Beginning from the point in step one, draw a horizontal line to the right until intersecting the vertical reference line.
3. From the intersection of the horizontal line from step two and the reference, draw a line parallel to the angled chart lines down to the right until reaching the takeoff weight and make a mark.
4. From the mark in step three draw another horizontal line to the next reference line and make a mark.

TAKEOFF DISTANCE OVER 50 FT OBSTACLE - SHORT FIELD EFFORT

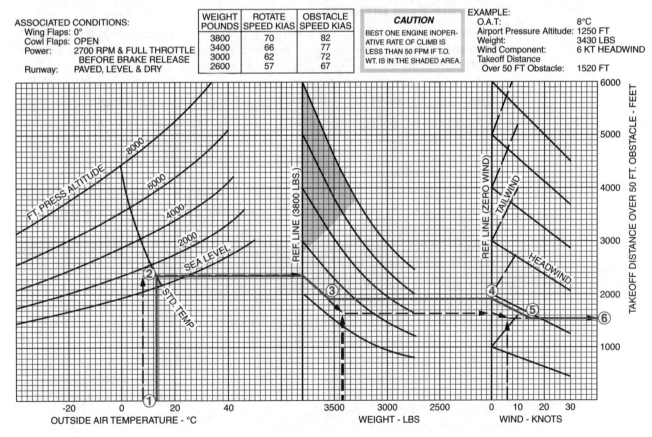

Figure 14-5. Takeoff distance over 50-foot obstacle.

Prior to the next step the headwind or tailwind for the takeoff runway must be determined using a headwind/crosswind chart and the observed winds. Refer back to Figure 14-4 (step 4 under the Takeoff Ground Roll calculations) and follow the same steps to determine the headwind or tailwind.

5. Starting at the mark from step four, draw a line parallel the wind lines (upward for tailwind and downward for headwind) to the known headwind/tailwind component and make a mark. In this example, the headwind component is approximately 14 knots and the crosswind component is approximately 6 knots.
6. The final step is to draw a horizontal line to the edge of the chart, which will correspond to the takeoff distance.

Takeoff distance over 50–foot obstacle: 1,550 ft.

After calculating the takeoff distance, you can reference the runway lengths to determine if the runways are long enough. The regulations don't specify the minimum runway length required for 14 CFR Part 91 aircraft, but it is good practice to ensure that the aircraft is capable of reaching 50 feet over the runway surface (or clearway if one exists) and is able to clear obstacles at the departure end of the runway. Once you have determined that the takeoff can be safely conducted on the required runway, it's time to move on to the next performance parameter: accelerate–stop distance.

Step 3. Accelerate-Stop and Accelerate-Go Distances

Accelerate-Stop Distance

Accelerate-stop distance is the distance required (from brake release) to accelerate (with full power on both engines) to V_R, experience an engine failure, and then decelerate to a full stop using maximum braking. Accelerate-stop distance calculations allow time for pilot recognition of the emergency.

Referencing Figure 14-6, there are 6 steps to determine the accelerate-stop distance:

1. Begin the chart at 13 degrees Celsius found on the KCEC METAR report and draw a vertical line up to the previously calculated pressure altitude of 301 feet.
2. Beginning from the point in step one, draw a horizontal line to the right until intersecting the vertical reference line.
3. From the intersection of the horizontal line from step two and the reference, draw a line parallel to the angled chart lines down to the right until reaching the takeoff weight and make a mark.
4. From the mark in step three draw another horizontal line to the next reference line and make a mark.

Prior to the next step the headwind or tailwind for the takeoff runway must be determined using a headwind/crosswind chart and the observed winds. Refer back to Figure 14-4 (step 4 under the Takeoff Ground Roll calculations) and follow the same steps to determine the headwind or tailwind.

5. Starting at the mark from step four, draw a line parallel the wind lines (upward for tailwind and downward for headwind) to the known headwind/tailwind component and make a mark. In this example, the headwind component is approximately 14 knots and the crosswind component is approximately 6 knots.
6. The final step is to draw a horizontal line to the edge of the chart; which will correspond to the accelerate and stop distance.

Accelerate–stop distance: 1,590 ft.

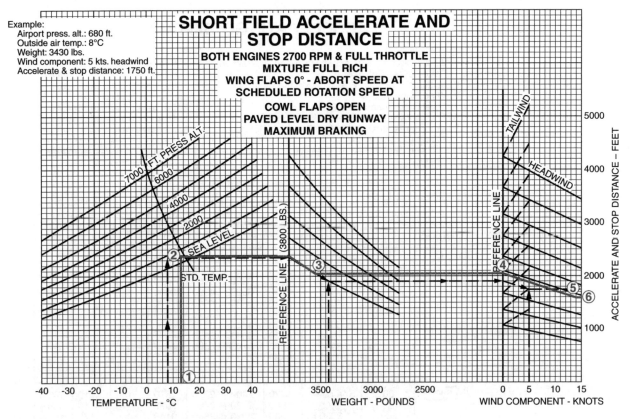

Example:
Airport press. alt.: 680 ft.
Outside air temp.: 8°C
Weight: 3430 lbs.
Wind component: 5 kts. headwind
Accelerate & stop distance: 1750 ft.

SHORT FIELD ACCELERATE AND STOP DISTANCE

BOTH ENGINES 2700 RPM & FULL THROTTLE
MIXTURE FULL RICH
WING FLAPS 0° - ABORT SPEED AT
SCHEDULED ROTATION SPEED
COWL FLAPS OPEN
PAVED LEVEL DRY RUNWAY
MAXIMUM BRAKING

Figure 14-6. Accelerate-stop distance.

Once you've calculated the accelerate-stop distance, reference the runway required for departure and ensure that the runway length is equal to or longer than the accelerate-stop distance.

Accelerate-Go Distance

The Piper Seminole does not have sufficient single-engine performance to merit an accelerate-go performance calculation, but it is important to calculate this if the performance charts are available. For discussion purposes, *accelerate-go distance* is the distance required from brake release to accelerate to rotation speed (or decision speed if one is published), experience an engine failure, lift off, and reach an altitude of 50 feet above the ground.

In order to calculate the accelerate-go performance using Figure 14-7, using the Cessna 421 as an example, you will need to know the following: aircraft weight, pressure altitude of the departure airport, and outside air temperature. For this example, we will assume a takeoff weight of 6,500 pounds, a pressure altitude of 1,500 feet, and an outside air temperature of 16 degrees Celsius.

When working with numeric charts, it can be time-consuming to calculate the exact performance values. It is more efficient to round up to the next higher value if the parameters fall between two declared values in the chart. This does not compromise safety in any way as the values will be more conservative.

1. Starting on the left side of the table, find the aircraft weight that is closest to the aircraft takeoff weight. The aircraft in our example weighs 6,500 pounds, so start at the next highest weight published on the chart—6,800 in this case.

ACCELERATE GO DISTANCE

CONDITIONS:
1. 2235 RPM and 39.0 Inches Hg. Manifold Pressure Before Brake Release.
2. Mixtures – CHECK Fuel Flows In the White Arc.
3. Wing Flaps – UP.
4. Level Hard Surface Dry Runway.
5. Engine Failure At Engine Failure Speed.
6. Propeller Feathered and Landing Gear Retracted During Climb.
7. Maintain Engine Failure Speed Until Clear of Obstacle.

NOTE:
1. If full power is applied without brakes set, distances apply from point where full power is applied.
2. Decrease distance 6% for each 10 knots headwind.
3. Increase distance 2% for each 1 knots of tailwind.
4. Distance in boxes represent rates of climb less than 50 ft/min.

WEIGHT - POUNDS	ENGINE FAILURE SPEED - KIAS	PRESSURE ALTITUDE - FEET	TOTAL DISTANCE TO CLEAR 50-FOOT OBSTACLE - FEET						
			-20°C -4°F	-10°C +14°F	0°C 32°F	+10°C +50°F	+20°C +68°F	+30°C +86°F	+40°C +104°F
7450	100	Sea Level	2390	2770	3290	4120	5800	12,210	------
		1000	2550	2980	3590	4630	7020	------	------
		2000	2740	3220	3950	5280	9100	------	------
		3000	2940	3500	4390	6190	13,540	------	------
		4000	3170	3830	4940	7570	------	------	------
		5000	3440	4220	5670	9990	------	------	------
		6000	3750	4710	6710	15,590	------	------	------
		7000	4120	5340	8330	------	------	------	------
		8000	4570	6190	11,350	------	------	------	------
		9000	5130	7430	------	------	------	------	------
		10,000	5870	9480	------	------	------	------	------
6800	96	Sea Level	1770	2000	2270	2670	3180	4010	5770
		1000	1880	2120	2460	2870	3470	4510	7070
		2000	2000	2290	2640	3100	3820	5170	9360
		3000	2150	2450	2830	3370	4240	6080	14,690
		4000	2290	2620	3050	3690	4780	7480	------
		5000	2450	2810	3310	4060	5490	9990	------
		6000	2620	3030	3600	4530	6480	16,070	------
		7000	2810	3270	3950	5120	8040	------	------
		8000	3020	3560	4370	5900	10,930	------	------
		9000	3270	3890	4890	7040	------	------	------
		10,000	3550	4280	5560	8880	------	------	------
6200	91	Sea Level	1380	1530	1710	1930	2200	2570	3120
		1000	1460	1620	1810	2050	2380	2800	3420
		2000	1540	1720	1930	2210	2550	3030	3780
		3000	1630	1820	2080	2360	2740	3290	4220
		4000	1730	1960	2210	2530	2960	3610	4780
		5000	1860	2080	2360	2720	3210	3980	5540
		6000	1970	2220	2520	2920	3500	4450	6650
		7000	2100	2370	2710	3160	3840	5050	8470
		8000	2240	2540	2910	3430	4250	5860	12,200
		9000	2390	2720	3150	3750	4760	7060	------
		10,000	2560	2930	3410	4130	5420	9060	------
5600	86	Sea Level	1070	1180	1300	1440	1610	1820	2090
		1000	1130	1240	1370	1530	1710	1940	2240
		2000	1190	1310	1450	1620	1820	2070	2430
		3000	1260	1390	1540	1720	1930	2240	2610
		4000	1330	1470	1630	1820	2090	2390	2820
		5000	1400	1550	1730	1960	2230	2570	3050
		6000	1490	1650	1860	2090	2380	2760	3330
		7000	1580	1770	1980	2230	2550	2990	3650
		8000	1690	1880	2110	2380	2740	3240	4050
		9000	1800	2000	2250	2550	2960	3540	4540
		10,000	1910	2140	2400	2740	3200	3890	5170

Figure 14-7. Accelerate-go distance for the Cessna 421.

2. Move over to the column labeled Pressure Altitude and choose the nearest pressure altitude. In this example, the pressure altitude is 1,500 feet, so round up to the 2,000 foot pressure altitude line.
3. Move across to the next column that corresponds to the temperature that is nearest to the current outside air temperature. In our example, the air temperature is 16 degrees Celsius, so we would round up to the +20 degree Celsius column and read the number provided. This is the calculated accelerate-go distance.

In our example, we arrive at an **accelerate-go distance of 3,820 feet**.

Step 4. Climb Performance—One Engine Operating

One-engine inoperative climb performance is the maximum climb performance with one engine failed, propeller feathered, landing gear up, and the aircraft flown with zero sideslip.

Referencing Figure 14-8, follow these steps to determine the one engine operating climb performance:

1. Begin the chart at 13 degrees Celsius found on the KCEC METAR report and draw a vertical line up to the previously calculated pressure altitude of 301 feet.
2. Beginning at the point found in step one, draw a horizontal line to the right until it intersects with the line corresponding to the takeoff weight of the aircraft.

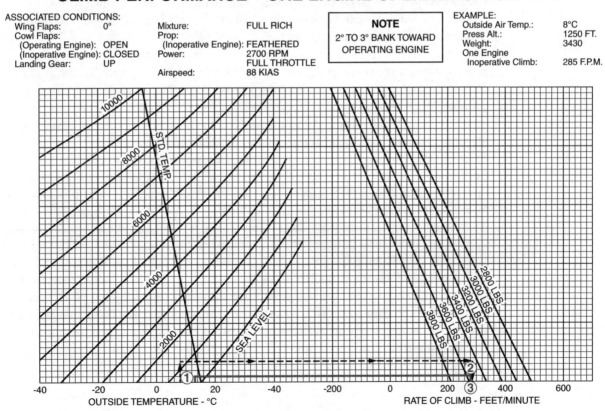

Figure 14-8. Climb performance with one engine operating and gear up—single-engine climb

3. Starting at the intersection determined in step two, draw a vertical line down to the bottom scale of the chart. The point where it intersects will tell you the rate of climb in feet per minute.

In this example calculation, we find that the **OEI climb performance is 280 fpm**.

Once you've calculated one-engine inoperative climb performance, look carefully at the climb gradient requirements of the departure airport and runway being used. The 14 CFR Part 91 regulations do not specify a minimum climb performance for departing from an airport, but it is good practice to take single engine climb performance into account when planning a flight, especially for departures into instrument meteorological conditions (IMC).

In many cases, the single-engine climb performance will not be sufficient to meet the climb gradient requirements of an obstacle departure procedure (ODP) or to simply clear obstacles on departure. If that is the case, you need to consider the surrounding terrain, weather conditions, and other departure runway options. The key to effective planning is to consider all available options while in the flight planning stage.

SID = standard instrument departure

In addition to considering initial takeoff single-engine climb performance, it's important to consider the effect of an engine failure during a higher-altitude climb (such as during a SID).

Some departure procedures (for example, O'Hare Six Departure) require a specific climb gradient. You should consider these climb gradient requirements and have a contingency plan in case the aircraft is unable to meet these requirements during single-engine operations. Be aware of the surrounding terrain and obstructions, and have a pre-planned route that will lead away from the highest obstructions.

Based on the calculated one-engine inoperative performance, you will not be able to continue along the original planned route, but where will you go? It's equally important to have a return plan. In some cases, the departure airport may not be the most suitable airport to return to in the event of an emergency. If this is the case, choose a suitable return airport during the preflight planning.

With all performance charts, it's very important to take into consideration the associated conditions listed at the top of the charts. These conditions give the pilot an idea of the aircraft configuration that is required in order to meet the performance values calculated in the charts. The associated conditions for single-engine climb performance are of utmost importance to the pilot. There are significant performance "penalties" for any configuration outside of these associated conditions. The Piper Seminole POH shows the performance "penalties" for other configurations (Figure 14-9). For example, if the pilot doesn't retract the landing gear while operating single-engine, the calculated 280 fpm climb performance will be reduced by 250 fpm. This will result in a 30 fpm rate of climb. Even worse, if a pilot does not properly feather the inoperative engine propeller with the landing gear extended, the performance penalty will now be an additional 200 fpm, resulting in a descent of 170 fpm. It is extremely important to be aware of the associated conditions, and when the aircraft performance margin is narrow, follow the proper checklists and procedures to ensure maximum performance is attained.

3.9j Summary of Factors Affecting Single Engine Operations.

Significant climb performance penalties can result from landing gear, flap, or windmilling propeller drag. These penalties are approximately as listed below:

Landing gear extended/Flaps Up .... - 250 ft./min.
Flaps extended 25°/Gear Down .... - 490 ft./min.
Flaps extended fully/Gear Down .... - 525 ft./min.
Inoperative engine propeller windmilling
(Gear and Flaps Up).. -200 ft./min.

WARNING
The propeller on the inoperative engine <u>must</u> be
feathered, the landing gear retracted, and the
wing flaps retracted for continued flight.

Figure 14-9. Seminole POH Performance Penalties Chart (Source: Seminole PA-44-180 POH.)

Step 5. Single-Engine Service Ceiling

The *single-engine service ceiling* in a multi-engine aircraft is the altitude at which the aircraft can maintain a 50 feet per minute rate of climb while flying with only one engine operating.

To determine the single engine service ceiling, follow the reverse process than that used in the previous example when calculating one-engine operating rate of climb. Referencing Figure 14-10, use the following 3 steps to determine the single-engine service ceiling:

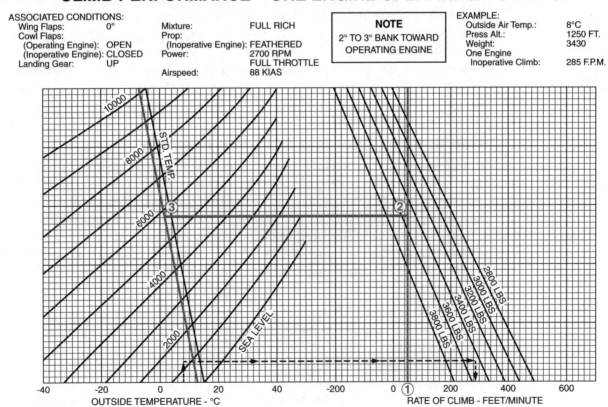

Figure 14-10. Climb performance with one engine operating and gear up—single-engine service ceiling.

1. Begin at the scale on the bottom right side of the chart. From the point representing a 50 feet per minute rate of climb, draw a vertical line up to where it intersects the line representing the current weight of the aircraft (3,550 lbs. in this case).
2. From the intersection determined in step one, draw a straight line towards the temperature and pressure values on the left side of the chart. Stop the line when you reach the approximate outside air temperature referenced from the scale on the bottom left side of the chart. The outside air temperature used for this example is 13 degrees Celsius and was obtained from the KCEC METAR report. If you don't know the outside air temperature, you can reference the standard temperature line shown on the chart.
3. Read the pressure altitude directly off the chart. In this example, we come up with a value of 5,800 feet. This is the single-engine service ceiling pressure altitude. To convert back to MSL, take the original pressure altitude correction and apply it to the single-engine pressure altitude.

$(29.92 - 29.68) \times 1,000 = 240$

To get pressure altitude at KCEC, you added 240 feet to field elevation. To move from pressure altitude back to MSL, subtract 240 feet from 5,800 feet.

$5,800 - 240 = 5,560$

OEI service ceiling: 5,560 ft. This is the single-engine service ceiling in mean sea level (MSL).

The single-engine service ceiling must be considered for the enroute phase of flight. Once you know the single-engine service ceiling, look through your route of flight to determine if you are capable of maintaining a minimum IFR altitude—ideally the minimum enroute altitude (MEA). If the MEA along your route of flight is above the calculated single-engine service ceiling, you'll need to consider other options. You might need to choose an enroute alternate airport that can be safely reached (above the minimum IFR altitude) in the case of an inflight engine failure. Mountain range crossings are of most concern when operating aircraft with low single-engine service ceilings. Be sure you have numerous safe options (potential enroute alternate airports that you can reach) in case the need arises.

Step 6. Time, Fuel and Distance to Climb

Time, fuel and distance to climb calculations are no different for multi-engine aircraft than they are for single-engine aircraft. The pilot must consider climb gradient requirements of SIDs or crossing restrictions along airways. Even climb performance with all engines operating may not be sufficient to meet certain crossing restrictions. If this is the case, the pilot must select contingencies.

Determining the time, fuel and distance from takeoff to cruise is a three-phase multi-step process using Figure 14-11.

Phase One
1. Start with the METAR temperature (13° Celsius) and draw a vertical line up to the previously calculated pressure altitude (301 feet) for the departure airport. Make a mark.
2. Starting at the mark from step one, draw a horizontal line that intersects each of the curved lines of Fuel, Time and Distance.
3. Write down the values of each intersection point referencing the scale at the bottom. In this example, the values are: Fuel = 0.5 gallon, Time = 1 minute, Distance = 1 nautical miles.

Phase Two

4. Start at the bottom of the chart with the winds aloft temperature (+1° Celsius) from the cruise altitude (9,000 feet) and draw a vertical line to the calculated pressure altitude (9,000 + 240 = 9,240 feet). Make a mark.

5. Starting from the mark in step one, draw a horizontal line toward the right that intersects each of the curved lines for Fuel, Time and Distance.

6. Write down the values of each intersection point referencing the scale at the bottom. In this example, the values are: Fuel = 5 gallons, Time = 11 minutes, Distance = 17 nautical miles.

Phase Three

7. Simply subtract the values determined in phase one from those in phase two. The result is the net fuel, time and distance from takeoff until reaching cruise. In our example, the values are **Fuel = 4.5 gallons, Time = 10 minutes, Distance = 16 nautical miles.**

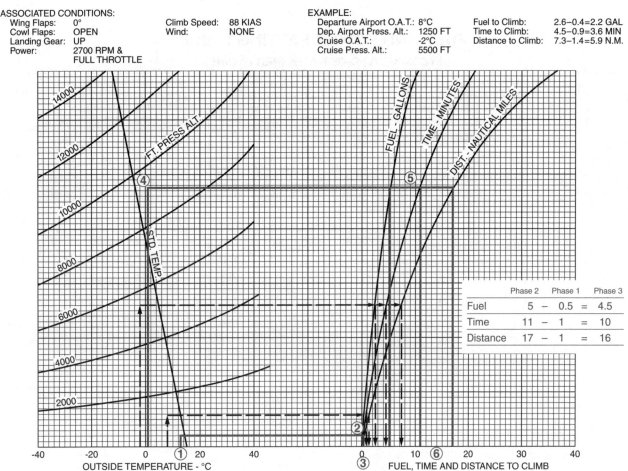

Figure 14-11. Time, fuel, and distance to climb.

Step 7. Cruise Performance

Cruise performance calculations for multi-engine aircraft are very similar to those for single-engine aircraft. Read the cruise performance charts carefully. Some cruise charts measure fuel burn for each engine, and some measure fuel burn for all engines operating. Be sure that you use the proper fuel burn for the flight. The Piper Seminole cruise performance charts provide a good example of this. Notice the highlighted area in the header, "(PER ENGINE)". This means the approximate fuel flow will need to be multiplied by two. Also, be sure to allow for non-standard temperatures if the charts offer a correction. The Piper Seminole cruise performance charts have a note at the bottom to indicate how non-standard temperature should be treated. It is very important to consider all of these factors so you're aware of exactly how much fuel is required for the flight.

For our example, use Figures 14-12 and 14-13 to determine the cruise power setting and true airspeed. Referring to Figure 14-12, with a pressure cruise altitude of 9,240 feet (determined in the previous section), select the percent horsepower desired. Sixty-five percent performance cruise at 2,300 RPM will be used for this example; the resulting RPM setting will be full throttle (FT).

FUEL AND POWER SETTING TABLE

LYCOMING (L) O–360–A1H6 (PER ENGINE)

Press. Alt. Feet	Std. Alt. Temp. °C	99 BHP–55% Rated Power Approx. Fuel Flow 8.7 G.P.H.* RPM AND MAN. PRESS.				117 BHP–65% Rated Power Approx. Fuel Flow 10.2 G.P.H.* RPM AND MAN. PRESS.				135 BHP–75% Rated Power Approx. Fuel Flow 11.7 G.P.H.* RPM AND MAN. PRESS.				Press. Alt. Feet
		2100	2200	2300	2400	2100	2200	2300	2400	2200	2300	2400	2500	
SL	15	22.3	21.7	21.1	20.6	24.9	24.2	23.5	22.9	26.7	26.0	25.2	24.6	SL
1000	13	22.0	21.3	20.8	20.3	24.6	23.8	23.2	22.6	26.3	25.6	24.9	24.3	1000
2000	11	21.7	21.0	20.5	20.0	24.2	23.5	22.9	22.3	25.9	25.3	24.6	24.0	2000
3000	9	21.3	20.7	20.2	19.8	23.9	23.2	22.6	22.0	25.6	25.0	24.4	23.7	3000
4000	7	21.1	20.5	20.0	19.5	23.5	22.8	22.3	21.8	FT	24.7	24.1	23.5	4000
5000	5	20.8	20.2	19.7	19.2	23.2	22.5	22.0	21.5	—	FT	23.8	23.2	5000
6000	3	20.5	19.9	19.4	19.0	22.9	22.2	21.7	21.3	—	—	FT	22.9	6000
7000	1	20.2	19.7	19.2	18.7	FT	21.9	21.5	21.0	—	—	—	FT	7000
8000	-1	20.0	19.4	18.9	18.5	—	FT	21.2	20.8					8000
9000	-3	19.7	19.1	18.7	18.2	—	—	FT	20.6					9000
10,000	-5	19.5	18.9	18.4	18.0	—	—	—	FT					10,000
11,000	-7	19.2	18.7	18.2	17.8									11,000
12,000	-9	FT	18.4	18.0	17.6									12,000
13,000	-11	—	FT	FT	17.4									13,000
14,000	-13	—	—	—	FT									14,000

NOTE: To maintain constant power, add approximately 1% Manifold Pressure for each 8°C above standard. Subtract approximately 1% for each 8°C below standard.

* PERFORMANCE CRUISE POWER

Figure 14-12. Fuel and power setting table.

Referencing Figure 14-13, three steps will be needed to determine the true airspeed.

1. Start at the bottom of the chart with the winds aloft temperature (+1° Celsius) from the cruise altitude (9,000 feet) and draw a vertical line to the calculated pressure altitude (9,000 + 240 = 9,240 feet). Make a mark.
2. Starting at the mark from step one, draw a horizontal line to the right until it intersects the 65% performance cruise line.
3. At the intersection of the horizontal line and the 65% performance cruise line, draw a vertical line down to the bottom of the chart. At the point where the line intersect the axis, read the corresponding true airspeed.

In our example, we arrive at an answer of **156 knots true airspeed (KTAS)**.

The true airspeed value will be used for filing flight plans.

It is possible that a fuel stop will be required for your planned flight. At times, winds and temperatures aloft prevent a non-stop flight. Don't assume you can make it non-stop just because you have been able to do so in the past. Fuel planning is quite possibly the most important preflight planning you can do and too often it is overlooked by the pilot. Heed this warning and always be aware of the fuel required for your flight.

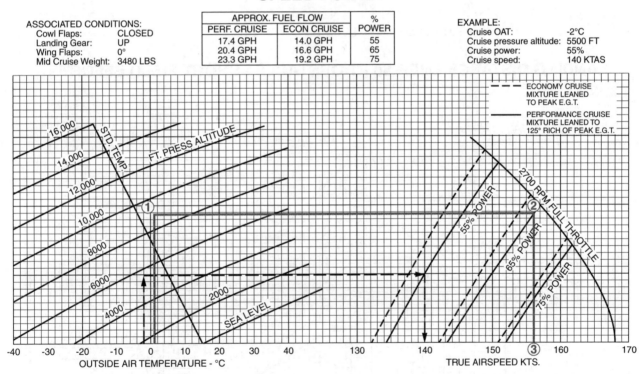

Figure 14-13. Speed power

Step 8. Landing Distance

Landing distance calculations in multi-engine aircraft also are very similar to those in single-engine aircraft. It is important to note the associated conditions that are required to meet the calculated landing distance. If the aircraft is operated outside of these associated conditions, the landing distance will increase, sometimes significantly. Approach speed, runway surface conditions, flap settings, and landing power settings all affect landing distance. The pilot must allow for any condition that is outside of the associated conditions shown on the landing distance chart. In some cases, no correction values are provided for varying runway surface conditions. This will require pilot judgment and "outside the box" planning.

Landing ground roll distance is the measurement from when the wheels touchdown on the runway surface to the point at which the aircraft comes to a complete stop. Landing ground roll distance is normally not calculated because it is included in the landing distance over 50-foot obstacle calculation.

Calculating landing distance requires you to determine what will be the pressure altitude at the destination. Referencing the weather report and the pressure altitude formula back at the start of our calculations (pp. 176–178), the following values are found:

$$(29.92 - 30.27) = -.35 \times 1000 = -350$$

Add −350 to KMFR field elevation:
−350 + 1,535 = 1,185

Pressure altitude = 1,185 ft.

LANDING DISTANCE OVER 50 FT OBSTACLE - SHORT FIELD EFFORT

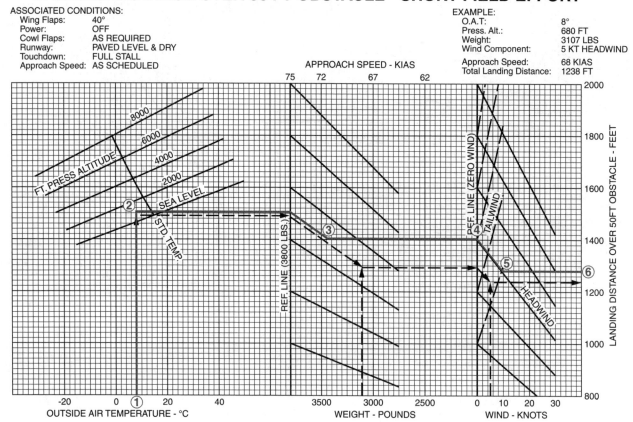

Figure 14-14. Landing distance over 50-foot obstacle.

Referencing Figure 14-14 (and the performance information on page 176), use the following five steps to determine the landing distance.

1. Begin on the chart at 8°C (found on the KMFR METAR report), and draw a vertical line up to the previously calculated pressure altitude of 1,185 feet.
2. Beginning from the point in step one, draw a horizontal line to the right until you intersect the vertical reference line.
3. From this intersection, draw a line parallel to the angled chart lines down until reaching the landing weight (3,450 lbs.) and make a mark.
4. From the mark in step three, draw another horizontal line to the right until intersecting the next reference line and make a mark.

Prior to the next step, the headwind or tailwind for the landing runway must be determined using a headwind/crosswind chart and the observed winds.

First corrections will need to be made for the differences between magnetic and true north. Runways are aligned in relationship to magnetic north but weather reports or forecasts in the textual format are reported in true north. To compensate for this difference, adjust the METAR winds to magnetic for maximum accuracy. As KMFR has a magnetic variation of 16E, 16 degrees will need to be subtracted from the METAR winds to change them to magnetic direction.

The reported winds in the METAR are 280 degrees at 18 knots. Subtracting the variation the magnetic winds will be 264 degrees at 18 knots.

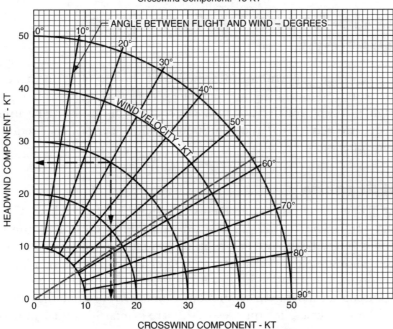

Figure 14-15. Wind components chart.

Now that the magnetic wind direction is known, it can be used in the crosswind chart with the following steps:

    a. Determine the angular difference between the runway and the wind direction. The runway is 322 degrees minus wind direction of 264 degrees, resulting in the angular difference of 58 degrees.

    b. On the crosswind chart the straight lines radiating from the 0 on the vertical axis are numbered from 0 to 90 degrees; this is the angular difference between the runway and magnetic winds.

    c. From the 60-degree line, draw a straight line that radiates outward and upward paralleling the existing lines.

    d. The arcing lines on the chart ranging from 0 to 70 knots represent the wind speed. Using the known wind speed of 18 knots at KMFR, follow the arced line until it intersects the straight line that was previously drawn and make a mark.

    e. Starting at the mark from step four, draw a horizontal line to the left until reaching the edge of the chart. The number that is intersected represents the headwind component.

    f. Starting again at the mark from step four, draw a vertical line down until reaching the bottom of the chart; the number that is intersected is crosswind component.

5. Starting at the mark from step four, draw a line parallel the wind lines (upward for tailwind and downward for headwind) to the known headwind/tailwind component and make a mark. For this example, the headwind component is 10 knots and will need consideration during landing performance computations.

6. The final step is to draw a horizontal line to the edge of the chart which will correspond to the landing distance.

In this example, the **landing distance over a 50-foot obstacle is 1,280 feet**.

Scenario-Based Performance Calculations

Scenarios give us the opportunity to demonstrate the use of performance calculations in practical, real-world flight experiences. A scenario gives you a guided tour into the flight planning and decision making required for multi-engine aircraft. This particular scenario was chosen to demonstrate a unique performance requirement of multi-engine operations.

A Flight Scenario

This scenario describes a flight from Reno, NV (KRNO) to Oakland, CA (KOAK) in a Cessna 421C. The Cessna 421 is a very capable medium-sized multi-engine aircraft, but as you will find out below, it has limitations. This scenario was chosen in order to demonstrate the preflight planning of a departure from a high-density-altitude airport in mountainous terrain. Additionally, you will have to consider high minimum enroute altitudes (MEAs) in mountainous terrain along the route of flight.

The performance charts for the Cessna 421 are primarily tabular in nature. This provides a good example of how tabular performance chart calculations differ from graphical performance chart calculations. The one important characteristic of tabular charts is the requirement for approximation and interpolation. Approximation is the process of utilizing the next highest (most conservative) value when values are in between published numbers. In some cases, approximation will yield a number that is overly conservative; when that occurs, interpolation will be required. The Cessna 421 POH offers the following guidance with respect to interpolation and approximation:

"If the approximation method yields a value larger than can be tolerated, a more exact value should be determined using the interpolation method."

In short, if the minimum performance requirements and the calculations are very close, it may be necessary to interpolate between the values provided within the charts. Interpolation requires a significant amount of time to calculate and tends to leave ample room for error; therefore do not rush this process. For takeoff and landing distance values, approximation will likely be sufficient. The accelerate-stop, accelerate-go, single-engine climb performance, and single-engine service ceiling calculations will likely require interpolation.

Properly planning a cross-country flight can be a daunting task. It may be easier to break the process into steps, as outlined below.

1. Retrieve the required charts

In order to properly plan this cross-country flight, you will need to have all the required charts available. Locate the following:

- Airport diagrams—for departure and arrival airports
- Instrument approach charts—for departure and arrival airports
- Enroute charts—low altitude IFR charts, sectional charts for departure and arrival areas (if terrain will be a factor)
- *Airport/Facility Directory*—for departure and arrival airports
- Aircraft performance charts (typically found in Section 5 of the POH)

See Pages 207–235, "Appendix to Chapter 14: Flight Scenario Figures" for the flight and weather briefings, charts, and illustrations that are to be used with this scenario.

2. Build the Route

Departure	Arrival	Connect (Cruise)
ODPs	STARs	Preferred Routes
SIDs	Direct a Fix	Direct
Textual DPs	Vector	Airways
Standard Instrument DP		

When building the route, it's best to start with the departure, then move on to the arrival, and then complete with the cruise. At this point the route is general, and it may need modification based on specific weather data (see Figure 14A-1) and performance calculations. Before starting to build the route, your first step should be to determine if there are any ATC-preferred routes between your departure and destination airports. Preferred routes are rare (typically they are used between airports with high traffic) but they are important to consider. Preferred routes can be found in the *Airport/Facility Directory* (A/FD) or enroute and approach charts available from the FAA's AeroNav Products division.

Departure

In planning the departure, first determine if the airport has an obstacle departure procedure (ODP) by referencing the airport diagram (Figure 14A-2) or the AeroNav takeoff minimums procedures (Figure 14A-5). An ODP will be published for an airport if there are obstacles that require an aircraft to climb at more than 200 feet per NM (FPNM). It is important to know that ODPs are not regulatory requirements of aircraft operating under 14 CFR Part 91; however, aircraft operating under Part 91 are strongly encouraged to file and fly an ODP (if one is available) at night, during marginal visual meteorological conditions (VMC), and IMC. Regardless of weather conditions, the presence of an ODP will be indicative of obstacles in the area of the departure airport and you should take this into consideration when planning your flight.

Standard instrument departure procedures (SIDs) are primarily designed for system enhancement and to reduce pilot and controller workload. SIDs are typically only issued for airports that have significant traffic, and they vary depending on runways in use and the direction the aircraft is flying from the departure airport. It can be difficult to pick an appropriate SID for your route of flight, especially if there are multiple SIDs or the runway in use is not known beforehand.

If your airport of departure does not have an ODP or a SID, you can skip the following departure instructions.

For this particular scenario, there is an ODP for all runways (Figure 14-A5). There also are a number of SIDs to choose from (Figures 14A-3 and 14A-4). At the departure time (1900Z) the winds are calm, giving you the possibility to choose which runway to use. The climb gradient requirements of departing runways 16 left or right are higher than departing 34 left or right. For this reason, choosing 34 left or right would be beneficial. If you have the choice, request a departure from 34 left or right, assuming the winds stay calm.

Next, choose a SID that best fits your route of flight. The Mustang Seven Departure (Figure 14-A3) ends at the FMG VOR, which is on the Victor 6 airway. This is a best-fit SID for our route of flight. The important thing to note about this departure procedure is that it requires a climbing hold over the FMG VOR until the aircraft reaches the MEA for our route. We will need to take this into account in the distance required to reach our altitude further along in our flight planning.

Arrival

The next step in planning an IFR cross-country is to determine what arrival procedure to use. Primarily used at busy airports, an arrival procedure's purpose is to simplify clearance delivery procedures and facilitate the transition between the enroute phase and the instrument approach phase. Much like SIDs, standard terminal arrival routes (STARs) tend to vary based on the inbound course to the destination airport as well as the runways in use at the airport. Choosing the appropriate STAR can be difficult; try to discuss this with pilots who are familiar with your destination airport to determine the best-fit STAR to choose. In the worst case, pick the arrival that best fits your route. If ATC needs to change your arrival, they will issue a new arrival in your pre-departure clearance or while you're en route.

If your destination airport does not have a STAR, you can skip this step. Additionally, you need to consider the aircraft capabilities with respect to the specific requirements of each STAR. In some cases, the STAR has much higher MEAs for certain routes. Sometimes these high MEAs can be reduced for aircraft with area navigation (RNAV) capability; however, when transitioning over areas of significant terrain, it is best to select an airway structure (Victor airways) or be aware of off-route obstacle clearance altitudes (OROCA) for your route of flight.

For the route of flight in this scenario, there is an arrival into Oakland that begins at the FMG VOR. This is a likely candidate for your route of flight; however, you need to consider the altitude requirements for this leg. The MEA for the FMG transition is FL220, which is too high for your particular aircraft. There are a couple other STARs that begin over the FMG VOR, but again they have MEAs that are too high. When transitioning the mountains, it is better to choose a Victor airway that is roughly along your route of flight. For this reason, don't choose a STAR into the Oakland airport; instead choose an airway structure that will take you to the Oakland airport.

En route

Once you have chosen the departure procedure and the arrival procedure (if necessary), you now need to connect the end of the departure procedure with the beginning of the arrival procedure. If there are no departure procedures or arrival procedures, then you need to connect the departure airport with the arrival airport. The enroute portion of the flight will largely depend on the navigation equipment and capabilities of your aircraft. An aircraft with only VOR and DME equipment will be required to plot a course from VOR to VOR or along Victor airways. An aircraft with GPS or other area navigation (RNAV) capability will be able to proceed direct.

Weather also plays an important role in enroute flight planning. For now, assume that weather is not a factor as the route can be easily amended to accommodate any weather patterns experienced. The most economical routing is direct. Due to the terrain along our route of flight, the most direct and safest route for us to follow is the Victor 6 airway from the FMG VOR (Figure 14A–10) all the way to the OAK VOR.

3. Weather for the Route

There are a multitude of resources available to get extensive route briefings via the internet. The three official sources are FSS, DUAT, and DUATS. The pilot should look at whether an alternate airport is required for the flight, and other hazardous weather conditions like icing and thunderstorms.

For this scenario, you will find the pertinent weather information in Figure 14-A1 in the Chapter 14 Appendix.

4. Enroute Performance Calculations

a. Determine cruising altitude.

When choosing a cruise altitude, a variety of factors should be considered: minimum IFR altitudes, winds, turbulence, cloud cover, and icing conditions. Start from the lowest altitude and work your way upwards. The minimum altitude a pilot would want to fly is the highest MEA for the route of flight. In this example, the highest MEA is between FMG and SWR on Victor 6 airway (Figure 14A–10): 13,000 feet.

Looking further into the weather, you can see that the cloud tops are around 14,000 feet with the freezing level around 10,000 to 12,000 feet in the area. Given this information, you should choose a cruise altitude above the cloud tops and correct for the direction of flight. For now, 16,000 feet seems best.

Next, look into the wind conditions and fuel burn to determine whether climbing higher will have significant fuel efficiency benefits. Looking at the wind, the wind conditions at 18,000 feet are less of a direct headwind. For this reason, choose 18,000 feet as your cruise altitude.

Looking at the cruise performance charts, you will notice that the true airspeed (TAS) increases at approximately 2 knots for every 1,000 feet of altitude gain, without an increase in brake horsepower (BHP) required or fuel burn.

From a TAS point of view, the higher the cruise altitude, the better; however, the pilot should be cognizant of the time required to reach this altitude, as in some cases the time to climb and the time to descend may not leave much time for the aircraft to spend at cruise. For this reason, we will choose the 18,000 foot cruising altitude. As you will soon find out, the time required to reach this altitude is reasonable.

b. Calculate time, fuel, and distance to climb.
   i. Now that you have chosen a cruising altitude, you need to calculate the time, fuel, and distance required to reach that altitude. Of particular interest will be the fuel required to climb, as the time and distance may depend on ATC clearances and obstacle departure procedures. In looking at the Time, Fuel, and Distance to Climb charts, you will notice that there are two options: one climbing at the best rate of climb, and one climbing at a cruise climb. Always choose the cruise climb performance (for better forward visibility and cooler engine temperatures) unless terrain or other obstacles require better climb performance. Also, you will notice that the chart requires knowledge of the aircraft weight, which we haven't yet calculated. Use a conservative weight here; in most cases, it is sufficient to assume maximum gross weight (Figure 14A-17).
   ii. Calculate pressure altitude of departure airport: 4,156 ft.
   iii. Determine time to climb: 19 − 3 = 16 minutes
   iv. Determine fuel to climb: 90 − 20 = 70 pounds
   v. Determine distance to climb: 45 − 38 = 7 NM
      For this example, we have determined the distance to climb from 13,000 feet to 18,000 feet, as we will climb up to 13,000 feet over the FMG VOR. We need to determine how much farther it will take to reach our cruising altitude after meeting the requirements of the Mustang Seven Departure procedure.

c. Calculate time, fuel, and distance to descend.
   i. Determine the time, fuel, and distance required to descend (Figure 14A-18).
   ii. Determine time to descend: 16 minutes
   iii. Determine fuel to descend: 52 pounds
   iv. Determine distance to descend: 55 NM (begin descent at or before SAC VOR)

d. Determine cruise performance and fuel burn.
   i. These tabular charts will require interpolation (Figure 14A-19). You'll notice that quite a few options are provided for propeller RPM and manifold pressure settings. Select an appropriate setting by consulting someone familiar with the aircraft. In most cases, select an intermediate (not the highest or the lowest) propeller RPM setting, and select a power setting that provides the highest TAS with the lowest fuel burn. If maximum range is desired, then select a lower power setting, and if minimum flight time is desired, select the maximum power setting. For this particular flight, we will choose 1,800 RPM (the most common cruise propeller RPM for this particular aircraft) and a power setting of 29.0 in. Hg. This yields 204 KTAS at a fuel flow of 215 pounds per hour.
   ii. Total distance for this route from the FMG VOR to KOAK is approximately 164 NM, 7 of which is used up climbing, and 55 of which is used for descending. The remainder of the flight will be at cruise, 102 NM. If there are specific altitude crossings required by STARs or other known ATC procedures, you

can make adjustments as necessary. Remember, the lower the aircraft and higher the power setting, the higher the fuel burn.

iii. Input wind to determine ground speed, time, and fuel required for the cruise portion of the flight. The fuel required for the cruise portion of this flight is 18.7 gallons. We will be at cruise for approximately 32 minutes.

Sample Navigation Log – KRNO to KOAK							
	Mag Course	True Course	True Wind	Ground Speed	Distance	Time Req'd	Fuel Req'd
Climb							
FMG	054	070			4	0:16	11.7
Top of Climb	218	234			7		
Cruise							
SWR	218	234	310@20	199	29	0:09	5.0
SAC	218	234	300@18	199	75	0:23	13.7
Descent							
REJOY	195	212			55	0:16	8.7
KOAK	137	154					
TOTALS					163	1:04	39.1

Table 14-2. Sample navigation log—KRNO to KOAK.

5. Calculate Weight and Balance

Cessna 421C Weight & Balance							
Payload Computations				Item	Weight	Arm	Moment/100
Item Occupants	Weight	Arm	Moment/100	Basic Empty Weight	4729	154.58	7310.00
				Payload	1135	160.65	1823.35
Seat 1	180	137.00	246.60	Zero Fuel Weight	5864	155.75	9133.35
Seat 2	180	137.00	246.60	Fuel Load - Main Tanks	1236		1991.00
Seat 3	170	175.00	297.50	Fuel Load - Locker Tanks			
Seat 4	170	175.00	297.50	Ramp Weight	7100	156.68	11124.35
Seat 5	145	218.00	316.10	Taxi Fuel	-50		
Seat 6	145	218.00	316.10	Takeoff Weight	7050	156.61	11041.35
Cargo Avionics		32.00	0.00	Fuel Burn	234		392.00
Nose	145	71.00	102.95	Landing Weight	6816	156.24	10649.35
Wing Lockers		186.00	0.00				
Bay A		266.00	0.00				
Bay B		282.00	0.00				
Payload	1135	160.65	1823.35				

Table 14-3. Cessna 421C weight and balance.

6. Calculate takeoff and landing performance and fill out the TOLD card

For these calculations, use a conservative approximation:

   a. Calculate takeoff distance (Figure 14A-20): 2,200 ft. ground roll / 2,900 ft. to clear 50 feet.

   b. Calculate accelerate-stop distance (Figure 14A-21): 4,310 feet

   c. Calculate accelerate-go distance (Figure 14A-22): 8,000 feet

   d. Calculate single-engine rate of climb (Figure 14A-23): 300 ft./minute @ 7,000 lbs.

   e. Calculate single-engine service ceiling (Figure 14A-24): 12,000 ft. @ 10°C OAT and 7,000 lbs.

   f. Calculate landing distance (Figure 14A-25): 660 ft. ground roll / 2,200 ft. to clear 50 feet.

Once the TOLD card data is calculated, look at the DP and make sure climb requirements can be met. Next, look at the cruise segment and ensure the aircraft can meet the MEA or OROCA requirements. Also take into consideration single-engine service ceiling and drift-down.

For this particular route, the takeoff distance and accelerate-stop performance values are within the limitations of your planned runways of departures and should not pose a significant risk. The accelerate-go performance is also within the runway limitations; however, the *single-engine rate of climb* is low enough that you need to consider what you will do if you lose an engine on departure from Reno. The climb gradient requirements of the ODP require a higher climb gradient than you are capable of attaining with one engine inoperative, especially with low ceilings and visibility.

To convert a gradient to a rate-of-climb requirement, determine the airspeed at which you will climb. Referencing the One Engine Inoperative Rate-of-Climb chart (Figure 14A-23) shows that the recommended climb airspeed is approximately 107 KIAS. Therefore, a climb gradient of 340 ft./NM will translate to a 5.7% climb gradient. The formula for calculating this is:

$$\left(\frac{\text{Climb gradient}}{6{,}076}\right) \times 100 = \text{Climb gradient (\%)}$$

$$\left(\frac{340}{6{,}076}\right) \times 100 = 5.6\%$$

To determine the rate of climb in feet per minute to achieve this climb gradient, use the following equation:

Climb Gradient (%) × Climb Airspeed (KIAS) = Climb Rate Required

5.6% × 107 KIAS = 600 feet per minute

From the above calculations you can see that the lowest required climb gradient for a departure from runway 34L at Reno will require a 600 fpm rate of climb. We are capable of meeting this climb gradient with both engines operating; however, we are not able to meet the climb gradient with one engine inoperative. This creates a challenging decision-making scenario. Recall from our earlier discussion that ODP requirements are not regulatory for Part 91 aircraft. However, we discussed the importance of considering these requirements when making our go/no-go decision. With the weather forecasting improved conditions after 2000Z, it would be best to delay the departure until the ceiling and visibility improve to at least 2700-3, which is listed as the "Climb in Visual Conditions" requirement of the ODP.

The next performance value that is a concern is your single-engine service ceiling. With a single-engine service ceiling of 12,000 feet, there is a portion of your route (from FMG to SWR VOR) during which the MEA is above the single-engine service ceiling. You will need to have a plan to implement in case you lose an engine at altitude along this portion of the route. Ideally, you would have an airport nearby along this portion of the route that you could descend to and safely land at. To the northwest of your route is the Truckee-Tahoe (KTRK) airport, which is a suitable airport (Refer back to Figure 14A-10). It would be beneficial to retrieve the approach charts and airport facility directory information for this airport so that you are prepared to land there should the need arise. Once you cross the SWR VOR, the MEAs drop sufficiently to allow more landing options, if the need arises further along in the flight.

7. File Flight Plan

The final step in the preflight planning process is to file your IFR flight plan (Figure 14A-26). This is a fairly simple process that is the same for all types of aircraft. Be sure that you have a copy of the flight plan that you have filed, as your clearance may be "cleared as filed...."

Review 14
Calculating Performance

Using the weight and weather provided, determine the performance values for a PA44-180 Piper Seminole. For these problems, reference Figures 14-16 through 14-22 on the following pages and work through the performance calculations on the various charts provided.

1. Takeoff weight............................3,500 lbs
   Airport ....KRAP (3,204 ft)
   Runway.................................32
   Weather: KRAP 011635Z AUTO 00000KT 10SM CLR 22/05A2962 RMK AO2

   Accelerate/stop distance: _____
   Takeoff ground roll distance: _____
   Takeoff distance over 50-ft obstacle: _____
   Obstacle speed: _____
   Climb performance – one engine operating (gear up): _____

2. Landing weight............................3,200 lbs
   Airport ....KBIL (3,652 ft)
   Runway.................................25
   Weather: KBIL 011653Z 27010KT 10SM SCT070 BKN100 16/04 A2997 RMK AO2SLP196 T00001039=

   Landing distance: _____
   Landing distance over 50-ft obstacle: _____
   Approach speed: _____

3. Aircraft weight............................3,400 lbs

Weather:	FT	3000	6000	9000	12000	18000	24000
	RAP	324216	315320	314507	3143-12	3143-28	3041-40

   One engine inoperative service ceiling: _____

Answers are provided in Appendix 2.

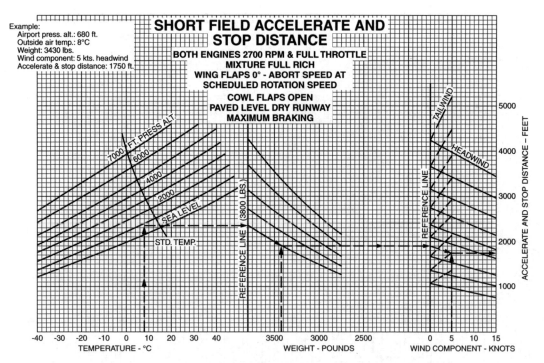

Figure 14-16. Accelerate-stop distance.

CLIMB PERFORMANCE – ONE ENGINE OPERATING – GEAR UP

ASSOCIATED CONDITIONS:

Wing Flaps:	0°	Mixture:	FULL RICH		
Cowl Flaps:		Prop:			
(Operating Engine):	OPEN	(Inoperative Engine):	FEATHERED		
(Inoperative Engine):	CLOSED	Power:	2700 RPM		
Landing Gear:	UP		FULL THROTTLE		
		Airspeed:	88 KIAS		

NOTE
2° TO 3° BANK TOWARD
OPERATING ENGINE

EXAMPLE:
Outside Air Temp.: 8°C
Press Alt.: 1250 FT.
Weight: 3430
One Engine
Inoperative Climb: 285 F.P.M.

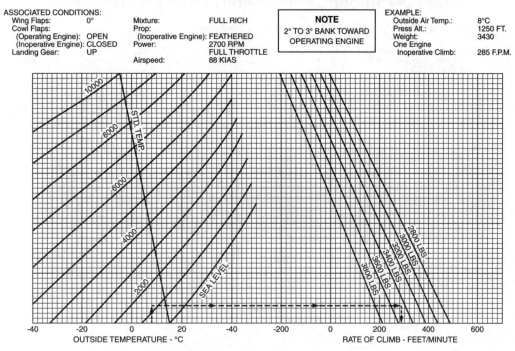

Figure 14-17. OEI climb perfomance.

TAKEOFF DISTANCE OVER 50 FT OBSTACLE - SHORT FIELD EFFORT

ASSOCIATED CONDITIONS:
Wing Flaps: 0°
Cowl Flaps: OPEN
Power: 2700 RPM & FULL THROTTLE
BEFORE BRAKE RELEASE
Runway: PAVED, LEVEL & DRY

WEIGHT POUNDS	ROTATE SPEED KIAS	OBSTACLE SPEED KIAS
3800	70	82
3400	66	77
3000	62	72
2600	57	67

CAUTION
BEST ONE ENGINE INOPER-ATIVE RATE OF CLIMB IS LESS THAN 50 FPM IF T.O. WT. IS IN THE SHADED AREA.

EXAMPLE:
O.A.T.: 8°C
Airport Pressure Altitude: 1250 FT
Weight: 3430 LBS
Wind Component: 6 KT HEADWIND
Takeoff Distance
Over 50 FT Obstacle: 1520 FT

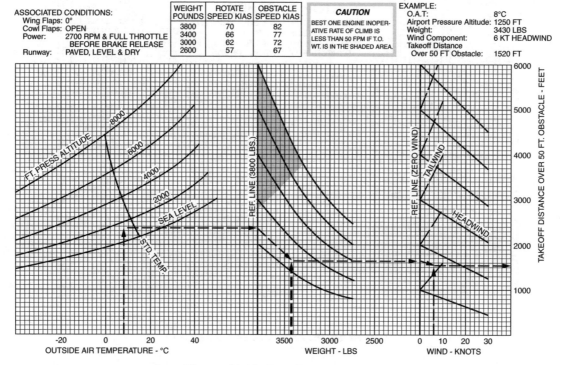

Figure 14-18. Takeoff, 50-ft obstacle.

TAKEOFF GROUND ROLL - SHORT FIELD EFFORT

ASSOCIATED CONDITIONS:
Wing Flaps: 0°
Cowl Flaps: OPEN
Power: 2700 RPM & FULL THROTTLE
BEFORE BRAKE RELEASE
Runway: PAVED, LEVEL & DRY

WEIGHT POUNDS	ROTATE SPEED KIAS
3800	70
3400	66
3000	62
2600	57

CAUTION
BEST ONE ENGINE INOPER-ATIVE RATE OF CLIMB IS LESS THAN 50 FPM IF T.O. WT. IS IN THE SHADED AREA.

EXAMPLE:
O.A.T.: 8°C
Airport Pressure Altitude: 1250 FT
Weight: 3430 LBS
Wind Component: 6 KT HEADWIND
Takeoff Ground Roll: 860 FT

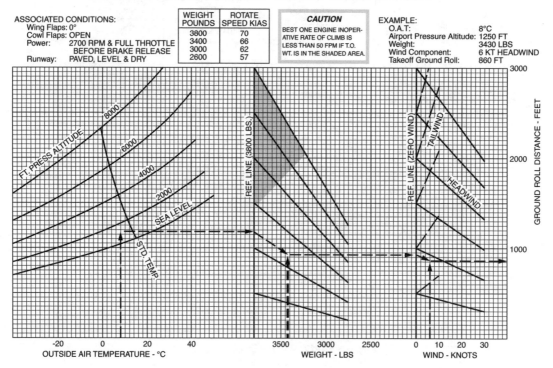

Figure 14-19. Takeoff ground roll.

LANDING DISTANCE OVER 50 FT OBSTACLE - SHORT FIELD EFFORT

ASSOCIATED CONDITIONS:
Wing Flaps: 40°
Power: OFF
Cowl Flaps: AS REQUIRED
Runway: PAVED LEVEL & DRY
Touchdown: FULL STALL
Approach Speed: AS SCHEDULED

EXAMPLE:
O.A.T.:   8°
Press. Alt.:   680 FT
Weight: 3107 LBS
Wind Component: 5 KT HEADWIND

Approach Speed: 68 KIAS
Total Landing Distance: 1238 FT

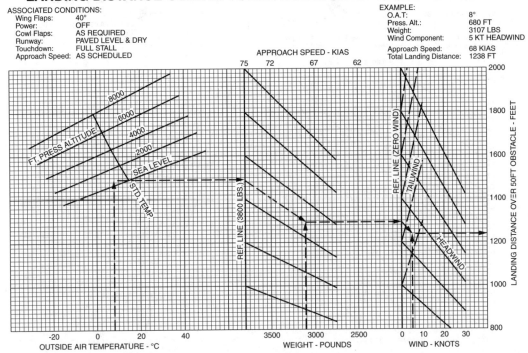

Figure 14-20. Landing, over 50-ft obstacle.

LANDING GROUND ROLL - SHORT FIELD EFFORT

ASSOCIATED CONDITIONS:
Wing Flaps: 40°
Power: OFF
Cowl Flaps: OPEN
Runway: PAVED LEVEL & DRY
Touchdown: FULL STALL

EXAMPLE:
O.A.T.:   8°
Press. Alt.:   680 FT
Weight: 3107 LBS
Wind Component: 5 KT HEADWIND
Landing Ground Roll: 542 FT

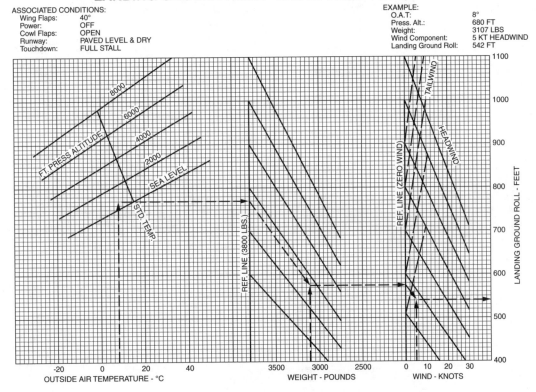

Figure 14-21. Landing ground roll.

CLIMB PERFORMANCE – ONE ENGINE OPERATING – GEAR UP

ASSOCIATED CONDITIONS:
Wing Flaps: 0°
Cowl Flaps:
  (Operating Engine): OPEN
  (Inoperative Engine): CLOSED
Landing Gear: UP

Mixture: FULL RICH
Prop:
  (Inoperative Engine): FEATHERED
Power: 2700 RPM
  FULL THROTTLE
Airspeed: 88 KIAS

NOTE
2° TO 3° BANK TOWARD OPERATING ENGINE

EXAMPLE:
Outside Air Temp.: 8°C
Press Alt.: 1250 FT.
Weight: 3430
One Engine
  Inoperative Climb: 285 F.P.M.

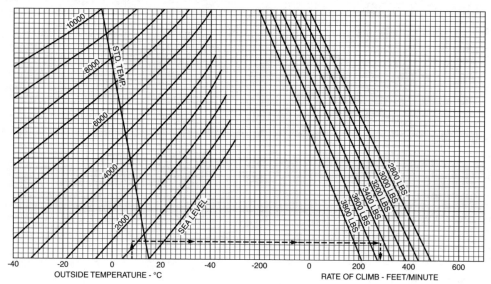

OUTSIDE TEMPERATURE - °C   RATE OF CLIMB - FEET/MINUTE

Figure 14-22. OEI service ceiling.

Appendix to Chapter 14
Flight Scenario Figures

Figure 14A-1. Flight and weather briefing (continues for three pages).

```
IFR DISPATCH RELEASE

AIRCRAFT ID: Cessna 421C - N421C
Departure: KRNO
EDT: 1900Z
Arrival: KOAK
ETA: 2005Z
Fuel Burn: 39 Gallons
Alternate: KSFO
Alternate Fuel: 15 Gallons
Reserve Fuel: 27 Gallons
Minimum Total Fuel: 81 Gallons
Contingency Fuel: 132 Gallons
Route: FMG V6 OAK

Aircraft Information:
BEW: 4729
CG: 154.58
Pilot: 180
Co-Pilot: 180
Passengers: 170, 170, 145, 145
Cargo: 145 lbs (Nose)
Fuel: 206 Gallons
PTOW: 7050
C.G.: 156.61
PLDW: 6816
C.G.: 156.24

FLIGHT BRIEFING FOR KRNO/KOAK

Recent Departure Weather
------------------------
KRNO 201755Z 00000KT 4SM -RA OVC009 10/08 A2967 RMK AO2 SLP061
KRNO 201655Z 00000KT 8SM -SHRA OVC006 10/8 A2966 RMK AO2 SLP059

Departure Terminal Forecast
---------------------------
TAF KRNO 201739Z 2018/2118 00000KT P6SM OVC050 VCSH TEMPO
2118/2120 SCT008 BKN010 RA FM210200 10004KT P6SM SCT080
BKN150FM211400 09005KT P6SM SCT090=

Departure D NOTAMs
------------------
```

Enroute AIRMETs

Enroute Weather

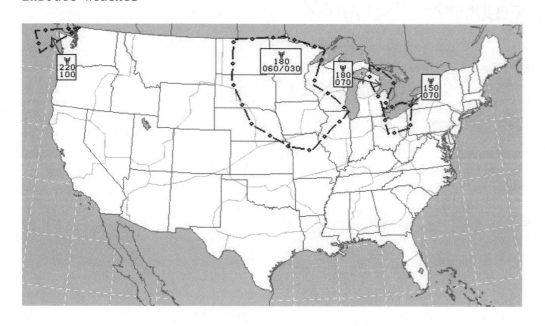

"Area Forecast - San Francisco Forecast Center"
Updated 1445 UTC 18

SFOZ WA 181445
AIRMET ZULU UPDT 2 FOR ICE AND FRZLVL VALID UNTIL 182100
AIRMET ICE...WA OR AND CSTL WTRS
FROM 30S YDC TO 120WNW ONP TO 140W TOU TO HUH TO 30S YDC
MOD ICE BTN 100 AND FL220. CONDS DVLPG 15-18Z. CONDS CONTG BYD
21Z THRU 03Z.

FRZLVL...RANGING FROM 065-165 ACRS AREA
 080 ALG YDC-60NNE GEG-50NNE GEG
 120 ALG 150W ONP-110SW HQM-40SE HQM-40SE YKM-30ESE BKE
 160 ALG 20S MZB-90SW LAX-140SSW RZS-180SSW RZS
 160 ALG 140SW SNS-30S PYE-60SE RBL-20NW FMG
....

SFOS WA 181301 AMD
AIRMET SIERRA UPDT 2 FOR IFR AND MTN OBSCN VALID UNTIL 181500
AIRMET IFR...WA OR
FROM 40SW SEA TO 40SSE SEA TO 40NNE OED TO 50WNW OED TO 50SSE
HQM TO 40SW SEA
CIG BLW 010/VIS BLW 3SM BR/FG. CONDS DVLPG 09-12Z. CONDS CONTG
BYD 15Z ENDG 18-21Z.
.
AIRMET MTN OBSCN...CA...UPDT
FROM 40NNE LAX TO 40WNW TRM TO 30SSE MZB TO 50SE LAX TO 20WNW
LAX TO 40NNE LAX
MTNS OBSC BY CLDS. CONDS CONTG BYD 15Z ENDG 15-18Z.
...NEW AIRMET...
....

```
SFOT WA 180845
AIRMET TANGO UPDT 1 FOR TURB VALID UNTIL 181500
NO SGFNT TURB EXP OUTSIDE OF CNVTV ACT.

....

SFOC FA 181045
SYNOPSIS AND VFR CLDS/WX
SYNOPSIS VALID UNTIL 190500
CLDS/WX VALID UNTIL 182300...OTLK VALID 182300-190500
WA OR CA AND CSTL WTRS

.
SEE AIRMET SIERRA FOR IFR CONDS AND MTN OBSCN.
TS IMPLY SEV OR GTR TURB SEV ICE LLWS AND IFR CONDS.
NON MSL HGTS DENOTED BY AGL OR CIG.

.
SYNOPSIS...ALF...BROAD UPR RDG WL CONT OVR THE WRN US..CNTRD OVR
CA WITH RDG NWD TO WRN WA. RDG WL SHFT SLOLY EWD. SHRTWV TROF
WELL OFF THE PAC NW CST WL MOV ENEWD APCHG SW BC-NW WA BY 03Z.
SFC...HI PRES RDG EXTDS FM THE NRN INTRMTN RGN THRU THE GRT
BASIN
AND WL MOV LTL WHILE SLOLY WKNG. TROF EXTDS FM SRN CA CSTL WTRS
TO NW CA WITH LTL CHG EXP.

.
WA CASCDS WWD
PAC CSTL SXNS...BKN060 TOPS 100 BKN CI. 17Z SCT060 SCT100 SCT-
BKN
CI. OTLK...MVFR CIG SHRA.
PUGET SOUND-INTR VLY...
NRN PTNS...BKN070-090 TOPS 130. 17Z SCT090 SCT-BKN CI. OTLK...
VFR
SHRA BECMG AFT 02Z MVFR CIG SHRA.
SRN PTNS...SCT080 SCT-BKN CI. OCNL VIS 3-5SM BR. 17Z BKN CI.
OTLK...VFR BECMG AFT 03Z VFR SHRA.
CASCDS...
NRN SXNS...BKN100-120 TOPS 160. 17Z SCT120 BKN CI. OTLK...VFR
SHRA BECMG AFT 03Z MVFR CIG SHRA.
SRN SXNS...SCT-BKN CI.OTLK...VFR BECMG AFT 03Z VFR SHRA.

.
WA E OF CASCDS
NRN HLF...BKN100-120 TOPS 160. 17Z SCT120 BKN CI. OTLK...VFR.
SRN HLF...SCT CI. 19Z SCT-BKN CI. OTLK...VFR.

.
OR CASCDS WWD
NRN CSTL SXNS...SCT CI. 17Z BKN CI. OTLK...MVFR

SRN CSTL SXNS...SKC OR SCT CI.OTLK...VFR.
WILLAMETTE VLY...OCNL VIS 3-5SM BR. 19Z SCT CI.
OTLK...MVFR.
SWRN INTR...SCT-BKN. OTLK...MVFR.
CASCDS...
NRN SXNS...SCT CI. 18Z BKN CI. OTLK...VFR.
SRN SXNS...SKC.OTLK...VFR.

.
OR E OF CASCDS
SKC OR SCT CI. OTLK...VFR.

.
NRN CA...STS-SAC-TVL LN NWD
OVC. OTLK...MVFR.

.
```

```
CNTRL CA
OVC. OTLK...MVFR.
.
SRN CA..VBG-NID-60NNW BIH LN SWD
CSTL SXNS...OVC005-008 SRN SXNS..BKN006-010 NRN SXNS. OTLK...
MVFR BECMG AFT
01Z MVFR CIG CSTLN S OF LAX.
INTR MTNS-MOJAVE-SRN DESERTS...SCT CI SRN SXNS..SKC NRN SXNS.
OTLK...VFR.
.
CSTL WTRS
CA...
NRN-CNTRL...BKN004-010 TOPS 140. OTLK...MVFR.
SRN...BKN005-010 TOPS 160. OTLK...VFR BECMG AFT 00Z MVFR CIG LAX
SWD.
....


Enroute 12 Hour Wind/Temp Aloft Forecast
-----------------------------------------
DATA BASED ON 180000Z
VALID 181200Z FOR USE 0900-1800Z. TEMPS NEG ABV 24000
FT30006000 900012000 18000 2400030000340003900
RNO11069900+12 2716+08 3120-07 3127-22 302839 293649 284756
SAC 1308 1509+19 9900+14 2206+09 3018-07 2812-21 282138 292848
283955
SFO 0906 0305+21 9900+14 1905+09 9900-06 2910-21 281638 282447
273455


Enroute Pilot Reports

N/A

Recent Destination Weather
--------------------------
KOAK 201955Z AUTO 08010KT 1SM OVC006 10/09 A2963 RMK AO2
 SLP058=
KOAK202055Z AUTO 09009KT 2SM OVC006 10/09 A2962 RMK AO2
 SLP053=

Destination Terminal Forecast
-----------------------------
TAF KOAK 201739Z 2018/2118 09008KT 2SM VCSH SCT008 BKN010
 FM210200 10004KT P6SM SCT080 BKN150
 FM211400 09005KT P6SM SCT090=

Destination D NOTAMs
--------------------


End of Briefing - Have a Good Flight.
```

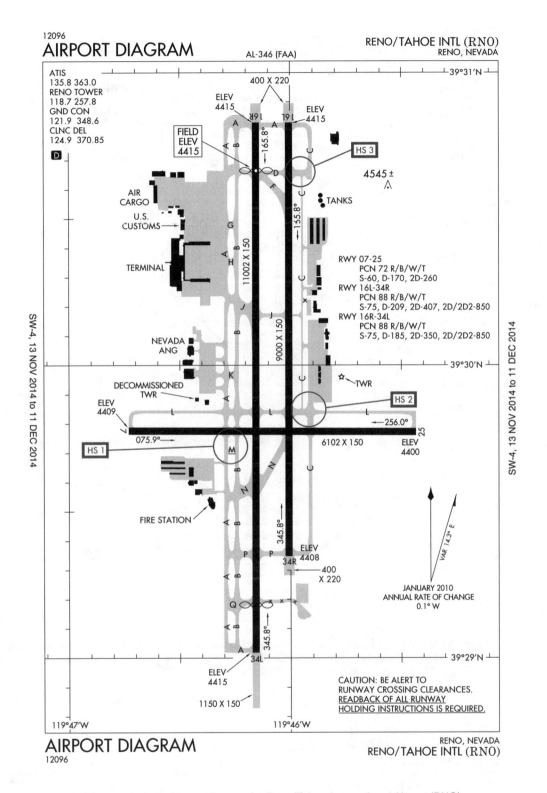

AIRPORT DIAGRAM

AL-346 (FAA)

RENO/TAHOE INTL (RNO)
RENO, NEVADA

ATIS
135.8 363.0
RENO TOWER
118.7 257.8
GND CON
121.9 348.6
CLNC DEL
124.9 370.85

D

ELEV
4415

400 X 220

ELEV
4415

−165.8°

FIELD
ELEV
4415

HS 3

4545 ±

155.8°

TANKS

AIR
CARGO

U.S.
CUSTOMS

RWY 07-25
PCN 72 R/B/W/T
S-60, D-170, 2D-260
RWY 16L-34R
PCN 88 R/B/W/T
S-75, D-209, 2D-407, 2D/2D2-850
RWY 16R-34L
PCN 88 R/B/W/T
S-75, D-185, 2D-350, 2D/2D2-850

TERMINAL

11002 X 150

9000 X 150

NEVADA
ANG

39°30'N

DECOMMISSIONED
TWR

TWR

HS 2

ELEV
4409

075.9°→

←256.0°

25

6102 X 150

ELEV
4400

HS 1

M

FIRE STATION

345.8°

VAR 14.3° E

JANUARY 2010
ANNUAL RATE OF CHANGE
0.1° W

ELEV
4408

34R

400
X 220

345.8°

39°29'N

34L

ELEV
4415

CAUTION: BE ALERT TO
RUNWAY CROSSING CLEARANCES.
READBACK OF ALL RUNWAY
HOLDING INSTRUCTIONS IS REQUIRED.

1150 X 150

119°47'W

119°46'W

39°31'N

SW-4, 13 NOV 2014 to 11 DEC 2014

SW-4, 13 NOV 2014 to 11 DEC 2014

AIRPORT DIAGRAM

RENO, NEVADA
RENO/TAHOE INTL (RNO)

Figure 14A-2. Airport diagram for Reno/Tahoe International Airport (RNO)

MUSTANG SEVEN DEPARTURE

SL-346 (FAA)

RENO/TAHOE INTL (RNO)
RENO, NEVADA

ATIS 135.8 363.0	
CLNC DEL	
124.9 370.85	
GND CON	
121.9 348.6	
RENO TOWER	
118.7 257.8	
NORCAL DEP CON	
119.2 279.55	
126.3 353.9	

TAKE-OFF OBSTACLE NOTES

Rwy 16L: Multiple antennas, trees, and light poles beginning 618' from DER, 131' left of centerline, up to 40' AGL/4449' MSL.
Terrain beginning 5189' from DER, 821' left of centerline, up to 5027' MSL.

Rwy 16R: Multiple antennas, trees, and light poles beginning 746' from DER, 380' left of centerline, up to 95' AGL/4510' MSL.
Terrain beginning 2784' from DER, 990' right of centerline, up to 288' AGL/4703' MSL.

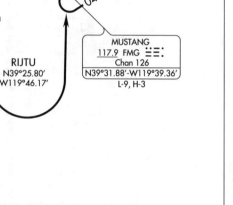

LOCALIZER 110.9
I-RNO ⠿⠿
Chan 46
N39°28.83'-W119°46.16'

RIJTU
N39°25.80'
W119°46.17'

MUSTANG
117.9 FMG
Chan 126
N39°31.88'-W119°39.36'
L-9, H-3

BACK COURSE
164°

221° R-041
041°

I-RNO 3

TAKE-OFF MINIMUMS

Rwy 7: NA- obstacles
Rwys 25, 34L/34R: NA- ATC.
Rwy 16L: Standard with minimum climb of 740' per NM to 8000 or, 600-1¼ with minimum climb of 525' per NM to 8000.
Rwy 16R: Standard with minimum climb of 740' per NM to 8000 or, 600-1¼ with minimum climb of 525' per NM to 8000.

NOTE: DME required.

NOTE: Chart not to scale.

DEPARTURE ROUTE DESCRIPTION

<u>TAKE-OFF RUNWAYS 16L/R:</u> Climb to 10000 or assigned altitude, via I-RNO south course to RIJTU/3 DME, then left turn direct FMG VORTAC. Climb in FMG holding pattern to depart FMG VORTAC at or above MEA/MCA for direction of flight. Expect clearance to requested altitude five minutes after departure.

MUSTANG SEVEN DEPARTURE
(FMG7.FMG) 11237

RENO, NEVADA
RENO/TAHOE INTL (RNO)

Figure 14A-3. The Reno Mustang Seven Departure.

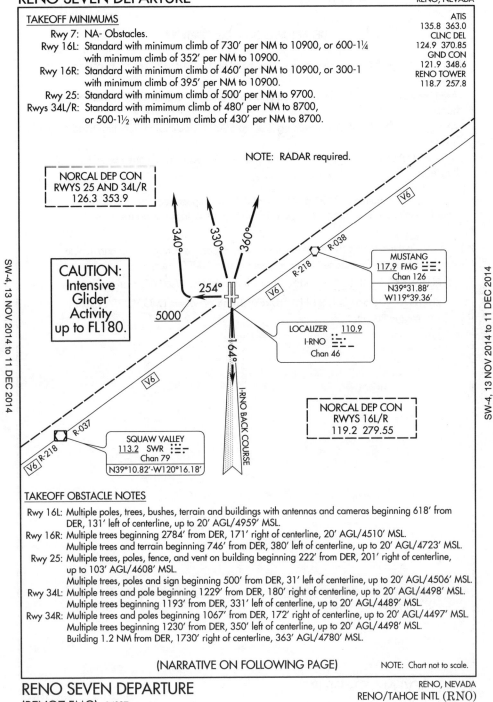

SL-346 (FAA)

RENO/TAHOE INTL (RNO)
RENO, NEVADA

RENO SEVEN DEPARTURE

TAKEOFF MINIMUMS

ATIS
135.8 363.0
CLNC DEL
124.9 370.85
GND CON
121.9 348.6
RENO TOWER
118.7 257.8

Rwy 7: NA- Obstacles.
Rwy 16L: Standard with minimum climb of 730' per NM to 10900, or 600-1¼ with minimum climb of 352' per NM to 10900.
Rwy 16R: Standard with minimum climb of 460' per NM to 10900, or 300-1 with minimum climb of 395' per NM to 10900.
Rwy 25: Standard with minimum climb of 500' per NM to 9700.
Rwys 34L/R: Standard with mimimum climb of 480' per NM to 8700, or 500-1½ with minimum climb of 430' per NM to 8700.

NOTE: RADAR required.

NORCAL DEP CON
RWYS 25 AND 34L/R
126.3 353.9

340° 330° 360°

CAUTION:
Intensive
Glider
Activity
up to FL180.

254°

5000'

164°

R-038

R-218

V6

MUSTANG
117.9 FMG
Chan 126
N39°31.88'
W119°39.36'

LOCALIZER   110.9
I-RNO
Chan 46

I-RNO BACK COURSE

NORCAL DEP CON
RWYS 16L/R
119.2 279.55

V6

R-037

R-218

V6

SQUAW VALLEY
113.2 SWR
Chan 79
N39°10.82'-W120°16.18'

TAKEOFF OBSTACLE NOTES

Rwy 16L: Multiple poles, trees, bushes, terrain and buildings with antennas and cameras beginning 618' from DER, 131' left of centerline, up to 20' AGL/4959' MSL.
Rwy 16R: Multiple trees beginning 2784' from DER, 171' right of centerline, 20' AGL/4510' MSL.
Multiple trees and terrain beginning 746' from DER, 380' left of centerline, up to 20' AGL/4723' MSL.
Rwy 25: Multiple trees, poles, fence, and vent on building beginning 222' from DER, 201' right of centerline, up to 103' AGL/4608' MSL.
Multiple trees, poles and sign beginning 500' from DER, 31' left of centerline, up to 20' AGL/4506' MSL.
Rwy 34L: Multiple trees and pole beginning 1229' from DER, 180' right of centerline, up to 20' AGL/4498' MSL.
Multiple trees beginning 1193' from DER, 331' left of centerline, up to 20' AGL/4489' MSL.
Rwy 34R: Multiple trees and poles beginning 1067' from DER, 172' right of centerline, up to 20' AGL/4497' MSL.
Multiple trees beginning 1230' from DER, 350' left of centerline, up to 20' AGL/4498' MSL.
Building 1.2 NM from DER, 1730' right of centerline, 363' AGL/4780' MSL.

(NARRATIVE ON FOLLOWING PAGE)

NOTE: Chart not to scale.

RENO SEVEN DEPARTURE
(RENO7.FMG) 14037

RENO, NEVADA
RENO/TAHOE INTL (RNO)

SW-4, 13 NOV 2014 to 11 DEC 2014

SW-4, 13 NOV 2014 to 11 DEC 2014

Figure 14A-4. The Reno Seven Departure. (Page 1 of 2)

▼

DEPARTURE ROUTE DESCRIPTION

<u>TAKEOFF RUNWAY 16L:</u> Climb on heading 164° and I-RNO localizer south course. Thence. . . .

<u>TAKEOFF RUNWAY 16R:</u> Climb on heading 164° and I-RNO localizer south course. Thence. . . .

<u>TAKEOFF RUNWAY 25:</u> Climb heading 254° to 5000 then climbing right turn heading 340°. Thence. . . .

<u>TAKEOFF RUNWAYS 34L/R:</u> Climb heading 330° CW 360° as assigned by ATC. Thence. . . .

. . . .All aircraft maintain FL190 or assigned altitude. Expect clearance to requested altitude 5 minutes after departure. Expect RADAR vectors to assigned route/fix.

<u>LOST COMMUNICATIONS:</u> If not in contact with departure control within one minute after takeoff, maintain assigned heading until passing 10000, thence. . . .

. . . .<u>RUNWAYS 16L/R DEPARTURES:</u> Turn left direct FMG VORTAC, then via assigned route.

. . . .<u>RUNWAYS 25 and 34L/R DEPARTURES:</u> Turn right direct FMG VORTAC, then via assigned route.

SW-4, 13 NOV 2014 to 11 DEC 2014

SW-4, 13 NOV 2014 to 11 DEC 2014

RENO SEVEN DEPARTURE   RENO, NEVADA

(RENO7.FMG) 14037   RENO/TAHOE INTL (RNO)

Figure 14A-4. The Reno Seven Departure. (Page 2 of 2)

RENO/TAHOE INTL (RNO)
TAKEOFF MINIMUMS AND (OBSTACLE)
DEPARTURE PROCEDURES
AMDT 4 07354 (FAA)

TAKEOFF MINIMUMS: **Rwy 7,** NA-terrain. **Rwy 16L,** std. w/ min. climb of 730' per NM to 8000, or 600-1¼ w/ min. climb of 480' per NM to 8000, or 2700-3 for climb in visual conditions. **Rwy 16R,** std. w/ the following minimum climb requirements: 210 knots or less, 385' per NM to 8000; more than 210 knots, 420' per NM to 8900, or 2700-3 for climb in visual conditions. Resume normal speed after passing FMG VORTAC. **Rwy 25,** std. w/ min. climb of 470' per NM to 7800, or 2700-3 for climb in visual conditions. **Rwy 34L,** std. w/ min. climb of 320' per NM to 7000, or 2700-3 for climb in visual conditions. **Rwy 34R,** std. w/ min. climb of 480' per NM to 7000, or 500-1½ w/ min. climb of 320' per NM to 7000, or 2700-3 for climb in visual conditions.

DEPARTURE PROCEDURE: **Rwys 16L/R,** climb heading 164° to 6600 then climbing left turn direct FMG VORTAC, thence. . . or for climb in visual conditions: cross Reno/Tahoe Intl Airport at or above 7000 via heading 054° and FMG R-234 to FMG VORTAC, thence. . .**Rwy 25,** climb heading 254° to 5000 then climbing right turn direct FMG VORTAC, thence. . . or for climb in visual conditions: cross Reno/Tahoe Intl Airport at or above 7000 via heading 054° and FMG R-234 to FMG VORTAC, thence. . . **Rwys 34L/R,** climb heading 344° to 7000 then climbing right turn direct FMG VORTAC, thence. . . or for climb in visual conditions: cross Reno/Tahoe Intl Airport at or above 7000 via heading 054° and FMG R-234 to FMG VORTAC, thence. . .
. . .**All aircraft:** continue climb in FMG VORTAC holding pattern (northeast, left turn, 221° inbound) to cross FMG VORTAC at or above MEA/MCA for route of flight.

NOTE: **Rwy 16L,** multiple poles, trees, bushes and terrain beginning 618' from DER, 133' left of centerline, up to 20' AGL/4961' MSL.
Rwy 16R, multiple trees 2784' from DER, 171' right of centerline, up to 20' AGL/4510' MSL. Multiple trees and terrain beginning 746' from DER, 380' left of centerline, up to 20' AGL/4703' MSL. **Rwy 25,** multiple trees and poles beginning 829' from DER, 201' right of centerline, up to 103' AGL/4523' MSL. Building 6023' from DER, 456' right of centerline, 152' AGL/4608' MSL. Fence 222' from DER, 270' right of centerline, up to 5' AGL/4415' MSL. Multiple trees and poles beginning 500' from DER, 31' left of centerline, up to 20' AGL/4506' MSL. **Rwy 34L,** multiple trees and poles beginning 1229' from DER, 180' right of centerline, up to 20' AGL/4498' MSL. Multiple trees beginning 1193' from DER, 331' left of centerline, up to 20' AGL/4489' MSL. **Rwy 34R,** multiple trees and poles beginning 1067' from DER, 172' right of centerline, up to 20' AGL/4497' MSL. Multiple trees and poles beginning 1230' from DER, 350' left of centerline, up to 20' AGL/4498' MSL. Building 1.2 NM from DER, 1730' right of centerline, 363' AGL/4780' MSL.

Figure 14A-5. Takeoff minimums and (obstacle) departure procedures for Reno/Tahoe International Airport.

NAME	ALTERNATE MINIMUMS

RENO, NV
RENO/TAHOE
INTL (RNO).......................ILS Rwy 16R, 2100-7[1]
ILS or LOC/DME Rwy 34L[2]
LOC Rwy 16R[3]
RNAV (GPS) X Rwy 34L[4]
RNAV (GPS) X Rwy 34R[4]
RNAV (GPS) X Rwy 16L[5]
RNAV (GPS) X Rwy 16R[6]
RNAV (RNP) Y Rwy 16L[9]
RNAV (RNP) Y Rwy 16R[9]
RNAV (RNP) Z Rwy 16L[7]
RNAV (RNP) Z Rwy 16R[7]
VOR-D[8]

[1]LOC, NA.
[2]ILS,LOC, Categories A, B, 1000-2; Category C, 1000-2¾.
[3]Categories A, B, 1600-2; Categories C, D, 1600-3; Category E, 2400-3.
[4]Categories A,B, 1000-2; Category C, 1000-2¾; Category D, 1000-3.
[5]Categories A, B, 1400-2; Categories C, D, 1400-3.
[6]Categories A, B, 1800-2; Categories C, D, 1800-3.
[7]Categories A, B, C, 800-2½.
[8]Categories A, B, 1600-2; Categories C, D, 1600-3.
[9]Categories A, B, C, D, 800-2½.

Figure 14A-6. Alternate minimums for Reno/Tahoe International Airport.

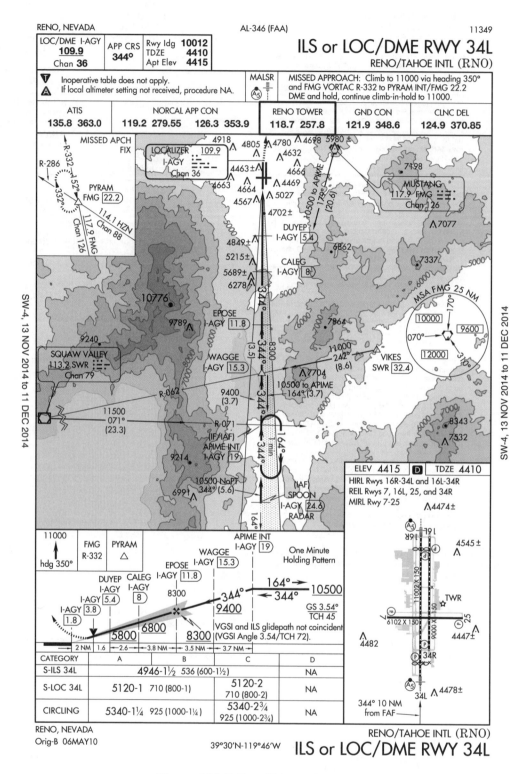

Figure 14A-7. Reno/Tahoe ILS RWY 34L

RENO/TAHOE INTL (RNO)(KRNO) P (ANG)   3 SE   UTC–8(–7DT)   N39°29.95′ W119°46.09′

4415   B   S4   **FUEL** 100LL, JET A1+
OX 1, 2, 3, 4   TPA—See Remarks   LRA   Class I, ARFF Index C   NOTAM FILE RNO
RWY 16R–34L: H11002X150 (CONC–GRVD)   S–75, D–185, 2D–350,
   2D/2D2–850 PCN 88 R/B/W/T   HIRL   CL
  RWY 16R: MALSR. PAPI(P4L)—GA 3.06° TCH 77′. Thld dsplcd 999′.
  RWY 34L: MALSR. PAPI(P4L)—GA 3.54° TCH 72′. Thld dsplcd 990′.
  Ground.
RWY 16L–34R: H9000X150 (CONC–GRVD)   S–75, D–209, 2D–407,
   2D/2D2–850 PCN 88 R/B/W/T   HIRL   CL
  RWY 16L: REIL. PAPI(P4L)—GA 3.0° TCH 75′.
  RWY 34R: REIL. PAPI(P4L)—GA 3.0° TCH 75′.
RWY 07–25: H6102X150 (CONC–GRVD)   S–60, D–170, 2D–260
  PCN 72 R/B/W/T   MIRL
  RWY 07: REIL. PAPI(P4L)—GA 3.2° TCH 48′. Pole.
  RWY 25: REIL. PAPI(P4L)—GA 3.0° TCH 45′. Tree.
RUNWAY DECLARED DISTANCE INFORMATION
  RWY 07: TORA–6102   TODA–6102   ASDA–5854   LDA–5854
  RWY 25: TORA–6102   TODA–6102   ASDA–6102   LDA–6102
MILITARY SERVICE: FUEL A, A+ (C775–858–7300.) (NC–100LL, A1+)
AIRPORT REMARKS: Attended continuously. CAUTION: Intsv glider activity
  invof arpt and surrounding areas up to 18.000′. Waterfowl all
  quadrants all seasons. Concentrated NW of Rwy 16R and East of Rwy
  16L. Twy M clsd to air carrier acft. Twy J east of rwy 16L–34R clsd to air carrier acft. Twy A btn N Twy B and Twy D clsd
  to acft with wingspan greater than 149′. Twy C btn Twy L and Twy D clsd to air carrier acft. Twy C btn Twy L and Twy D
  rstd to acft 60,000 lbs or less. TPA—5215(800) single engine, 5415(1000) larger/high performance acft. Noise sensitive
  area all quadrants. All coml acft ctc gnd ctl for advisories prior to push back on the terminal ramp. Pilots of turbojet acft
  use recommended NS ABTMT procedures, avbl on req. Pilots of non–turbojet acft use best abatement procedures and
  settings. Avoid as much as feasible flying over populated areas. Pure jet touch and go low apch and practice instrument
  apchs are prohibited, acft over 12500 lbs rqr prior written apvl for trng flts, for further info ctc arpt ops 1–877–736–6359.
  24 hrs PPR for tran acft parking with wingspans greater than 75′. LRA PPR call 775–784–5585, no after hrs ldg without
  prior arrangement. Glider/soaring ops 30–50 miles South of arpt dur VFR wx and mountain wave wind cond 1900Z‡ to
  SS. Rwy 25 PAPI not to be used byd 2 NM due to rapidly rising mountainous terrain. Rwy 34L and Rwy 34R PAPI not to
  be used byd 6 NM due to high terrain. For MIRL Rwy 07–25 0600–1330Z‡, HIRL Rwy 16L–34R and cntrln lgts
  0800–1330Z‡ ctc twr. Touchdown RVR and rwy visibility value Rwy 16R. Flight Notification Service (ADCUS) avbl.
  NOTE: See Special Notices—Glider/Soaring Activities around the Reno–Tahoe Intl Arpt, Continuous Power Facilities.
AIRPORT MANAGER: 775-328-6400
WEATHER DATA SOURCES: ASOS (775) 324–6659
COMMUNICATIONS: D–ATIS 135.8   775–348–1550 **UNICOM** 122.95
  RCO 122.2 122.5 (RENO RADIO)
Ⓡ **NORCAL APP/DEP CON** 126.3 (220°–035°) 119.2 (036°–219°)
  TOWER 118.7 **GND CON** 121.9 **CLNC DEL** 124.9
AIRSPACE: CLASS C svc ctc **APP CON** svc renother times ahoe intl.
  CLASS C svc continuous ctc **APP CON**
RADIO AIDS TO NAVIGATION: NOTAM FILE RNO.
  MUSTANG (H) VORTACW 117.9   FMG   Chan 126   N39°31.88′ W119°39.36′   234° 5.5 NM to fld. 5949/16E.
  VORTAC unusable:
    200°–230° byd 30 NM blo 13,000′
  ILS/DME 110.9   I–RNO   Chan 46   Rwy 16R.   Class ID.   Localizer backcourse unusable byd 20° left of course.
  ILS/DME 109.9   I–AGY   Chan 36   Rwy 34L.   Class IE.   LOC front course unusable inside DUYEP (3.6 NM) above
    8,500′ MSL; at threshold above 6,400′ MSL.

Figure 14A-8. Airport/Facility Directory for RNO

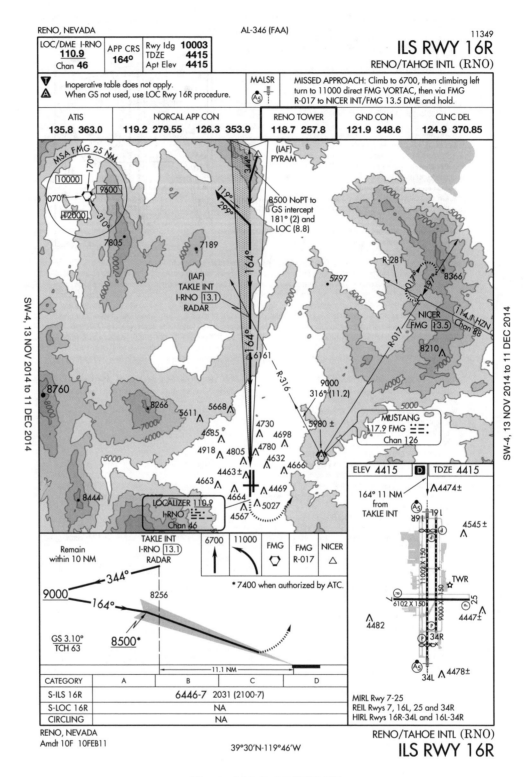

Figure 14A-9. ILS RWY 16R

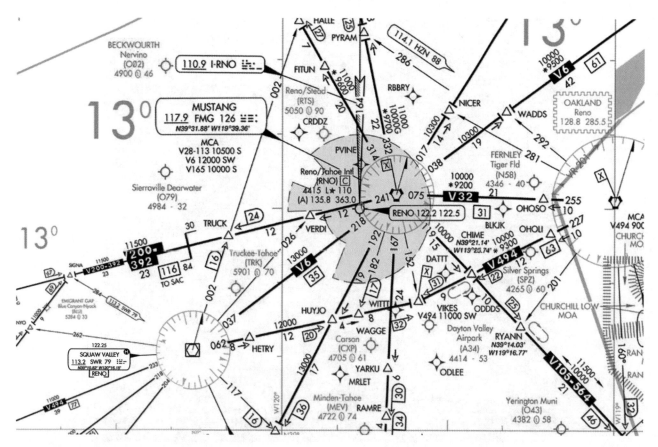

Figure 14A-10. Highest MEA on the route is between FMG and SWR—13,000 feet. (From the Enroute Low-Altitude Chart)

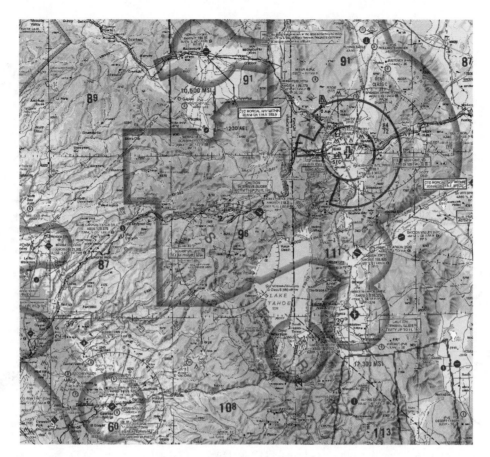

Figure 14A-11. VFR Sectional

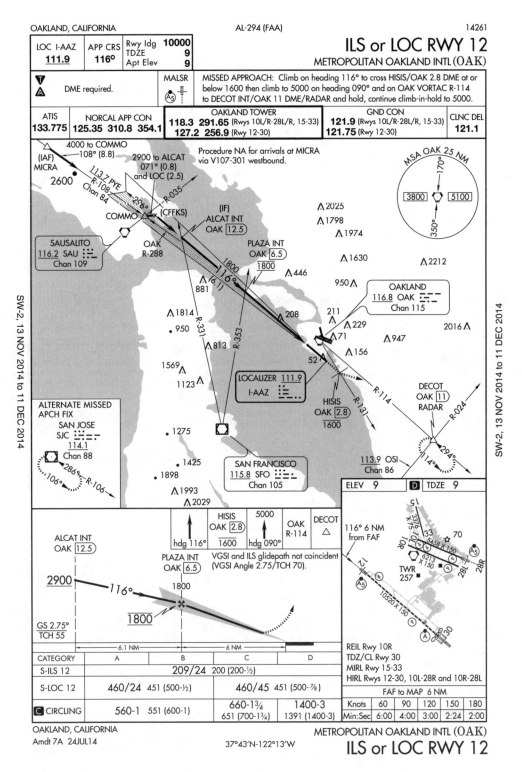

Figure 14A-12. Oakland ILS RWY 12

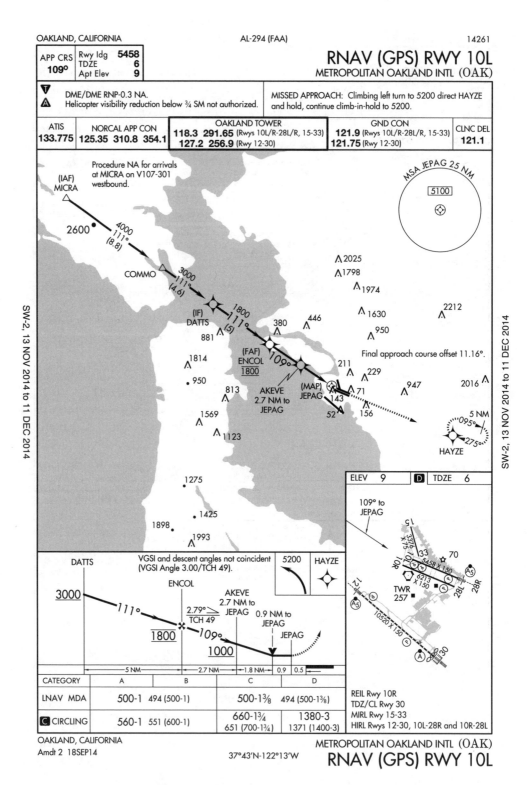

Figure 14A-13. Oakland RNAV RWY 10L

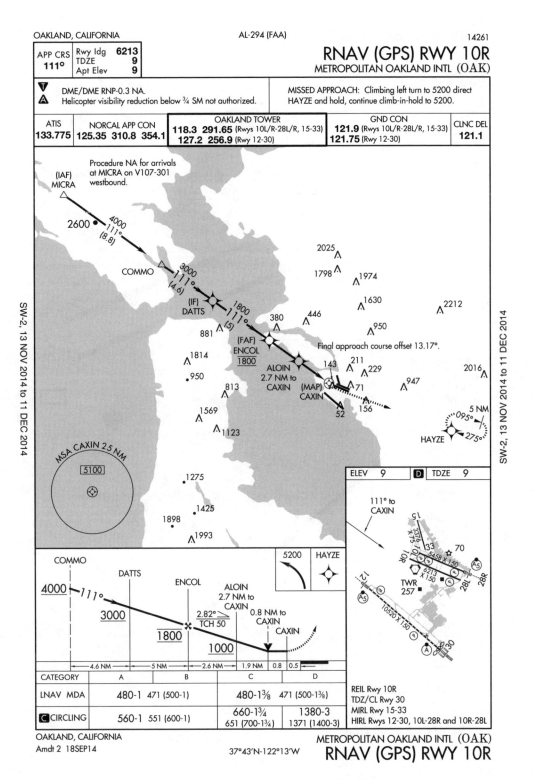

OAKLAND, CALIFORNIA   AL-294 (FAA)   14261

APP CRS	Rwy Idg	6213
111°	TDZE	9
	Apt Elev	9

RNAV (GPS) RWY 10R
METROPOLITAN OAKLAND INTL (OAK)

▽ DME/DME RNP-0.3 NA.
⚠ Helicopter visibility reduction below ¾ SM not authorized.

MISSED APPROACH: Climbing left turn to 5200 direct HAYZE and hold, continue climb-in-hold to 5200.

ATIS	NORCAL APP CON	OAKLAND TOWER	GND CON	CLNC DEL
133.775	125.35 310.8 354.1	118.3 291.65 (Rwys 10L/R-28L/R, 15-33) 127.2 256.9 (Rwy 12-30)	121.9 (Rwys 10L/R-28L/R, 15-33) 121.75 (Rwy 12-30)	121.1

SW-2, 13 NOV 2014 to 11 DEC 2014

OAKLAND, CALIFORNIA
Amdt 2 18SEP14

37°43'N-122°13'W

METROPOLITAN OAKLAND INTL (OAK)
RNAV (GPS) RWY 10R

Figure 14A-14. Oakland RNAV RWY 10R

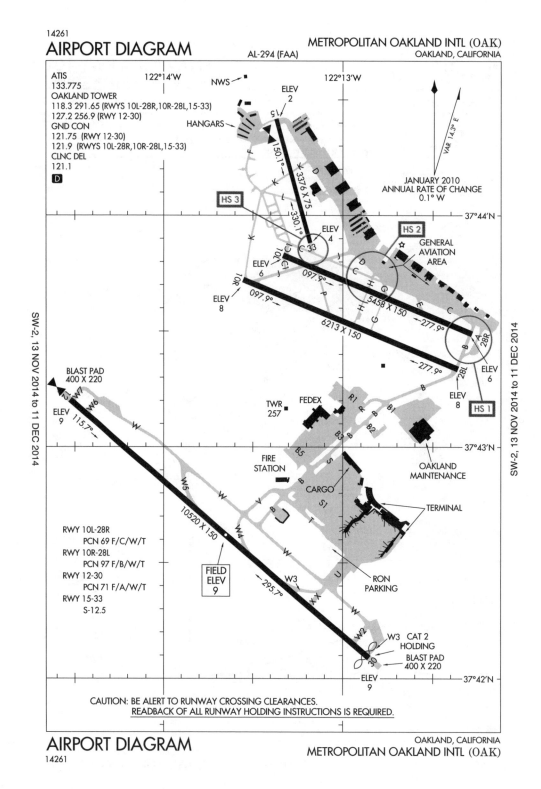

Figure 14A-15. Airport diagram for Metropolitan Oakland International Airport.

OAKLAND

METROPOLITAN OAKLAND INTL   (OAK)(KOAK)   4 S   UTC–8(–7DT)   N37°43.28′ W122°13.27′   SAN FRANCISCO
  9   B   S4   **FUEL** 100LL, JET A   OX 1, 2, 3, 4   TPA—See Remarks   LRA   Class I, ARFF Index D   H–3B, L–2F, 3B, A
  NOTAM FILE OAK.   IAP, AD

  RWY 12–30: H10520X150 (ASPH–GRVD)   PCN 71 F/A/W/T   HIRL   CL
    RWY 12: MALSR. PAPI(P4L)—GA 2.75° TCH 70′. Rgt tfc.
    RWY 30: ALSF2. TDZL. PAPI(P4L)—GA 3.0° TCH 71′. Thld dsplcd 115′.
  RWY 10R–28L: H6213X150 (ASPH–GRVD)   PCN 97 F/B/W/T   HIRL
    RWY 10R: REIL. PAPI(P4L)—GA 3.0° TCH 50′.
    RWY 28L: PAPI(P4L)—GA 3.0° TCH 71′.
  RWY 10L–28R: H5458X150 (ASPH–GRVD)   PCN 69 F/C/W/T   HIRL
    RWY 10L: PAPI(P4R)—GA 3.0° TCH 49′.
    RWY 28R: MALSR. PAPI(P4L)—GA 3.0° TCH 57′. Bldg. Rgt tfc.
  RWY 15–33: H3376X75 (ASPH)   S–12.5   MIRL
    RWY 33: Rgt tfc.

  RUNWAY DECLARED DISTANCE INFORMATION
    RWY 12: TORA–10000 TODA–10000 ASDA–10000 LDA–10000
    RWY 30: TORA–10000 TODA–10000 ASDA–10000 LDA–10000
  AIRPORT REMARKS: Attended continuously. Rwy 15–33 CLOSED to air carrier acft. Birds on and invof arpt. Ops superintendent 510–563–6432, cell 510–715–6286, 24 hour ops 510–563–3361. Acft with experimental or limited certification having over 1,000 horsepower or 4,000 pounds are restricted to Rwy 12–30. TPA—Rwy 28L 606(597), TPA—Rwy 28R 1006(997). 24 hr Noise abatement procedure–turbojet and turbofan powered acft, turborops over 17,000 lbs, four engine reciprocating powered acft, and surplus Military acft over 12,500 lbs should not depart Rwy 28L and Rwy 28R or land on Rwy 10L and Rwy 10R. For noise abatement information ctc noise abatement office at 510–563–6463. 1000′ clearways Rwy 12 and Rwy 30. Twy A, Twy E, Twy G, Twy H between Rwy 28R and Twy C max acft weight 150,000 lbs. Twy G and Twy H between Rwy 28L and Rwy 28R, max acft weight 12,500 lbs. Twy P max acft weight 24,000 lbs single, 40,000 lbs dual. Twy C between Rwy 28R and Twy G and Twy B, Twy J, and Twy D max acft weight 900,000 lbs. Twy C between Twy G and Twy J max acft weight 25,000 lbs single, 175,000 lbs dual, 400,000 lbs tandem. Twy C between Twy J and Twy F max acft weight 25,000 lbs single, 150,000 lbs dual. 155,000 lbs tandem (dual tandem not authorized). Twy K between Twy D and intersection Twy F, Twy L, Twy K max acft weight 25,000 lbs single, 115,000 lbs dual, 140,000 lbs tandem. Twy K between Rwy 10R and intersection Twy F, Twy L, Twy K max acft weight 25,000 lbs single, 115,000 lbs dual, 140,000 lbs tandem. 45,000 lbs dual, tandem not authorized. Twy K between Rwy 10R and intersection Twy F, Twy L, Twy K max acft weight 25,000 lbs single, 45,000 lbs dual, tandem not authorized. Preferential rwy use program in effect 0600–1400Z‡. North fld preferred arrival Rwy 27L, north fld preferred departure Rwys 09R or 27R. If these Rwys unacceptable for safety or twr instruction then Rwy 12–30 must be used. Noise abatement procedures not applicable in emerg or whenever Rwy 12–30 is closed due to maintenance, safety, winds or weather. 400′ by 220′ blast pad Rwy 12 and Rwy 30. Rwys 30, 28R and 28L distance remaining signs left side. Rwy 10L–28R and Rwy 10R–28L have centerline reflectors. 100′ lgtd microwave antenna twr located 1320′ wsw of OAK VORTAC, south of upwind end of Rwy 28L. Rwy 10L–28R and Rwy 10R–28L have centerline reflectors. 100′ lgtd microwave antenna twr located west–southwest of OAK VORTAC, south of upwind end of Rwy 28L. Ldg fee may apply for Rwy 12–30, rwy commercial ops and tiedown, ctc afld ops 510–563–3361. Flight Notification Service (ADCUS) avbl.
  AIRPORT MANAGER: 510–563–6436
  WEATHER DATA SOURCES: ASOS (510) 383–9514 **HIWAS** 116.8 OAK.
  COMMUNICATIONS: D–ATIS 133.775 (510) 635–5850 **UNICOM** 122.95
    OAKLAND RCO 122.2 122.5 (OAKLAND RADIO)
  (R) **NORCAL APP CON** 125.35 (East) 135.65 (South) 135.1 (West) 134.5 120.9
  (R) **NORCAL DEP CON** 135.1 (West) 120.9 (Northwest)
    OAKLAND TOWER 118.3 (Rwy 10L–28R, Rwy 10R–28L, Rwy 15–33) 127.2 (Rwy 12–30) 124.9
    GND CON 121.75 (Rwy 12–30)   121.9 (Rwy 10L–28R, Rwy 10R–28L, Rwy 15–33) **CLNC DEL** 121.1
  AIRSPACE: CLASS C svc ctc APP CON
  RADIO AIDS TO NAVIGATION: NOTAM FILE OAK.
    OAKLAND (H) VORTACW 116.8   OAK   Chan 115   N37°43.56′ W122°13.42′   at fld. 13/17E.   **HIWAS.**
    TACAN AZIMUTH unusable:
      018°–065° byd 30 NM blo 10,000′
      335°–351° byd 30 NM blo 10,000′
      351°–018° byd 20 NM blo 10,000′
    DME unusable:
      335°–065° byd 30 NM blo 8,000′
    ILS 111.9   I–AAZ   Rwy 12.   Class IE.   Ry 11 glideslope deviations are possible when critical areas are not required to be protected. Acft operating invof glideslope transmitter.
    ILS 109.9   I–OAK   Rwy 28R.   Class IE.
    ILS/DME 108.7   I–INB   Chan 24   Rwy 30.   Class IIIE.
  COMM/NAV/WEATHER REMARKS: Emerg frequency 121.5 not avbl at twr.

SW, 13 NOV 2014 to 08 JAN 2015

Figure 14A-16. Airport/Facility Directory for OAK

TIME, FUEL AND DISTANCE TO CLIMB – CRUISE CLIMB

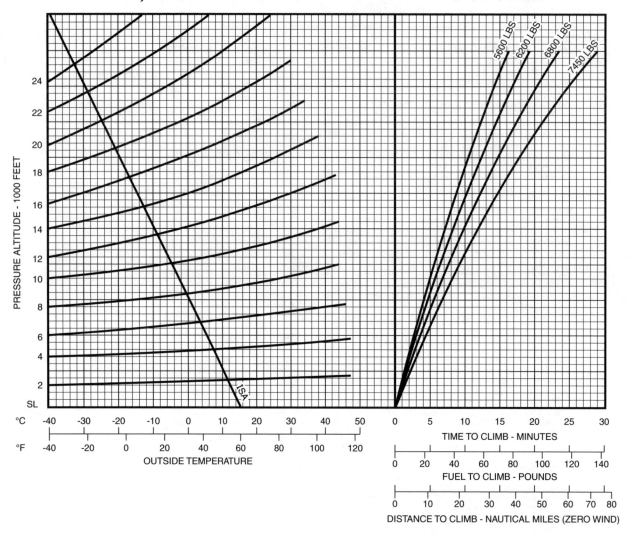

Figure 14A-17. Time, Fuel, Distance to Climb – Cruise Climb chart for Cessna 421C

TIME, FUEL AND DISTANCE TO DESCEND

CONDITIONS:
1. Power - 1800 RPM and 23 Inches Hg.
   Manifold Pressure (45% Power).
2. Fuel Flow - RECOMMENDED LEAN
   (Approximately 83.0
   Pounds Per Hour Per
   Engine).
3. Landing Gear - UP.
4. Wing Flaps - UP.
5. Airspeed - 180 KIAS.

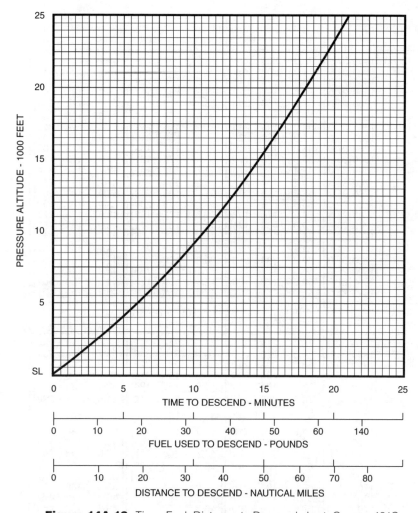

Figure 14A-18. Time, Fuel, Distance to Descend chart, Cessna 421C.

CRUISE PERFORMANCE
WITH RECOMMENDED LEAN MIXTURE

NOTE:
1. At 10,000 Feet, increase speed by 5 KTAS for each 1000 pounds below 7450 pounds.
2. At 15,000 feet, increase speed by 6 KTAS for each 1000 pounds below 7450 pounds.
3. Operations at peak EGT may be utilized with power settings within the boxes. The use of peak EGT results in a speed loss of approximately 4 KTAS and a range increase of approximately 8%.

ALTITUDE	RPM	MP	-25°C (-13°F)			-5°C (STD TEMP) (23°F)			15°C (59°F)		
			PERCENT BHP	KTAS	TOTAL LB/HR	PERCENT BHP	KTAS	TOTAL LB/HR	PERCENT BHP	KTAS	TOTAL LB/HR
10,000 FEET	1900	32.5	78.0	204	271	73.5	204	257	69.0	203	242
	1900	31.0	74.3	200	260	70.0	200	246	65.7	199	231
	1900	29.0	68.8	194	241	64.8	194	228	60.8	193	216
	1900	27.0	63.0	187	223	59.3	187	211	55.7	185	200
	1900	25.0	57.1	180	204	53.8	179	194	50.5	177	183
	1800	32.5	73.2	199	256	69.0	199	242	64.8	198	228
	1800	31.0	69.9	195	245	65.9	195	232	61.8	194	219
	1800	29.0	64.3	189	227	60.6	188	215	56.9	187	204
	1800	27.0	58.8	182	210	55.4	181	199	52.0	179	188
	1800	25.0	53.0	173	191	49.9	172	181	46.9	169	172
	1800	23.0	47.4	165	173	44.7	162	165	42.0	157	156
	1700	32.5	69.2	194	243	65.2	194	230	61.2	193	217
	1700	31.0	65.5	190	230	61.7	190	219	57.9	188	207
	1700	29.0	60.5	184	215	57.0	183	204	53.5	182	193
	1700	27.0	54.9	176	197	51.7	175	187	48.6	173	177
	1700	25.0	49.6	169	180	46.8	167	171	43.9	163	162
	1700	23.0	44.1	158	163	41.6	155	155	39.0	145	147
	1600	32.5	63.4	188	224	59.7	187	212	56.1	185	201
	1600	31.0	60.0	183	213	56.6	183	203	53.1	181	192
	1600	29.0	55.3	177	199	52.1	176	188	48.9	174	178
	1600	27.0	50.3	170	183	47.4	168	173	44.5	164	164
	1600	25.0	45.5	161	167	42.9	158	159	40.2	151	151

ALTITUDE	RPM	MP	-35°C (-30°F)			-15°C (STD TEMP) (6°F)			5°C (42°F)		
			PERCENT BHP	KTAS	TOTAL LB/HR	PERCENT BHP	KTAS	TOTAL LB/HR	PERCENT BHP	KTAS	TOTAL LB/HR
15,000 FEET	1900	32.5	78.0	214	271	73.5	214	257	69.0	213	242
	1900	31.0	74.3	210	260	70.0	210	246	65.7	208	231
	1900	29.0	68.8	203	241	64.8	203	228	60.8	201	216
	1900	27.0	63.0	196	223	59.3	195	211	55.7	193	200
	1900	25.0	57.1	187	204	53.8	186	194	50.5	183	183
	1800	32.5	73.2	209	256	69.0	208	242	64.8	207	228
	1800	31.0	69.9	205	245	65.9	204	232	61.8	203	219
	1800	29.0	64.3	198	227	60.6	197	215	56.9	195	204
	1800	27.0	58.8	190	210	55.4	189	199	52.0	186	188
	1800	25.0	53.0	181	191	49.9	179	181	46.9	174	172
	1800	23.0	47.4	171	173	44.7	166	165	42.0	153	156
	1700	32.5	69.2	204	243	65.2	203	230	61.2	202	217
	1700	31.0	65.5	199	230	61.7	198	219	57.9	197	207
	1700	29.0	60.5	192	215	57.0	191	204	53.5	189	193
	1700	27.0	54.9	184	197	51.7	183	187	48.6	179	177
	1700	25.0	49.6	175	180	46.8	172	171	43.9	165	162
	1600	32.5	63.4	196	224	59.7	195	212	56.1	194	201
	1600	31.0	60.0	192	213	56.6	191	203	53.1	188	192
	1600	29.0	55.3	185	199	52.1	183	188	48.9	180	178
	1600	27.0	50.3	177	183	47.4	174	173	44.5	167	164

Figure 14A-19. Cruise Performance With Recommended Lean Mixture (sheet 2 of 3).

NORMAL TAKEOFF DISTANCE

CONDITIONS:
1. 2235 RPM and 39.0 Inches Hg. Manifold Pressure Before Brake Release.
2. Mixtures – CHECK Fuel Flows In the White Arc.
3. Wing Flaps – UP.
4. Level, Hard Surface, Dry Runway.

NOTE:
1. If full power is applied without brakes set, distances apply from point where full power is applied.
2. Decrease distance 7% for each 10 knots headwind.
3. Increase distance 4% for each 2 knots tailwind.

WEIGHT - POUNDS	TAKEOFF TO 50-FT OBSTACLE SPEED - KIAS	PRESSURE ALTITUDE - FEET	–20°C (–4°F)		–10°C (14°F)		0°C (32°F)		10°C (50°F)	
			GROUND ROLL - FEET	TOTAL DISTANCE TO CLEAR 50 FEET	GROUND ROLL - FEET	TOTAL DISTANCE TO CLEAR 50 FEET	GROUND ROLL - FEET	TOTAL DISTANCE TO CLEAR 50 FEET	GROUND ROLL - FEET	TOTAL DISTANCE TO CLEAR 50 FEET
7450	100	Sea Level	1280	1610	1410	1780	1550	1980	1710	2200
		1000	1360	1710	1500	1890	1650	2100	1810	2340
		2000	1450	1810	1590	2000	1750	2220	1930	2490
		3000	1540	1920	1690	2120	1860	2300	2050	2650
		4000	1630	2030	1800	2260	1980	2520	2190	2830
		5000	1740	2160	1920	2400	2110	2680	2330	3020
		6000	1850	2300	2040	2560	2250	2860	2490	3230
		7000	1970	2440	2180	2720	2400	3060	2650	3460
		8000	2110	2610	2320	2910	2570	3270	2840	3720
		9000	2250	2780	2480	3110	2740	3510	3030	4010
		10,000	2410	2970	2660	3330	2930	3770	3250	4330
6800	96	Sea Level	1010	1280	1110	1410	1220	1550	1370	1750
		1000	1070	1350	1180	1490	1330	1670	1460	1850
		2000	1140	1430	1280	1610	1410	1770	1550	1970
		3000	1240	1540	1360	1700	1500	1880	1650	2090
		4000	1320	1630	1450	1800	1590	2000	1750	2220
		5000	1400	1730	1540	1910	1690	2120	1870	2360
		6000	1490	1840	1640	2030	1800	2260	1990	2520
		7000	1590	1950	1750	2160	1920	2400	2120	2690
		8000	1700	2080	1870	2300	2050	2560	2270	2880
		9000	1810	2210	1990	2460	2190	2740	2420	3080
		10,000	1930	2360	2130	2620	2350	2930	2590	3300
6200	91	Sea Level	810	1030	890	1130	980	1240	1070	1370
		1000	860	1090	950	1200	1040	1320	1140	1450
		2000	920	1150	1010	1270	1100	1390	1240	1570
		3000	980	1220	1070	1340	1200	1500	1320	1660
		4000	1040	1290	1160	1450	1280	1590	1400	1760
		5000	1130	1390	1240	1530	1360	1690	1490	1870
		6000	1200	1480	1320	1630	1450	1800	1590	1990
		7000	1280	1570	1400	1730	1540	1910	1690	2120
		8000	1360	1670	1500	1840	1640	2030	1810	2260
		9000	1450	1770	1600	1960	1750	2170	1930	2410
		10,000	1550	1890	1700	2080	1870	2310	2060	2570

Figure 14A-20. Normal Takeoff Distance chart.

ACCELERATE STOP DISTANCE

CONDITIONS:
1. 2235 RPM and 39.0 Inches Hg. Manifold Pressure Before Brake Release.
2. Mixtures – CHECK Fuel Flows In the White Arc.
3. Wing Flaps – UP.
4. Level, Hard Surface, Dry Runway.
5. Engine Failure at Engine Failure Speed.
6. Idle Power and Maximum Effective Braking After Engine Failure.

NOTE:
1. If full power is applied without brakes set, distances apply from point where full power is applied.
2. Decrease distance 3% for each 4 knots headwind.
3. Increase distance 5% for each 2 knots tailwind.

WEIGHT - POUNDS	ENGINE FAILURE SPEED - KIAS	PRESSURE ALTITUDE - FEET	TOTAL DISTANCE - FEET						
			-20°C -4°F	-10°C +14°F	0°C 32°F	+10°C +50°F	+20°C +68°F	+30°C +86°F	+40°C +104°F
7450	100	Sea Level	2900	3090	3290	3510	3750	4010	4300
		1000	3030	3240	3450	3680	3940	4210	4520
		2000	3180	3390	3620	3870	4140	4430	4760
		3000	3340	3560	3800	4060	4350	4670	5020
		4000	3500	3740	4000	4270	4580	4910	5290
		5000	3680	3930	4200	4500	4820	5180	5580
		6000	3860	4130	4420	4740	5080	5470	5900
		7000	4060	4350	4660	4990	5360	5770	6240
		8000	4280	4580	4910	5260	5660	6100	6600
		9000	4510	4830	5180	5560	5980	6450	6990
		10,000	4750	5090	5460	5870	6320	6830	7410
6800	96	Sea Level	2330	2480	2640	2850	3040	3240	3470
		1000	2440	2600	2800	2990	3190	3400	3650
		2000	2560	2760	2940	3130	3350	3580	3840
		3000	2710	2890	3080	3290	3520	3760	4040
		4000	2850	3040	3240	3460	3700	3960	4260
		5000	2990	3190	3400	3640	3890	4170	4490
		6000	3140	3350	3580	3830	4100	4400	4730
		7000	3300	3530	3770	4030	4320	4640	5000
		8000	3470	3710	3970	4250	4560	4900	5290
		9000	3650	3910	4180	4480	4810	5180	5590
		10,000	3850	4120	4420	4730	5090	5480	5920
6200	91	Sea Level	1890	2010	2140	2280	2430	2590	2790
		1000	1980	2110	2240	2390	2570	2750	2930
		2000	2080	2210	2350	2530	2700	2880	3090
		3000	2180	2320	2500	2660	2840	3030	3250
		4000	2280	2460	2620	2800	2980	3190	3420
		5000	2420	2580	2750	2940	3140	3360	3600
		6000	2540	2710	2890	3090	3300	3540	3800
		7000	2670	2850	3050	3250	3480	3730	4010
		8000	2810	3000	3210	3430	3670	3930	4230
		9000	2960	3160	3380	3610	3870	4150	4470
		10,000	3120	3330	3560	3810	4090	4390	4730
5600	86	Sea Level	1500	1600	1700	1800	1920	2040	2180
		1000	1570	1670	1780	1890	2010	2140	2290
		2000	1650	1750	1870	1980	2110	2250	2430
		3000	1730	1840	1960	2080	2220	2390	2560
		4000	1810	1930	2060	2190	2360	2520	2690
		5000	1900	2030	2160	2330	2480	2650	2830
		6000	2000	2130	2290	2440	2610	2790	2980
		7000	2100	2260	2410	2570	2750	2940	3150
		8000	2230	2380	2540	2710	2890	3090	3320
		9000	2350	2500	2670	2850	3050	3260	3500
		10,000	2470	2640	2820	3010	3220	3450	3700

Figure 14A-21. Accelerate Stop Distance chart.

ACCELERATE GO DISTANCE

CONDITIONS:
1. 2235 RPM and 39.0 Inches Hg. Manifold Pressure Before Brake Release.
2. Mixtures – CHECK Fuel Flows In the White Arc.
3. Wing Flaps – UP.
4. Level Hard Surface Dry Runway.
5. Engine Failure At Engine Failure Speed.
6. Propeller Feathered and Landing Gear Retracted During Climb.
7. Maintain Engine Failure Speed Until Clear of Obstacle.

NOTE:
1. If full power is applied without brakes set, distances apply from point where full power is applied.
2. Decrease distance 6% for each 10 knots headwind.
3. Increase distance 2% for each 1 knots of tailwind.
4. Distance in boxes represent rates of climb less than 50 ft/min.

WEIGHT – POUNDS	ENGINE FAILURE SPEED – KIAS	PRESSURE ALTITUDE – FEET	TOTAL DISTANCE TO CLEAR 50-FOOT OBSTACLE – FEET						
			-20°C -4°F	-10°C +14°F	0°C 32°F	+10°C +50°F	+20°C +68°F	+30°C +86°F	+40°C +104°F
7450	100	Sea Level	2390	2770	3290	4120	5800	12,210	------
		1000	2550	2980	3590	4630	7020	------	------
		2000	2740	3220	3950	5280	9100	------	------
		3000	2940	3500	4390	6190	13,540	------	------
		4000	3170	3830	4940	7570	------	------	------
		5000	3440	4220	5670	9990	------	------	------
		6000	3750	4710	6710	15,590	------	------	------
		7000	4120	5340	8330	------	------	------	------
		8000	4570	6190	11,350	------	------	------	------
		9000	5130	7430	------	------	------	------	------
		10,000	5870	9480	------	------	------	------	------
6800	96	Sea Level	1770	2000	2270	2670	3180	4010	5770
		1000	1880	2120	2460	2870	3470	4510	7070
		2000	2000	2290	2640	3100	3820	5170	9360
		3000	2150	2450	2830	3370	4240	6080	14,690
		4000	2290	2620	3050	3690	4780	7480	------
		5000	2450	2810	3310	4060	5490	9990	------
		6000	2620	3030	3600	4530	6480	16,070	------
		7000	2810	3270	3950	5120	8040	------	------
		8000	3020	3560	4370	5900	10,930	------	------
		9000	3270	3890	4890	7040	------	------	------
		10,000	3550	4280	5560	8880	------	------	------
6200	91	Sea Level	1380	1530	1710	1930	2200	2570	3120
		1000	1460	1620	1810	2050	2380	2800	3420
		2000	1540	1720	1930	2210	2550	3030	3780
		3000	1630	1820	2080	2360	2740	3290	4220
		4000	1730	1960	2210	2530	2960	3610	4780
		5000	1860	2080	2360	2720	3210	3980	5540
		6000	1970	2220	2520	2920	3500	4450	6650
		7000	2100	2370	2710	3160	3840	5050	8470
		8000	2240	2540	2910	3430	4250	5860	12,200
		9000	2390	2720	3150	3750	4760	7060	------
		10,000	2560	2930	3410	4130	5420	9060	------
5600	86	Sea Level	1070	1180	1300	1440	1610	1820	2090
		1000	1130	1240	1370	1530	1710	1940	2240
		2000	1190	1310	1450	1620	1820	2070	2430
		3000	1260	1390	1540	1720	1930	2240	2610
		4000	1330	1470	1630	1820	2090	2390	2820
		5000	1400	1550	1730	1960	2230	2570	3050
		6000	1490	1650	1860	2090	2380	2760	3330
		7000	1580	1770	1980	2230	2550	2990	3650
		8000	1690	1880	2110	2380	2740	3240	4050
		9000	1800	2000	2250	2550	2960	3540	4540
		10,000	1910	2140	2400	2740	3200	3890	5170

Figure 14A-22. Accelerate Go Distance chart.

RATE-OF-CLIMB – ONE ENGINE INOPERATIVE

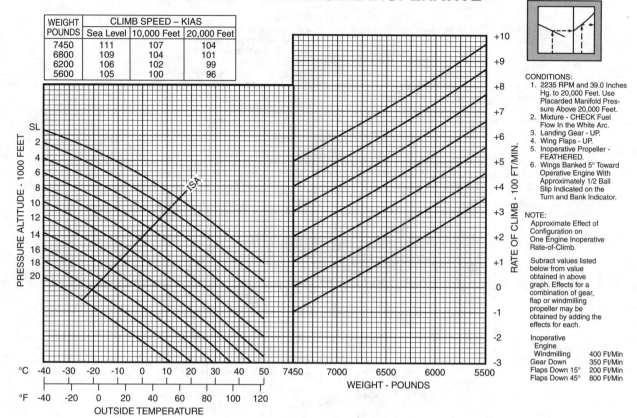

WEIGHT POUNDS	CLIMB SPEED – KIAS		
	Sea Level	10,000 Feet	20,000 Feet
7450	111	107	104
6800	109	104	101
6200	106	102	99
5600	105	100	96

CONDITIONS:
1. 2235 RPM and 39.0 Inches Hg. to 20,000 Feet. Use Placarded Manifold Pressure Above 20,000 Feet.
2. Mixture - CHECK Fuel Flow In the White Arc.
3. Landing Gear - UP.
4. Wing Flaps - UP.
5. Inoperative Propeller - FEATHERED.
6. Wings Banked 5° Toward Operative Engine With Approximately 1/2 Ball Slip Indicated on the Turn and Bank Indicator.

NOTE:
Approximate Effect of Configuration on One Engine Inoperative Rate-of-Climb.

Subract values listed below from value obtained in above graph. Effects for a combination of gear, flap or windmilling propeller may be obtained by adding the effects for each.

Inoperative Engine	
Windmilling	400 Ft/Min
Gear Down	350 Ft/Min
Flaps Down 15°	200 Ft/Min
Flaps Down 45°	800 Ft/Min

Figure 14A-23. Rate-of-Climb—One Engine Inoperative chart.

ONE ENGINE INOPERATIVE SERVICE CEILING

CONDITIONS:
1. One Engine Inoperative Climb Configuration.

NOTE:
1. One Engine inoperative service ceiling is the maximum altitude where the airplane has the capability of climbing 50 feet per minute with one engine inoperative and feathered.
2. Increase indicated service ceiling 100 feet for each 0.10 inches Hg. altimeter setting greater than 29.92.
3. Decrease indicated service ceiling 200 feet for each 0.10 inches Hg. altimeter setting less than 29.92.
4. This chart provides performance information to aid in route selection when operating under FAR 135.181 and 91.119 requirements.

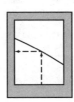

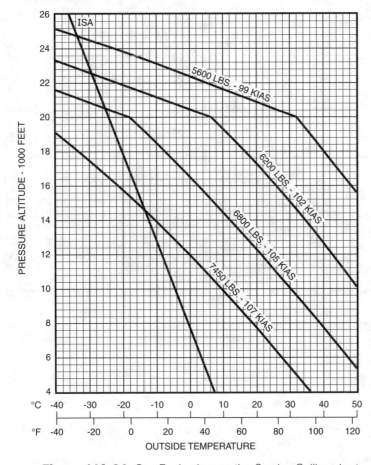

Figure 14A-24. One Engine Inoperative Service Ceiling chart.

NORMAL LANDING DISTANCE

CONDITIONS:
1. Throttles – IDLE at 50 feet above ground level.
2. Landing Gear – DOWN.
3. Wing Flaps – 45°.
4. Touchdown – FULL STALL.
5. Level, Hard Surface Runway.
6. Maximum Effective Braking.

NOTE:
1. If necessary to land with wing flaps UP, the approach speed should be increased above the normal approach speed by 12 knots. Expect total landing distance to increase by 35%.
2. Decrease total distances by 3% for each 4 knots headwind. For operations with tailwinds up to 10 knots, increase total distances by 8% for each 3 knots wind.

WEIGHT - POUNDS	SPEED AT 50-FT OBSTACLE KIAS	PRESSURE ALTITUDE - FEET	-20°C (-4°F)		-10°C (14°F)		0°C (32°F)		10°C (50°F)	
			GROUND ROLL - FEET	TOTAL DISTANCE TO CLEAR 50 FEET	GROUND ROLL - FEET	TOTAL DISTANCE TO CLEAR 50 FEET	GROUND ROLL - FEET	TOTAL DISTANCE TO CLEAR 50 FEET	GROUND ROLL - FEET	TOTAL DISTANCE TO CLEAR 50 FEET
7200	100	Sea Level	640	2210	660	2240	690	2260	710	2290
		1000	660	2230	690	2260	710	2290	740	2310
		2000	690	2260	710	2290	740	2310	770	2340
		3000	710	2280	740	2310	770	2340	790	2370
		4000	740	2310	770	2340	800	2370	820	2400
		5000	770	2340	800	2370	830	2400	860	2430
		6000	790	2370	830	2400	860	2430	890	2460
		7000	820	2400	860	2430	890	2460	920	2490
		8000	860	2430	890	2460	920	2500	960	2530
		9000	890	2460	920	2500	960	2530	990	2570
		10,000	920	2500	960	2530	1000	2570	1030	2610
6600	96	Sea Level	530	2100	550	2120	570	2140	590	2160
		1000	550	2120	570	2140	590	2160	610	2180
		2000	570	2140	590	2160	610	2180	630	2210
		3000	590	2160	610	2180	630	2210	660	2230
		4000	610	2180	630	2210	660	2230	680	2250
		5000	630	2210	660	2230	680	2260	710	2280
		6000	660	2230	680	2260	710	2280	730	2310
		7000	680	2250	710	2280	740	2310	760	2340
		8000	710	2280	740	2310	760	2340	790	2360
		9000	740	2310	760	2340	790	2370	820	2400
		10,000	760	2340	790	2370	820	2400	850	2430

Figure 14A-25. Normal Landing Distance chart.

U.S. DEPARTMENT OF TRANSPORTATION FEDERAL AVIATION ADMINISTRATION	(FAA USE ONLY) ☐ PILOT BRIEFING ☐ VNR ☐ STOPOVER		TIME STARTED	SPECIALIST INITIALS
FLIGHT PLAN				

1. TYPE	2. AIRCRAFT IDENTIFICATION	3. AIRCRAFT TYPE/ SPECIAL EQUIPMENT	4. TRUE AIRSPEED	5. DEPARTURE POINT	6. DEPARTURE TIME		7. CRUISING ALITITUDE
VFR					PROPOSED (Z)	ACTUAL (Z)	
X IFR	N421C	C421C/G	204 KTS	KRNO	2000Z		16,000
DVFR							

8. ROUTE OF FLIGHT

FMG.V6.OAK

9. DESTINATION (Name of airport and city)	10. EST. TIME ENROUTE		11. REMARKS
	HOURS	MINUTES	
KOAK	1.	04	

12. FUEL ON BOARD		13. ALTERNATE AIRPORT(S)	14. PILOT'S NAME, ADDRESS & TELEPHONE NUMBER & AIRCRAFT HOME BASE	15. NUMBER ABOARD
HOURS	MINUTES			
05.	30		17. DESTINATION CONTACT/TELEPHONE (OPTIONAL)	3

16. COLOR OF AIRCRAFT	CIVIL AIRCRAFT PILOTS. FAR Part 91 requires you file an IFR flight plan to operate under instrument flight rules in controlled airspace. Failure to file could result in a civil penalty not to exceed $1,000 for each violation (Section 901 of the Federal Aviation Act of 1958, as amended. Filing of a VFR flight plan is recommended as a good operating practice. See also Part 99 for requirements concerning DVFR flight plans.
W/GD	

FAA Form 7233-1 (8-82)
Electronic Version (Adobe)

CLOSE VFR FLIGHT PLAN WITH _____ FSS ON ARRIVAL

Figure 14A-26. Sample Flight Plan Form KRNO to KOAK.

Regulations

15

🔍 *Chapter Focus on Certificate Limitations*

Becoming a commercial pilot is an exciting and rewarding experience, one of the first of many milestones in a pilot's career. Commercial certification opens up a whole new world of flying possibilities, but with those possibilities comes more responsibility and regulation.

The world of commercial aviation is heavily regulated by the FAA, requiring pilots to learn and interpret regulations to ensure they are operating within the limitations. One of the hardest transitions into commercial flying is determining what you can do legally for hire with your new Commercial Pilot Certificate.

Commercial pilots need to understand the privileges and limitations they operate within, and how these apply to real-world commercial operations. With this knowledge, the pilot can navigate the complex world of commercial aviation.

New commercial pilots often ask the question, "What can I do with my new commercial pilot certificate?" The simple answer is "you can fly for hire." However, the field of commercial aviation is not quite that simple. There are four pathways that commercial pilots generally take:

1. 14 CFR Part 119 (commonly being a CFI)
2. 14 CFR Part 121—Airlines
3. 14 CFR Part 135—Scheduled and unscheduled
4. 14 CFR Part 91 (Subpart K)—Corporate and fractionals

Getting a clear picture of these pathways requires understanding some basic terminology and the definition of flying for hire.

Key Terms

(in the order they appear in this chapter)

common carrier
private carriage
holding out
commercial operator
air carrier
air transportation
compensation

Terminology in the Regulations

Common Carriage/Common Carrier

A carrier—pilot or operator—becomes a *common carrier* when it "holds itself out" to the public or a segment of the public and is willing to offer transportation to any person who wants it. There are four (4) elements defining common carriage:

1. Holding out
2. Transporting persons or property
3. From place to place
4. For compensation

If any of the above is not met, the operation is considered private carriage.

Private Carriage

Carriage for hire that does not involve holding out is *private carriage*, sometimes called contract carriage.

Holding Out

Holding out is a phrase used to describe advertising the availability of services. This can mean physically advertising (via newspaper or website, for example) or it can mean showing a willingness to offer a service. The latter form of advertising is much more indirect and difficult to identify or define.

Commercial Operator

A person who operates an aircraft for compensation or hire is considered a *commercial operator*. When determining whether or not an operation is for compensation or hire, the test applied is whether the carriage by air is merely incidental to the person's other business, or is in itself a major enterprise for profit.

Air Carrier

An *air carrier* is a person who undertakes directly by lease or other arrangement to engage in air transportation.

Air Transportation

Air transportation is defined, for the purpose of the regulations, as interstate, overseas or foreign air transportation or the transportation of mail by air for compensation or hire.

Commercial Pilot Privileges and Limitations

Most pilots who intend to fly professionally usually go on to get their CFI certificate and ratings and teach in order to build the necessary hours to get hired by a 14 CFR Part 121 airline or 14 CFR Part 135 operation. This is probably the easiest and most traveled path taken to the airlines. However, if you choose not to get your flight instructor certificates, or want to fly persons or property for compensation or hire, you need to understand what you can and can't do. Commercial operations outside of the typical 14 CFR Part 121 and Part 135 operations can be confusing. This section will explain commercial pilot privileges and limitations and provide examples of legal and non-legal operations.

Privileges

As a commercial pilot you may act as pilot-in-command (PIC) carrying persons or property for compensation or hire. This is the basic regulation covering all commercial pilots. This regulation does not allow you to operate an aircraft as PIC under 14 CFR Part 135 or 14 CFR Part 121 unless it meets the particular requirements of those sections. 14 CFR Part 119 provides a list of commercial pilot activities that are allowed with a commercial pilot certificate, and that do not fall under the criteria of 14 CFR Part 135 or 121.

The FAA views *compensation* with a broad perspective. In past NTSB rulings, compensation has been defined as more than an exchange of money. Services exchanged will be considered compensation if they are quid pro quo, which means that an equal exchange of services was made. Some examples are:

1. Exchange of money (most likely)
2. Exchange of products
3. Exchange of services
4. Flight time (logged or not)
5. Goodwill or an expectation of goodwill

Limitations

If a commercial pilot does not hold an instrument rating in the same category and class (e.g., AMEL), then the pilot will have a limitation on his or her certificate that reads:

"the carriage of passengers for hire on cross-country flight in excess of 50 NM or at night is prohibited…"

The limitation can be removed by passing the requirements in 14 CFR §61.65.

14 CFR Part 119

14 CFR Part 119 applies to air carriers or commercial operators intending to operate in air commerce (and to charge for services). Part 119 does not apply if common carriage is not involved (holding out your services).

14 CFR Part 119 provides the requirements a person needs to meet to obtain and hold a certificate that allows that person to operate under Part 121 and 135. This includes operations specifications for each kind of operation and the class and size of aircraft to be operated. The exclusions are what the newly minted commercial pilot should focus on. 14 CFR Part 119 does not apply to:

- Operations conducted under Part 91 subpart K—fractional ownership fleet operators (i.e., NetJets)
- Student instruction—if you hold your instructor certificate
- Nonstop commercial air tours (such as Grand Canyon tours)
- Ferry or training flights
- Crop dusting
- Banner towing
- Aerial photography or survey (you cannot transport a photographer)
- Firefighting
- Helicopter operations in construction or repair work (transportation to and from the site)
- Powerline or pipeline patrol
- Nonstop flights conducted within 25 SM of the airport of takeoff for the purpose of parachute jumping
- Emergency mail service
- Flying candidates for elections (the rule refers to 14 CFR §91.321)

A new commercial pilot is likely to have only 250–300 hours of flight time when they receive a commercial pilot certificate. With new regulations in place, commercial pilots will have to wait until they have at least 1,000 hours (1,500 hours if the school attended is not certified) to fly for a Part 121 commercial airline. Most commercial pilots will build time by getting their flight instructor certificate and ratings and teaching students how to fly. However, some may want to take other flying jobs on the 14 CFR Part 119 exclusion list, or fly corporate 14 CFR Part 91. The following case studies are very helpful for understanding what commercial pilots can and can't do for hire.

Case Studies

Case 1

You recently moved to Seattle, Washington, for a new job opportunity with Microsoft. After settling into your house you hear a knock at the door. You open it and your new neighbor, Jim, introduces himself and welcomes you to the neighborhood. After chatting about the neighborhood and schools, Jim asks what you do. You reply that you work for Microsoft designing their flight simulator software. You also mention that you are a commercial pilot and like to fly on the side when you have time.

Jim says he is a contractor and just so happens to be looking for an airplane for flying around to meet with suppliers. He asks if you would be interested in helping him find the right airplane and flying it for him on occasion. He offers a finder's fee for the airplane and season tickets to the Seahawks. Jim will compensate you $50 per flight hour, and $25 an hour for all other duties. You will be an employee of his corporation, Hawks Contracting and Construction.

Based on this information, can you fly for Jim as a commercial pilot?

The answer is yes. Since Jim owns the airplane and is compensating you to be the pilot, this falls under private carriage. If you had owned the airplane and "held out" your services to Jim after meeting him, then that would no longer be private carriage—it would be considered a Part 135 operation, which involves common carriage. In that case, you would have to go through the requirements of 14 CFR Parts 119 and 135 and become a certified air carrier.

Case 2

John owns a very successful toxic waste diving company and enjoys personal flying and flying for business. He holds a Commercial Pilot Certificate with ASEL, AMEL, and an instrument rating. John, his wife, and two children live in Crescent City, California, and have four season tickets to the Seattle Seahawks.

John and his wife were planning on taking the kids and flying to Seattle to watch the Seahawks season opener against the 49ers. However, John's wife is not feeling well and will not be able to make the trip. John remembers his neighbor Dan is a huge 49ers fan so he decides to ask him if he would like to go. Dan is excited about the trip and they both agree Dan will cover aircraft costs, and John will give him the ticket for the game. Is this legal?

The answer is no, it is not legal. In this case John owns the airplane and is receiving compensation for the flight because Dan is paying all the costs related to the aircraft. The only way this can work is if Dan and John split the costs (pro rata). They have established a common purpose (Seahawks game) and just need to split costs to make the flight legal. Examples of direct operating costs that can be split are hanger, fuel, and tie-down fees.

Case 3

Jack is a professional golfer and owns his own airplane, which he flies to golf tournaments regularly. He holds a Commercial Pilot certificate with ASEL, AMEL, and instrument airplane ratings.

Jack is just about to leave a golf tournament and return to his home in Crescent City, California, when his agent asks if he can take a father and daughter with him. The agent tells Jack they need to see a specialist at Sutter Coast Hospital and they would be willing to pay fuel costs. Is this legal?

The answer is no, it is not legal. Jack and his two passengers don't have a common purpose and the pro-rata share has not been established because the passengers are paying all of the fuel costs. To make this operation legal, a common purpose would have to be established and they would need to split fuel costs. Before pro-rata can occur, a common purpose must be established.

Case 4

Silas owns multiple surf and skate shops along the coast of Northern California and Oregon. He wants to be able to get to multiple stores in one day and is getting tired of the driving. An airplane would make things a lot easier on his schedule and allow him to make multiple store stops in one day.

His friend Ben runs the local FBO in Crescent City, California, and has an airplane he is willing to lease to Silas. Ben says he will lease him the airplane along with a pilot. Ben does not have a 14 CFR Part 135 certificate. Can he legally lease Silas the plane and pilot?

No. This is considered a wet lease. In this particular case the plane and pilot cannot come from the same source. Ben could lease Silas the aircraft with no pilot, which is called a dry lease. A dry lease would be legal, but a wet lease would not be legal unless Ben applied for and received a 14 CFR Part 135 operating certificate.

In all four cases, a pilot should ask the following questions:

1. Who has operational control of the aircraft?
2. Is there a common purpose?
3. What costs are considered pro-rata?

Commercial Airlines—14 CFR Part 121

In the past, getting hired by a regional airline required meeting a minimum number of hours that was set by the number of pilots available to hire (the market). In certain cases, pilots who had just received their commercial pilot certificates (with around 300 hours) were being hired as co-pilots to fly for regional airlines. With the new FAA regulations, this is no longer a reality.

The new qualifications apply to the second-in-command (first officer) and pilot-in-command (PIC). First officers must hold an ATP certificate to fly in 14 CFR Part 121 operations. To obtain an ATP certificate the applicant must have 1,500 hours and be age 23 or older.

In certain cases a pilot may qualify for a restricted ATP certificate if they are at least 21 years of age and meet any of the following three conditions:

1. A military pilot with at least 750 hours who has not been taken off flight duty for proficiency or disciplinary reasons.
2. A pilot who attends an accredited institution of higher education (defined by 14 CFR §61.1) with a minimum of 1,000 hours* of flight time. The pilot must have

A person who applies for a restricted ATP under 14 CFR §61.160 must meet all the requirements of §61.159, except that the 500 hours of cross-country flight time is reduced to 200 hours.

obtained a bachelor's degree and completed 60 semester credit hours of aviation and aviation-related coursework and hold a commercial pilot certificate with an airplane category and instrument rating. The flight training must have been completed as part of an approved Part 141 curriculum at the institution, or a Part 141 pilot school that has a training agreement established with the institution.

*If a person has less than 60 credits, but more than 30, the minimum flight time requirement is 1,250 hours. This situation can occur in some Aviation Management degree programs. Each institution will be different and should be consulted to determine into exactly which category their degree program would place you.

3. A pilot who holds an associate's degree with an aviation major from an institution of higher education, has a minimum of 1,250 hours, and has completed at least 30 semester credit hours of aviation and aviation-related coursework. The pilot must hold a commercial pilot certificate with an airplane category and instrument rating. The flight training must have been completed as part of an approved Part 141 curriculum at the institution, or a Part 141 pilot school that has a training agreement established with the institution.

Commercial pilots are advised to seek information from the institution at which they received their training. Each individual's situation will vary and only the specific institution and training program can determine exactly what category of minimums the pilot falls into.

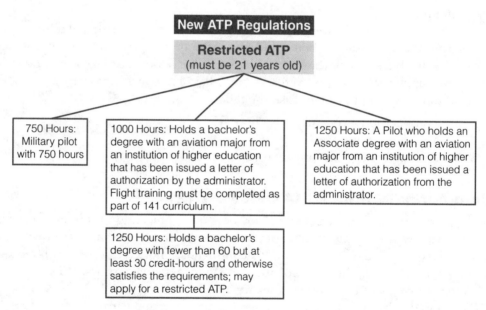

Figure 15-1. New 14 CFR Part 121 first officer requirements.

14 CFR Part 135

To act as PIC under 14 CFR Part 135, a commercial pilot generally needs to meet the requirements of having an instrument rating, 1,200 total hours, 500 hours of cross-country flight time, 100 hours of night, and 75 hours of instrument (50 of which must be actual). If the aircraft used for Part 135 is a turbojet and has 10 or more passenger seats, the PIC must hold an Air Transport Pilot certificate.

14 CFR Part 91 Subpart K

14 CFR Part 91 Subpart K was designed to regulate the growing fractional ownership market. Companies like NetJets and Citation Air fall under this category of operation. Part 91 (K) is designed to give corporations access to the benefits of corporate travel with more regulation than a traditional corporate flight department. To act as PIC in Part 91 (K) operations, the pilot needs a minimum of 1,500 hours; if the aircraft flown is a multi-engine turbine, the PIC must hold an Air Transport Pilot certificate.

Conclusion

A multi-engine rating expands options in terms of aircraft performance and pilot privileges. This multi-engine rating can be added to a private pilot certificate to enhance personal flying options; more often it is added to the commercial pilot certificate to expand opportunities as a professional pilot.

While the process of becoming a professional pilot has not changed significantly, the minimum qualifications to earn and exercise an ATP certificate have changed such that pilots will be spending more time as a commercial pilot before moving up the ladder to earning an ATP certificate. This chapter provides general guidelines—yet due to the complexity of the rules, commercial pilots should consult directly with the school where they receive their training and degree in order to more fully understand their options and goals for putting the new multi-engine rating to work.

Review 15
Regulations

1. Describe the difference between common carriage and private carriage.

2. Define "holding out."

3. List 5 examples of what is considered compensation.

4. What does "quid pro quo" mean?

5. What limitation is placed on a commercial pilot certificate if the pilot does not hold an instrument rating in the same category and class?

6. What is the purpose of 14 CFR Part 119?

7. What commercial operations are excluded from 14 CFR Part 119?

8. What is the difference between a dry and wet lease?

9. *Situation 1*—Your former college roommate has a very successful internet consulting business and wants to buy an airplane to help her visit more clients when she travels around the country. You meet up at a local restaurant to discuss her plan. She says the local FBO offered to lease her an airplane and also provide the pilot.
   a. Is this a legal commercial operation?
   b. Why is it legal or not legal? Explain using material in the chapter and the regulations.

10. *Situation 2*—Your neighbor owns his own Beechcraft Baron and uses it for personal and business use. He sometimes gets busy and wants someone else to fly the plane. He asks you to fly for him on the occasions he does not want to fly himself. He offers you Seattle Seahawks season tickets as payment.
    a. Is this a legal commercial operation?
    b. Why is it legal or not legal? Explain using material in the chapter and the regulations.

    Answers are provided in Appendix 2.

Appendix 1
Glossary

absolute ceiling. The altitude at which a climb is no longer possible.

accelerated slipstream. The airflow accelerated rearward by the propeller producing thrust.

accelerate-go distance. The distance required to accelerate to a decision speed with all engines at takeoff power, experience an engine failure at the decision speed, and continue the takeoff on the remaining engine(s). The runway required includes the distance required to climb to 35 feet, by which time one-engine inoperative takeoff climb speed must be attainted.

accelerate-stop distance (ASD). The distance required to accelerate to a decision speed with all engines at takeoff power, experience an engine failure at V_1, and abort the takeoff and bring the airplane to a stop using braking action only (use of thrust reversing is not considered).

accelerator pump. A component of a carbureted engine that forces additional fuel through the main discharge nozzle when the throttle is moved towards the open (full-power) position. This helps the engine accelerate more quickly and smoothly.

accumulator. A device that stores oil under pressure.

actuator. A system component that converts fluid pressure into linear movement.

ailerons. Primary flight control surfaces mounted on the trailing edge of an airplane wing, near the tip. Ailerons control roll about the longitudinal axis.

air bleed. A component of a carbureted engine that draws air from the float chamber and delivers it to the discharge nozzle to maintain proper fuel and air mixture (mostly during idle or low power settings).

air carrier. A person (generally a company) that undertakes directly, by leads or other arrangements, to engage in air transportation.

air data computer (ADC). The unit that feeds static and ram air pressure to the PFD and MFD in a glass cockpit installation.

air transportation. In the FAA regulations, this refers to interstate, overseas, or foreign air transportation, or the transport of mail by aircraft.

alternator control unit. A component found on aircraft engines with alternators that serves the following functions: protects against system overvoltage, ensures consistent output over a wide range of alternator RPM, and shares entire electrical load equally on dual-fed aircraft.

alternator. A device that converts rotational energy into electrical energy in the form of alternating current (AC). Most aircraft alternators transform the AC electricity into direct current (DC) electricity. Due to the design of an alternator, it is able to produce sufficient power at low RPM. A generator must be spun much faster than an alternator to achieve sufficient power.

ampere (amp). A measurement of the amount of electricity traveling through a circuit over a given time period (typically one hour).

annunciator. A warning light that provides the pilot an awareness of an abnormal aircraft system state. A yellow annunciator (caution) indicates an abnormal system state that may require pilot attention. A red annunciator (warning) indicates an abnormal system status that requires immediate pilot attention.

anti-feathering pins. Spring-loaded pins that prevent a propeller from feathering on engine shutdown. The purpose of anti-feathering pins is to make engine starts less demanding on the aircraft systems.

anti-ice. A system of preventing the formation of ice accretion on an aircraft surface.

anti-servo tab. An adjustable tab attached to the trailing edge of a stabilator that moves in the same direction as the primary control. It is used to make the stabilator less sensitive.

arm. The distance from a datum to the applied force.

ashless dispersant oil. A mineral-based type of lubricating oil used in reciprocating engines. The additives in this oil allow ash deposits resulting from combustion to be dispersed in the oil and returned to the oil filter and sump, where they will not contaminate the engine and damage engine components.

attitude and heading reference system (AHRS). A three-axis sensor that provides aircraft heading, attitude, and yaw information, replacing mechanical gyros for this purpose. The AHRS is integrated into the electronic flight instrument systems (EFIS).

aviator's breathing oxygen. Oxygen that meets certain standards to ensure that it is safe to be taken to altitude; only aviator's breathing oxygen meets this specification. Simply put, impurities and water vapor are removed from the oxygen to prevent freezing.

basic empty weight (BEW). Basic empty weight includes the standard empty weight plus optional and special equipment that has been installed.

battery. A device that stores chemical energy and is capable of converting chemical energy into electrical energy.

blanketing (aerodynamic). This refers to when the relative wind airflow is disturbed by another aircraft surface (such as parts of the fuselage, wing or engines), reducing the control effectiveness of the "blanketed" flight control areas.

bleed hole. A small hole in an oil or hydraulic powered system that is used by maintenance to remove air from the system. Any air within a hydraulic system will significantly reduce the effectiveness of the system.

blower fan. An electrically powered fan that increases the speed of airflow going through the heater and into the cabin. Blower fans are necessary when the aircraft is on the ground where there is little relative airflow. Once an aircraft is airborne, most heating systems will automatically turn off the blower fan.

bottom dead center (BDC). The physical position of the piston within the cylinder of a reciprocating engine when the piston is at the lowest point of its range of travel.

brake caliper. The brake component that holds the brake pads around the brake rotor. The caliper transfers the hydraulic force from the brake fluid to the brake pads.

brake cylinder. An actuator that transfers the pilot's toe pressure into hydraulic force, which in turn squeezes the brake pads against the rotors.

brake rotor. Also known as the brake disc, this is the circular component of the brake system that the brake pads "squeeze" in order to slow the aircraft wheels and slow the aircraft.

bus bar (bus). An electrical power distribution point to which several circuits may be connected. It is often a solid metal strip having a number of terminals installed on it.

carburetor. A device that mixes air and fuel entering an internal combustion, piston, reciprocating engine.

center of gravity (CG). The point at which an airplane would balance if it were possible to suspend it at that point. It is the mass center of the airplane, or the theoretical point at which the entire weight of the airplane is assumed to be concentrated. It may be expressed in inches from the reference datum, or in percentage of mean aerodynamic chord (MAC). The CG location depends on the distribution of weight in the airplane.

check valve. A valve that allows fluid to flow in only one direction. A check valve is commonly used to lock fluid into one portion of a closed system.

circuit breaker. A circuit-protecting device that opens the circuit in case of excess current flow. A circuit breaker differs from a fuse in that it can be reset without having to be replaced.

combustion heater. A heater that burns fuel from the aircraft fuel tanks.

commercial operator. A person who operates an aircraft for compensation or hire.

common carrier. A carrier that holds out to the public its services (this can be a pilot or an operator), and is willing to offer transportation to any person who wants it.

compensation. An exchange of money or services.

compression stroke. The movement of the piston returning to the top of the cylinder compressing the fuel and air mixture into the combustion chamber of the cylinder head. During this stroke, both the intake and exhaust valves are closed.

compressor. The "pump" that increases the pressure of the intake air. In most cases the compressor is a round, fan-shaped object that rapidly changes the velocity of the air when it is spun at high speed. There are a few different types of compressors in use today. Centrifugal compressors are by far the most common compressors used in modern turbocharged aviation engines.

constant-speed propeller. A controllable-pitch propeller whose pitch is automatically adjusted in flight by a governor to maintain a constant RPM through varying airspeed ranges.

continuous flow oxygen system. A system that supplies a constant supply of pure oxygen to a rebreather bag which dilutes the pure oxygen with exhaled gases and thus supplies a healthy mix of oxygen and ambient air to the mask. Primarily used in passenger cabins of commercial airliners.

controllable-pitch propeller. A propeller with adjustable pitch propeller blades. The blade angle is typically adjusted by the pilot and/or the governor. Most often, engine oil is used to physically move the propeller blades.

conventional twin. Twin-engine aircraft in which both propellers turn in the same direction—clockwise from the pilot's perspective.

counter-rotating twin. Twin-engine aircraft in which the propellers turn in the opposite direction, typically toward each other (left engine turns clockwise and the right engine counter-clockwise).

crankshaft. The part of a reciprocating piston engine that translates the linear action of the piston (up and down) into a rotational (circular) force. The crankshaft produces the rotational force that drives the propeller of a piston-powered, reciprocating aviation engine.

critical engine. The engine whose failure has the most adverse effect on directional control.

cylinder head temperature (CHT). A measurement of the temperature at the top of the cylinder.

datum. An imaginary vertical plane or line from which all measurements of arm are taken. The datum is established by the manufacturer. Once the datum has been selected, all moment arms and the location of CG range are measured from this point.

deck pressure. The measurement of the air pressure, in inches of mercury, in the intake manifold prior to the throttle valve.

deep stall. A stall in which the airflow over the horizontal tail surface is blanketed by the disturbed airflow from the wings and fuselage. This will diminish elevator or stabilator control, making recovery difficult.

deice. A system of removing ice accretion from a surface of the aircraft.

density controller. Provides the normalizing feature of the turbocharger. As the deck pressure decreases, the density controller will increase the oil pressure to the exhaust by-pass valve, which in turn closes the waste gate. As the waste gate closes, the turbine spins faster and the compressor increases the pressure of the intake air which will result in a higher deck pressure and manifold pressure. The density controller is designed to work only during full power.

detonation. The sudden release of heat energy from fuel in an aircraft engine caused by the fuel and air mixture reaching its critical pressure and temperature. Detonation occurs as a violent explosion rather than a smooth burning process.

differential ailerons. Control surface rigged such that the aileron moving up moves a greater distance than the aileron moving down. The up aileron produces extra parasite drag to compensate for the additional induced drag caused by the down aileron. This balancing of the drag forces helps minimize adverse yaw.

differential braking. The practice of applying more brake pressure to one wheel in an effort to help turn the aircraft.

differential pressure controller. The differential pressure controller is designed to limit the boost—increased pressure of intake air—during partial power applications.

diluter-demand oxygen system. An oxygen system that delivers oxygen mixed or diluted with air in order to maintain a constant oxygen partial pressure as the altitude changes.

diode. An electric component that allows electricity to pass in only one direction.

directional control. Control about the vertical axis of an aircraft. The vertical tail is the primary contributor to directional control, causing an airplane in flight to align with the relative wind.

drag. The net aerodynamic force parallel to the relative wind, usually the sum of two components: induced drag and parasite drag.

dual-fed. An aircraft electrical system that has two normal sources of electricity (one alternator or generator on each engine).

elevator. The horizontal, moveable primary control surface in the tail section, or empennage, of an airplane. The elevator is hinged to the trailing edge of the fixed horizontal stabilizer.

exhaust bypass valve. The object that controls the waste gate. Most exhaust bypass valves are controlled by engine oil pressure.

exhaust gas temperature (EGT). A measurement of the air leaving the combustion chamber, measured downstream in the exhaust manifold before the air leaves through the exhaust stack.

exhaust stroke. This movement of the piston from bottom dead center back up to top dead center with the exhaust valve open forces the spent fuel and air mixture through the exhaust port and into the exhaust manifold.

external power. A source of electricity that is not part of the normal aircraft electrical system.

feather. To feather a propeller blade is to rotate it around its pitch-change axis so it becomes parallel to the line of flight.

feathering propeller. A controllable pitch propeller with a pitch range sufficient to allow the blades to be turned parallel to the line of flight to reduce drag and prevent further damage to an engine that has been shut down after a malfunction.

fixed-pitch propeller. A propeller with fixed blade angles.

floor load limit. The maximum weight the floor can sustain per square inch or foot, as provided by the manufacturer.

Fowler flap. A type of secondary flight control surface that is mounted on the trailing edge of the airplane wing, inboard of the ailerons. The Fowler flap moves outward and downward on tracks, increasing both camber and the surface area of the wing surface.

freezing drizzle. Drizzle is precipitation at ground level or aloft in the form of liquid water drops that have diameters less than 0.5 mm and greater than 0.05 mm. Freezing drizzle is drizzle that exists at air temperatures less than 0°C (supercooled), remains in liquid form, and freezes upon contact with objects on the surface or airborne.

freezing rain. Rain is precipitation at ground level or aloft in the form of liquid water drops which have diameters greater than 0.5 mm. Freezing rain is rain that exists at air temperatures less than 0°C (supercooled), remains in liquid form, and freezes upon contact with objects on the ground or in the air.

Frise ailerons. Aileron having the nose portion projecting ahead of the hinge line. When the trailing edge of the aileron moves up, the nose projects below the wing's lower surface and produces some parasite drag, decreasing the amount of adverse yaw.

fuel cross-feed. A system that allows either engine on a twin-engine airplane to draw fuel from any fuel tank.

fuel injection. A method of mixing the fuel with air for combustion directly in the cylinder where the combustion will take place.

fuel transfer. A system that allows fuel to be delivered from one fuel tank to another fuel tank within the aircraft fuel system.

fuel vent. An opening in the fuel tank that allows air or fuel to pass out of or into the tank. Without a fuel vent, a fuel tank could rupture with a decrease in pressure.

fuse. A circuit-protecting device that opens the circuit in case of excess current flow. A fuse differs from a circuit breaker in that it cannot be reset without being replaced.

gear down snubber orifice. Slows the release of hydraulic pressure as it equalizes at the emergency gear valve. This slows gear extension to prevent damage to the landing gear system.

gear warning horn. A system which audibly alerts the pilot that the landing gear is not in a safe position for landing. The gear warning horn will also activate if the landing gear handle is retracted while the aircraft is still on the ground.

gear warning light. Anytime the gear is not in a safe position, this panel light will illuminate.

generator. A device that converts rotational energy into electrical energy in the form of alternating current (AC) or direct current (DC). The generator is designed opposite to an alternator; however, the same effect is achieved. A generator must be spun much faster than an alternator in order to produce sufficient power.

global positioning system (GPS). Navigation system that uses satellite rather than ground-based transmitters for location information.

governor. A control that controls the rotational speed of a device. On a constant speed propeller, the governor boosts the pressure of engine oil to control the RPM of the propeller.

ground effect. Occurring within approximately one wing span from the ground, ground effect results from a reduction in upwash, downwash, and wingtip vortices, and provides a corresponding decrease in induced drag.

high pressure control valve. A relief valve that prevents damage to the gear system that could occur due to excessively high pressure during gear retraction.

holding out. Advertising the availability of goods and services.

horizontal component of lift. One of two components that make up total lift when the airplane is banked. The other component is the vertical component of lift.

horizontal situation indicator (HSI). A flight navigation instrument that combines the heading indicator with a CDI in order to provide the pilot with better situational awareness of location with respect to the course line.

induced airflow. The volume of air accelerated behind a propeller producing thrust.

induction. The clean intake air that enters a combustion engine to be mixed with fuel and used for combustion.

intake stroke. The movement of the piston descending from the top of the cylinder to the bottom of the cylinder, increasing the volume of the cylinder. During this movement, a mixture of fuel and air is drawn into the cylinder through the intake port.

intercooler. A device used to reduce the temperature of the compressed air before it enters the fuel metering device. The resulting cooler air has a higher density, which permits the engine to be operated at a higher power setting.

keel effect. A weathervane tendency similar to the keel of a ship, exerting a steadying influence on the aircraft laterally about the longitudinal axis.

known icing conditions. Atmospheric conditions in which the formation of ice is observed or detected in flight.

landing distance. The distance required to complete a landing from a height of 50 feet above the runway until the aircraft has stopped on the landing surface.

landing ground roll distance. The distance required to stop after touching down on the landing surface.

landing weight. The takeoff weight of an aircraft less the fuel burned and/or dumped enroute.

lift. A component of the total aerodynamic force on an airfoil, acting perpendicular to the relative wind.

limit switch. A switch that activates or deactivates an electrically powered system by the proximity of an object.

low-pitch stop. A physical stop that prevents a propeller from reaching to shallow (or negative) blade angles. A propeller is against the low-pitch stop if the actual propeller RPM is below selected propeller RPM.

low pressure control valve. A spring-loaded poppet valve which will relieve pressure within an oil or hydraulic system. The valve can be preset to open at specific pressures, depending upon system requirements. It is called a low-pressure control valve when it is set to open at lower pressure; for example, extending the gear in a hydraulic landing-gear system.

magneto. A self-contained, engine-driven unit that supplies electrical current to the spark plugs; it is completely independent of the airplane's electrical system. There are normally two magnetos per engine.

manifold (absolute) pressure (MAP). The (absolute) pressure of the fuel and air mixture within the intake manifold, usually indicated in inches of mercury (in. Hg).

mineral oil. A type of lubricating oil that is purely petroleum-based with no additives.

moment. The product of the weight of an item multiplied by its arm. Moments are expressed in pound-inches (lb-in). Total moment is the weight of the airplane multiplied by the distance between the datum and the CG.

multi-function display (MFD). Small screen (CRT or LCD) in an aircraft that can be used to display information, such as GPS moving maps, airport data, weather information, terrain proximity, and aircraft engine and systems information, replacing several analog-type indicators. Often an MFD will be used in concert with a primary flight display.

negative ground. *See* positive/negative ground.

normally aspirated. A reciprocating piston engine that uses ambient (normal, unpressurized outside air) for combustion.

oil cooler. A radiator that circulates the oil through a coil so that the oil can be cooled using ambient airflow.

one engine inoperative rate of climb. The rate of climb of a multiengine aircraft with one engine inoperative.

Otto cycle. The thermodynamic cycle that describes the function of a typical reciprocating piston engine. It can be broken down into four basic steps (or strokes): intake, compression, combustion, exhaust.

over-temperature limit switch. An electrical switch that deactivates an electrical device once a predetermined temperature has been reached. Combustion heaters have over-temperature limit switches as a safety measure.

oxygen regulator. Manually adjustable device used to reduce cylinder pressure to torch pressure and to keep the oxygen pressure constant in an oxygen delivery system.

payload. The weight of occupants, cargo and baggage.

performance speeds. Designated speeds for a specific flight condition.

P-factor (or, propeller factor). A tendency for an aircraft to yaw to the left due to the descending propeller blade on the right producing more thrust than the ascending blade on the left. This occurs when the aircraft's longitudinal axis is in a climbing attitude in relation to the relative wind.

plain flap. A type of secondary flight control surface that is mounted on the trailing edge of the airplane wing, inboard of the ailerons. The plain flap deflects downwards into the airflow below the wing, increasing the camber of the wing surface.

positive/negative ground. An electrical ground is a wire attached to an electrical conductor (solid, clean, metal or copper component) that prevents a buildup of static electricity within electrical components. A positive ground system sends a grounding wire from the positive side of the battery and the starter receives the negative wire. A negative ground system sends a grounding wire from the negative side of the battery and the starter receives the positive wire. Negative ground is the standard format in most aircraft and automotive applications.

power enrichment system. A component of a carbureted engine that enriches the fuel and air mixture (adds more fuel to the air) during full throttle operations.

power stroke. The beginning of the second revolution, this is the movement of the cylinder from top dead center back down to bottom dead center. This movement is initiated by the ignition of the fuel and air mixture. Both the intake and exhaust valves are closed during this stroke.

pressure control valve (high pressure or low pressure). A spring-loaded poppet valve which will relieve pressure within an oil or hydraulic system. The valve can be preset to open at specific pressures depending upon system requirements.

pressure switch. A switch that activates or deactivates an electrically powered system once a predetermined fluid pressure is reached.

pressure-demand oxygen system. A demand oxygen system that supplies 100 percent oxygen at sufficient pressure above the altitude where normal breathing is adequate. Also referred to as a pressure breathing system.

primary flight controls. The controls that cause the airplane to move about its three axes of pitch, roll and yaw. These include the aileron, elevator, and rudder.

primary flight display (PFD). A display that provides increased situational awareness to the pilot by replacing the traditional six analog instruments used for instrument flight with an easy-to-scan display providing the horizon, airspeed, altitude, vertical speed, trend, trim, and rate of turn, among other key relevant indications.

private carriage. Carriage for hire that does not involve holding out.

propeller synchronization. A condition in which all of the propellers have their pitch automatically adjusted to maintain a constant RPM among all of the engines of a multi-engine aircraft.

propeller synchrophasing. A condition in which the propellers nearest the fuselage of a multi-engine aircraft are sequenced so that at any given time, only one propeller tip is passing the fuselage. This creates a more even noise within the cockpit.

propwash. The volume of air accelerated behind a propeller producing thrust.

pushrod. The control surface that forces the intake of exhaust valves open. The pushrod is moved by the camshaft.

ramp weight/taxi weight. The weight of the aircraft with all fuel and with payload on board. Ramp weight can be calculated by taking the zero fuel weight and adding all of the usable fuel on board.

rate-of-change controller. The rate-of-change controller limits the rate of boost during power application to prevent the system from overshooting the pilot-selected power setting.

revolutions per minute (RPM). A measurement of the number of revolutions a propeller or other rotating surface makes within one minute.

rudder authority. The ability of the rudder to generate adequate moment under specific conditions through the law of the lever.

rudder. The moveable primary control surface mounted on the trailing edge of the vertical fin, or empennage, of an airplane. Movement of the rudder rotates the airplane about its vertical axis.

secondary flight controls. The controls that supplement the primary flight controls to assist the pilot in operating an airplane. Secondary flight controls include flaps, trim, and flight spoilers.

service ceiling. The maximum density altitude where the best rate-of-climb airspeed will produce a 100 feet-per-minute climb at maximum weight while in a clean configuration with maximum continuous power.

shock cooling. Cooling a piston-powered reciprocating, combustion engine too quickly. This typically occurs when power is reduced rapidly, and can result in physical damage to the cylinder head(s).

shuttle valve. A valve that allows fluid to flow one of two directions depending upon system requirements.

single-engine absolute ceiling. The altitude at which a multi-engine airplane can no longer climb with one engine inoperative.

single-engine operations. Multi-engine operations with only one engine operative.

single-engine rate of climb. The climb rate of a multi-engine aircraft with only one engine operative.

single-engine service ceiling. The altitude at which a multiengine airplane can no longer climb at a rate greater than 50 feet-per-minute with one engine inoperative.

slotted flap. A type of secondary flight control surface that is mounted on the trailing edge of the airplane wing, inboard of the ailerons. The slotted flap deflects downwards, increasing the camber of the wing surface. It also redirects some of the airflow below the surface of the wing over the upper surface of the flap, preventing airflow separation and in turn increasing the lift produced by the wing surface.

snubber. A restriction within a hydraulic system that slows the movement of a hydraulic actuator.

spiraling slipstream. The slipstream of a propeller-driven airplane that rotates around the airplane. This slipstream strikes the left side of the vertical fin, causing the aircraft to yaw slightly.

split flap. A type of secondary flight control surface that is part of the underside of the trailing edge of the airplane wing, inboard of the ailerons. The split flap deflects downwards into the airflow below the wing, increasing the camber of the wing surface.

spoiler. High-drag devices that can be raised into the air flowing over an airfoil, reducing lift and increasing drag. Spoilers are used for roll control on some aircraft. Deploying spoilers on both wings at the same time allows the aircraft to descend without gaining speed. Spoilers are also used to shorten the ground roll after landing.

squat switch. An electrical switch mounted on one of the landing gear struts. It is used to sense when the weight of the aircraft is on the wheels.

stabilator. A single-piece horizontal tail surface on an airplane that pivots around a central hinge point. A stabilator serves the purposes of both the horizontal stabilizer and the elevators.

starter contactor. A relay (electrical switch) that connects the battery to the starter in order to start the engine.

station. A location in the airplane that is identified by a number designating its distance in inches from the datum. The datum is, therefore, identified as station zero. An item located at station +50 would have an arm of 50 inches.

supercharged. A reciprocating piston engine that increases the pressure of the intake air well above standard, sea-level atmospheric pressure (30 in. Hg) prior to combustion.

synthetic oil. Lubricant that consists of chemical compounds that are artificially made.

tail down force. A force exerted by the horizontal stabilizer to counteract aircraft nose-down tendency and provide longitudinal stability.

takeoff distance (TOD). The distance required to complete an all-engines-operative takeoff from brake release to the 35-foot height. It must be at least 15% less than the distance required for a one-engine inoperative engine takeoff. This distance is not normally a limiting factor as it is usually less than the one-engine inoperative takeoff distance.

takeoff ground roll distance. The distance required to complete an all-engines-operative takeoff from brake release until the aircraft leaves the ground.

takeoff weight. The weight of an aircraft just before beginning the takeoff roll. It is the ramp weight less the weight of the fuel burned during start and taxi.

taxi weight. *See* ramp weight/taxi weight.

thermal relief. A poppet-valve that will relieve pressure within an oil or hydraulic system if the fluid expands as a result of high temperature.

thrust. The forward aerodynamic force produced by a propeller, fan, or turbojet engine as it forces a mass of air to the rear, behind the aircraft.

thrust centerline. An imaginary line passing through the center of the propeller hub, perpendicular to the plane of the propeller rotation.

thrust vector. The resultant forward aerodynamic force produced by a propeller blade as it forces a mass of air rearward.

tie bus. A switch that connects two or more bus bars. It is usually used when one generator fails and power is lost to its bus. By closing the switch, the operating generator powers both buses.

top dead center (TDC). The physical position of the piston within the cylinder of a reciprocating engine when the piston is at the highest point of its range of travel.

torque. Forces that produce a twisting or rotating motion.

turbocharged. A reciprocating piston engine that increases the pressure of the intake air prior to combustion.

turbo-normalized. A turbocharging system that maintains sea level power as the aircraft climbs to altitude.

V_A. The design maneuvering speed. The maximum speed at which full, abrupt control movement can be used without overstressing the airframe.

valve. A tapered, disk-shaped plug, which controls the flow of air and fuel through the intake and exhaust ports. Each cylinder contains at least two valves, located at the top of the cylinder (also referred to as the cylinder head). The valves are held closed by a spring, and are forced open by the push rod.

venturi. An effect that reduces the static pressure of a fluid (air included) as it flows through a constricted section of a pipe.

V_{FE}. The maximum speed with the flaps extended. The upper limit of the white arc.

V_{LE}. Landing gear extended speed. The maximum speed at which an airplane can be safely flown with the landing gear extended.

V_{LO}. Landing gear operating speed. The maximum speed for extending or retracting the landing gear if using an airplane equipped with retractable landing gear.

V_{LOF}. Lift off speed. The speed at which the airplane leaves the surface.

V_{MC} demonstration. A flight maneuver in which the pilot demonstrates intentional loss of directional control and proper recovery technique.

V_{MC}. Minimum control airspeed. This is the minimum flight speed at which a light, twin-engine airplane can be satisfactorily controlled when an engine suddenly becomes inoperative and the remaining engine is at takeoff power.

V$_{MCG}$. Minimum control speed on the ground. This is the minimum calibrated airspeed during the takeoff run at which, when the critical engine is suddenly make inoperative, it is possible to maintain control of the airplane using the rudder control alone. This speed is not required to be published in aircraft certified under 14 CFR Part 23 and less than 6,000 pounds.

V$_{NE}$. The never-exceed speed. Operating above this speed is prohibited since it may result in damage or structural failure. The red line on the airspeed indicator.

V$_{NO}$. The maximum structural cruising speed. Do not exceed this speed except in smooth air. The upper limit of the green arc.

volt. A measurement of the electric potential and electromotive force.

V$_R$. Rotation speed. The speed that the pilot begins rotating the aircraft prior to lift-off.

V$_{S0}$. The stalling speed or the minimum steady flight speed in the landing configuration. In small airplanes, this is the power-off stall speed at the maximum landing weight in the landing configuration (gear and flaps down). The lower limit of the white arc.

V$_{S1}$. The stalling speed or the minimum steady flight speed obtained in a specified configuration. For most airplanes, this is the power-off stall speed at the maximum takeoff weight in the clean configuration (gear up, if retractable, and flaps up). The lower limit of the green arc.

V$_{SSE}$. Safe, intentional one-engine inoperative speed. The minimum speed to intentionally render the critical engine inoperative.

V$_X$. Best angle-of-climb speed. The airspeed at which an airplane gains the greatest amount of altitude in a given distance. It is used during a short-field takeoff to clear an obstacle.

V$_{XSE}$. Best angle of climb speed with one engine inoperative. The airspeed at which an airplane gains the greatest amount of altitude in a given distance in a light, twin-engine airplane following an engine failure.

V$_Y$. Best rate-of-climb speed. This airspeed provides the most altitude gain in a given period of time.

V$_{YSE}$. Best rate-of-climb speed with one engine inoperative. This airspeed provides the most altitude gain in a given period of time in a light, twin-engine airplane following an engine failure.

waste gate. A butterfly valve located inside the exhaust pipe that can direct exhaust gas over the turbine wheel, or direct exhaust gas around the turbine wheel and out the exhaust pipe into the atmosphere.

weight. A measure of the force of gravity acting upon a body. One of the four main forces acting on an aircraft, acting downward through the aircraft's center of gravity toward the center of the Earth opposing lift.

windmilling. When an engine fails in flight, there is enough aerodynamic force (relative wind) to continue to rotate the propeller—this is called windmilling. It creates additional aerodynamic drag, which can be reduced by feathering the propeller.

zero sideslip. A maneuver in a twin-engine airplane with one engine inoperative that involves a small amount of bank and slightly uncoordinated flight to align the fuselage with the direction of travel and minimize drag.

zero fuel weight. The weight of an aircraft with all payload but without fuel.

Appendix 2
Answers to Review Questions

Section I Multi-Engine Systems

Review 1: Flight Controls

1. Elevator/stabilator, rudder, and ailerons

2. An elevator is hinged to the horizontal stabilizer—which means that part of the horizontal stabilizer moves, and the other portion is fixed. The stabilator replaces the entire horizontal stabilizer, and the entire horizontal stabilizer surface moves. This design is generally found on Piper aircraft.

3. The anti-servo tab is designed to make the control surface harder to move. The anti-servo tab is a small tab attached to the stabilator or rudder that moves with the control surface in the same direction—but farther—making the control forces feel heavier to the pilot. Its purpose is to prevent the pilot from overstressing the aircraft by applying sudden and abrupt control deflection.

4. When the aircraft enters the initial stall, there generally is enough airflow over the stabilator to remain streamlined with the relative airflow. As the stall deepens and the airload on the stabilator decreases, the stabilator is driven by the elevator down spring to the nose-down position. The purpose is to prevent the stall from deepening.

5. Differential ailerons are designed to reduce adverse yaw and reduce the likelihood of the wing tips stalling. This is accomplished by restricting the travel of the downward aileron. Frise-type ailerons are designed to reduce the effects of adverse yaw. This is done by protruding the bottom of the upward-traveling aileron into the relative wind, causing drag opposite to the direction the aircraft is trying to yaw. The ailerons can be combined, offering the benefits of both design types.

These can be combined to offer the benefits of both design types.

6. The pilot should use power to control the pitch of the aircraft. The centerline of thrust will determine the direction of pitch when power changes are made. Bank can also be used to reduce pitch.

7. Very simply put, if you yaw, you roll; if you roll, you yaw—you can't have one without the other. For example, if the pilot pushes the right rudder, the left wing speeds up and rolls. This is also referred to as Dutch roll.

8. Generally, the first step is to press and hold the trim interrupt switch (if installed). The second step is to pull the trim circuit breaker. The pilot can also increase or decrease power to counteract the trim force if necessary.

9. Flaps and trim.

10. Plain flaps are hinged to the aft portion on the wing and provide lift and drag. Split flaps are hinged on the underside of the wing; this type of flap produces mostly drag and very little lift. Fowler flaps increase lift significantly by increasing the surface area of the wing, and they also produce a considerable amount of drag. Slotted flaps allow high-pressure air from below the wing to travel through a slot to the upper surface of the wing, which energizes the boundary layer and delays the onset of a stall.

11. At low angles of deflection the split flap will create an increase in lift, but also a considerable increase in drag. At high deflection angles (higher flap settings) the split flap will create negligible lift but a high amount of drag.

12. Spoilers are most often used to control rate of descent without increasing airspeed. Some aircraft use spoilers for roll control, which has the advantage of eliminating adverse yaw. To turn right, for example, the spoiler on the right wing is raised, destroying some of the lift and creating more drag on the right. The

right wing drops, and the aircraft banks and yaws to the right. Deploying spoilers on both wings at the same time allows the aircraft to descend without gaining speed. Spoilers are also deployed to help reduce ground roll after landing. By destroying lift, they transfer weight to the wheels, improving braking effectiveness.

13. The approach speeds will be higher than normal, leading to a longer-than-normal landing distance.

14. In systems that use individual flap panels, there is a flap position monitor that measures the position of each flap panel during extension or retraction. If the flap positions are asymmetric, the system will stop flap movement and lock out further flap control.

Review 2: Powerplant

1. Shock cooling is when the engine temperature decreases rapidly. This is usually caused by reducing the power in descent and descending at a too-high rate. In extreme cases shock cooling can cause cracks in the engine block, leading to expensive repairs and a decrease in reliability.

2. Fuel and air are the two main ways to cool the engine. Enriching the mixture decreases the cylinder head temperature. In most light twins, the pilot can control airflow over the engine by changing airspeed and adjusting the cowl flaps.

3. The engine will continue to run even if one magneto fails.

4. Carbureted engines mix the fuel and air in the carburetor, while fuel injection directly injects fuel into the intake manifold. Fuel injection mixes the fuel and air more precisely than a carburetor. Carburetors are also susceptible to carburetor ice.

5. Turbocharging provides the engine compressed air that increases the manifold pressure to a value higher than normally produced. For example, at sea level on a standard day, a Piper Seminole will produce about 29–30 in. Hg. If the engine is turbocharged, it could produce 38–40 in. Hg.

6. Turbocharging compresses engine air to a value higher than normally produced. For example, at sea level on a standard day the pressure will be 29.92 inches, and a turbocharged engine will compress the air to 40 inches. Turbo-normalizing works a little differently; with the same sea-level example (standard day, pressure = 29.92 in.), as a turbo-normalized aircraft climbs, the engine will compress the air to *maintain* sea-level pressure, 29.92.

7. The tachometer.

8. Generally, yes. Typically, the mixtures are set rich to help with starting. Leaning prevents fouling of the spark plugs.

9. Yes, the magnetos are engine driven and have nothing to do with the electrical system. The ignition system in a car is run by the electrical system.

10. Mineral oil is used to break-in the engine; generally the limitation is 50 hours or until the oil burn stabilizes. Ashless dispersant oil is used after mineral oil; it cleans, cools, and lubricates. Ashless dispersant is mineral oil, but with chemicals added to it that help keep the engine clean by suspending soot and dirty carbon in the oil—this is the reason why oil turns black after a period of time. Straight mineral oil does not have these added chemicals, making it good for engine break-in, but little else.

11. Fuel is stored in the float chamber prior to being distributed through the discharge nozzle. As the fuel level in the chamber drops, so does the float, allowing fuel to re-enter and fill the chamber. As the chamber fills with fuel, the float rises back up to the top, cutting off the fuel-flow into the chamber. The fuel then exits the float chamber through the nozzle into the venturi, where it is mixed with air and distributed to the cylinders. The amount of fuel and air reaching the cylinders is controlled within the venturi through the throttle valve, which is directly connected to the throttle lever in the aircraft.

12. The ice inside the carburetor could partially melt, move further downstream, and refreeze at a place where full carburetor heat cannot melt it.

13. Once engine oil reaches a certain temperature, the oil is sent through the cooler to reduce the temperature.

14. To clean, cool, and lubricate.

15. I = Fuel injected
O = opposed cylinders
360 = displacement in cubic engines.
If an L proceeds IO, it means it is a left-turning (counter-rotating) engine.

16. After idling on the ground for long periods of time, and/or not leaning the mixture properly.

17. To maintain the proper stoichiometric ratio—leaning to the ideal mixture of fuel/air for the altitude.

18. During ground operations, the throttle valve is slightly open, which creates a vacuum. After engine start, the MAP drops from ambient pressure to a lower pressure. When power is applied on the runway, the throttle valve opens and the pilot transitions from RPM to MAP since the vacuum is gone.

19. The exhaust gas temperature change is immediate and accurate. CHT is accurate but the change occurs slowly, because it is measuring the temperature of the engine's metals, which change at different rates.

Review 3: Propeller Systems

1. Propellers on a multi-engine aircraft are full-feathering.

2. Generally there are five:
   • Nitrogen charge
   • Counterweights
   • Oil pressure
   • Aerodynamic twisting force
   • Feathering spring(s)

3. Low pitch, high RPM—Oil pressure and aerodynamic twisting force
High pitch, low RPM—Nitrogen, counterweights, and springs

4. If oil pressure is lost in a multi-engine aircraft, the propeller will move to the fail-safe position: feathered (minimum drag). In single-engine aircraft, the propeller moves to the low pitch, high RPM position, in which case the pilot may have limited control over engine RPM. In a single-engine airplane, any chance to control the engine RPM is vital, because an engine failure will likely lead to a forced landing. In most cases, multi-engine airplanes generally have the option of flying to a suitable airport.

5. Change blade angle (adjustable pitch) and maintain selected RPM (constant speed).

6. The speeder spring is adjusted by moving the propeller control levers. The pilot valve moves when the speeder spring moves, allowing oil to flow to or from the propeller dome (adjustable pitch). The flyweights maintain the selected RPM by moving out as centrifugal force increases (airloads increasing on blades) and in when centrifugal force decreases (airloads decreasing on blades). The flyweights are connected to the speeder spring, which moves the pilot valve and allows oil to flow to or from the propeller dome (constant speed).

7. The unfeathering accumulator is designed to save wear and tear on the starter on multi-engine training aircraft. It stores high-pressure oil in a long metal cylinder when the pilot moves the propeller control to the feathered position. When the pilot moves the propeller control out of the feathered position, high-pressure oil is released by the accumulator and sent to the propeller dome to push the propeller out of the feathered position. In most cases the pilot will not have to use the starter during an inflight restart.

8. Their purpose is to prevent the propeller blades from moving into the feathered position during engine shutdown on the ground. When the propeller is in the feather position during engine start, it puts increased stress on the aircraft electrical system.

9. An average of 200 to 300 fpm.

Review 4: Fuel

1. Typical types of aviation fuel (AVGAS) are diesel, 100 LL, and Jet-A. Some aircraft also have the ability to use automotive gas.

2. There has been a push for more efficient and environmentally friendly fuels, and alternatives being used or researched, including diesel and biofuels.

3. There are three usual types of containers used for fuel storage: bladder, integral, and rigid removable tanks. Bladder tanks are made of synthetic rubber and are flexible bags that can be replaced easily without having to remove large sections of aircraft skin. An integral tank, often called a "wet wing," uses empty space in the wing and aircraft structure to store fuel. Rigid removable tanks are generally welded aluminium. The structure of the aircraft must be built around them, and the tanks themselves do not provide any structural support. Replacing a rigid removable tank is a lengthy and expensive process.

4. Aircraft can change altitude quickly, so to prevent damage, efficient fuel venting is necessary. There are typically two types: recessed fuel vents and probe vents. Fuel vents provide positive pressure on the fuel in the tank—equalizing the pressure—preventing a vacuum from being created. Recessed vents, also known as NACA fuel vents, prevent ice particles from entering the vent by recessing it into the wing surface. Probe vents are very simple and protrude into the relative wind; they can be heated or unheated.

5. Use Figure 4-4 as an example. (Refer to your aircraft's POH for a specific fuel schematic.)

6. Fuel cross-feed allows the engine on one side to draw fuel from the opposite tank (e.g., left tank, right engine). Fuel transfer is moving fuel from tank to tank to reduce or prevent imbalance. The Piper Seminole includes a fuel cross-feed feature.

7. Electric-driven, and engine-driven.

8. One limitation of cross-feeding is that it often can only be used during straight-and-level cruise. Pilots must be aware of this limitation and take appropriate fuel management actions early.

9. A fuel vent allows the air pressure in the fuel tank to equalize with the surrounding ambient air, preventing the tank from expanding or collapsing, whereas a fuel sump is a normally closed port which allows the pilot to drain any water or sediment from the lowest point in the fuel system.

10. Combustion heaters can burn as much as 3 gallons of fuel per hour.

11. Once the aircraft has reached desired cruise altitude and accelerated to cruise speed, and you've leaned the mixture, complete a fuel check; then, a fuel check should be conducted each hour thereafter.

Review 5: Landing Gear and Hydraulics

1. There are typically two types of landing gear systems: hydraulic and electric. Hydraulic systems have an electrically-driven hydraulic pump that pushes hydraulic fluid into actuators, which extends and retracts the landing gear. Electrical gear systems consist of a motor with levers and cranks, which extend and retract the gear. The hydraulic system is more popular because of its ease of use for emergency gear extension.

2. (See Figure 5-4.)

3. V_{LE}—maximum speed at which you can extend the landing gear.
V_{LO}—maximum speed at which you can operate with the gear down and locked.
V_{LR}—maximum speed at which you can retract the landing gear.

   V_{LO} and V_{LE} generally are gear-door limitations. V_{LR} is a pump pressure issue, meaning above this speed undue pressure is put on the pump, causing wear and premature failure.

4. Squat switches are used to prevent inadvertent retraction of the landing gear on the ground.

5. The limit switches activate the gear warning horn and the gear position lights.

6. The pressure switch shuts off the hydraulic pump when a certain pressure has been reached. The pressure remains stable, holding the gear up until the pilot moves the selector to the down position.

7. The gear warning horn is activated to alert the pilot when the gear is in an unsafe position. Typically, this horn is activated if the selector is moved to the up position while the aircraft is on the ground, the throttles are brought to idle with the gear in the up position, or the flaps are moved past a normal approach setting. Training aircraft will have a gear warning mute switch installed that can be used at altitude while flight training maneuvers are being conducted.

8. There are two primary methods of emergency gear extension, depending on the type of landing gear system installed on the aircraft. In aircraft with hydraulically-actuated gear extension, the primary method of emergency gear extension is by relieving hydraulic pressure and allowing the landing gear to free-fall. The second method of extension, for aircraft with mechanical gear systems, is a hand crank by which the pilot will manually extend the landing gear.

9. The hydraulic brake system uses hydraulic pressure created by foot brakes on the rudder pedals. This pressure is delivered to brake pads on each main wheel via hydraulic lines. The brake pads "squeeze" a brake rotor that is attached to each main wheel, slowing the wheel and the aircraft.

10. *Aborted Takeoff*—If the brakes fail while trying to abort the takeoff, the pilot should respond by reducing power to idle, bringing the mixtures to idle cutoff, and directing the aircraft—using rudder pressures—towards an area that will result in minimal damage to the aircraft and surrounding property. It may be necessary to continue beyond the end of the runway surface, in which case the pilot should ensure that all fuel is shut off, including fuel pumps, to minimize the potential of a fire.

   Landing—Similar to a brake failure during an aborted takeoff, the pilot should respond by reducing power to idle, bringing the mixtures to idle cutoff, and directing the aircraft towards an area that will result in minimal damage.

   During Taxi—If the brakes fail during taxi, the pilot can use rudder pressure to turn the aircraft from side to side to dissipate energy. Additionally, the pilot must ensure the power levers are at idle and bring the mixtures to idle cutoff; then, direct the aircraft towards an open area to minimize damage.

Review 6: Electrical

1. Primary cell batteries are not rechargeable; an example is a traditional Energizer or Duracell AA battery. Secondary cell batteries are rechargeable batteries.

2. In volts and amps.

3. If I have an electrical load of 60 amps, the battery will last 1 hour. With a load of 15 amps, the battery will last 4 hours.

4. Multiple buses make the aircraft safer by allowing essential equipment to be powered by different sources. Also, if a bus has a short, the bus can be isolated from the system.

5. In colder temperatures the chemical process in the battery slows, and therefore its rated output will not match actual output. For example, if it is –10°F outside and the battery is rated at 100 amps/hour, it might be able to operate at 80 amps/hr.

6. Alternators are smaller, lighter, and generally better built than generators. Because an alternator is simple and better built, it can turn at a faster speed than a generator, which makes alternators fully functioning at idle ground speeds.

7. The magnets within the alternator do not produce much electricity on their own. For this reason, the alternator magnets are coiled with a wire, which has electric current flowing through it (called the alternator field). This amplifies the intensity of the magnets. The alternator will not produce electricity without power flowing through the alternator field.

8. The ACU regulates alternator voltage, controls load sharing if two or more alternators are

operating, and takes the alternator offline if an overvoltage condition exists.

9. A diode is an electrical check valve that allows flow in only one direction.

10. Alternator taken off-line by the ACU or the pilot turning the alternator switch off.

11. The aircraft is running on battery power only.

12. Opens the electrical circuit to prevent damage to the equipment if fire or an electrical fault exists.

13. Generally, the pilot should wait 2–3 minutes prior to resetting the circuit breaker. If the circuit breaker protects a fuel system component, it is advisable not to reset the circuit breaker.

14. Dual-fed means multiple alternators or generators are present.

15. Negative ground means the negative side of the battery is grounded to the aircraft airframe. A positive ground system would work for certain electrical equipment, but devices that are sensitive to the direction of flow (i.e., diodes) would be damaged in this type of system.

16. The 70-amp system, restricted to 60 amps, contains more wire coil windings, which reduces the operating temperature of the alternator.

17. An ammeter shows the total load in amperage placed on the electrical system and total load in amperage drawn from the battery in the event of an alternator failure (shown as a negative amp indication); therefore, the pilot can use it to determine the health of an alternator.

18. A contactor (also known as a relay) is an electrically powered switch. There are two types of contactors: those that require electrical power to open, and those that require electrical power to close. The benefit of a contactor over a switch is that they will automatically go to their unpowered state when power is taken away from them. This allows electrical components to be "shed" or removed from the electrical system when power is removed. Most multi-engine aircraft contactors are the powered-closed type, except for the avionics contactor, which is typically powered-open.

19. Most light multi-engine aircraft have what is termed a "hot" EPU. Once the EPU is plugged in and turned on, the aircraft buses are powered without switching the battery on. The specific procedure can be found in Sections 3 and 7 of the POH.

20. Items such as Hobbs meters, clocks, and lights can be powered without turning the battery master switch on.

21. With the EPU connected and on, engage the starter and turn on the battery. If cranking speed increases, the battery is at a higher rate than the EPU.

22. See Figure 6-10. Refer to your aircraft's POH for the specific aircraft information.

Review 7: Environmental

1. In the case of a heater over-temp, the heater over-temperature annunciator will illuminate. If this occurs in flight, the pilot should turn the heater off and leave the air vent open until the annunciator light goes out.

2. Small ice accumulations—no thicker or rougher than a piece of coarse sandpaper—can reduce lift by up to 30 percent and increase drag up to 40 percent.

3. Engine surging, decrease in performance while in level cruise flight, or engine failure.

4. *Deicing* is the removal of ice after it has accumulated, and *anti-icing* is the prevention of ice formation.

5. Most multi-engine aircraft with propeller deice systems use electrically heated pads placed on the leading edge of the propeller blades.

6. In the Piper Seminole, a small combustion engine provides heat for the cabin.

7. Air conditioners are typically electrically powered and require extra engine power, depleting aircraft performance. The Piper Seminole does not have adequate engine power to justify an air conditioner.

8. Immediately turn off the heater, open all fresh air intakes, and land as soon as is practical.

9. Exit the icing conditions immediately.

10. Icing that is observed or detected in flight.

11. Thermal, mechanical, or chemical.

12. By checking the Pilot's Operating Handbook.

13. A device installed on aircraft to condition the air prior to entering the cabin (air conditioning).

Review 8: Oxygen

1. *Diluter-demand*—as altitude increases, partial pressure decreases (oxygen per square foot). The system increases oxygen as altitude increases to keep the amount of oxygen the same.

   Pressure-demand—pressure in the mask is greater than ambient pressure, making it easier to breathe in. This type of mask is generally used in aircraft that fly at high altitudes unpressurized (e.g., fighter jets).

   Continuous flow—this type of mask continuously provides oxygen, regardless of whether the person wearing the mask is inhaling or exhaling.

2. Preflight usually consists of checking the oxygen level, making sure there are enough masks for all the occupants, checking that each mask works, and ensuring that the occupants can operate the masks.

3. Hypoxia is a condition in which the body is deprived of adequate oxygen, resulting in degraded mental and physical performance.

4. The mask inflates and deflates quickly, allowing the pilot to put the mask on quickly and with one hand.

5. 14 CFR §91.211.

6. Aviator's breathing oxygen is 99.9% pure oxygen to prevent freezing in the line. There are three grades of oxygen—aviation, medical, and welding; yet medical and welding oxygen generally meet U.S. aviation requirements and can be used in aircraft, because they contain little to no moisture.

7. Cabin altitudes above 14,000 MSL, up to and including 15,000 MSL.

8. When you are "pressure breathing" you feel the same sensation as if sticking your head out the window of a vehicle while traveling on a freeway. Air is forced into the lungs without effort (a passive process). The user has to force air out of the lungs (with active effort) in order to complete the breathing cycle. This is completely opposite of the normal breathing process.

9. A nasal-cannula mask can only be used up to 18,000 feet because the flow of oxygen is insufficient to provide adequate oxygen content in the lungs at higher altitudes.

10. Most crew oxygen masks will have a built-in microphone to allow the pilot to continue radio communications while wearing the mask. This microphone must be turned on with a switch located somewhere in the cockpit, and you must be able to locate this switch very quickly.

Review 9: Flight Instruments, Avionics, and Warning Systems

1. Attitude and heading reference system.

2. Attitude indicator, heading indicator, and turn coordinator.

3. Air data computer.

4. Airspeed indicator, altimeter, and vertical speed indicator.

5. Red "X" marks, and in some cases, textual instructions are displayed over the affected instrument(s) on the display.

6. During an AHRS failure, the pilot should immediately use the backup attitude indicator for pitch and bank information. In the event the ADC fails, the backup airspeed indicator and altimeter should be used.

7. The backup attitude indicator can be powered by the electrical system or a vacuum system.

8. A magnetometer senses the earth magnetic field and delivers the information directly to the AHRS, then displays the aircraft's current magnetic heading.

9. Most manufacturers of engine indication systems have videos and computer-based instruction software available to help you become familiar with the functions of their systems—pilots must take time to get to know their particular system prior to the first flight with it.

10. It removes the possibility of reverse sensing.

Section II Aerodynamics

Review 10: Multi-Engine Aerodynamics and V-Speeds

1. Induced airflow is propwash flowing over the wings or tail directly impacting the lift produced by the airfoil.

2. In a conventional twin aircraft, both propellers will turn in the same direction. Routinely, this will be clockwise from the pilot's perspective, placing the critical engine on the left. In a counter-rotating twin the propellers will turn toward each other. Typically, they will turn inward toward the fuselage. From the pilot's perspective, the left engine would be clockwise and the right engine would be counterclockwise. This configuration will eliminate the critical engine.

3.

Conventional Twin	Counter-rotating Twin
Pros	Pros
Reduced maintenance costs	No critical engine
Reduced part inventory	No left-turning tendencies
Cons	Cons
Critical engine	Higher maintenance costs
Significant left-turning tendencies	Increased parts inventory

4. • Increased climb performance
   • Increased cruise speeds
   • Increased ability to operate at higher altitudes
   • Increased safety through redundancy

5. Lift: Due to the loss of induced airflow over the affected wing and the naturally slower airspeed of the aircraft during single-engine operations, a higher angle of attack is needed to produce the required lift to counteract weight.

   Drag: Parasite drag will increase as a result of the failed engine. Even with a feathered propeller there will be a noticeable increase in the roll and yaw toward the failed engine due to parasite drag. The induced drag will increase because of the higher angle of attack and slower airspeed needed to maintain altitude with the failed engine.

   Thrust: Overall thrust or power available will be reduced by 50% and performance could see as much as an 80% decrease, due to the loss of excess thrust/power that would normally be produced by an operating second engine.

   Weight: When flying a multi-engine aircraft with an inoperative engine, it is recommended to use bank and rudder to counteract the forces of roll and yaw. This increase in bank will also increase the aircraft's load factor—essentially increasing the overall weight, which will require a slightly higher angle of attack to produce the needed lift. In addition, careful fuel-management planning may be needed to maintain proper aircraft balance as fuel is burned.

6. V_{MC} is the minimum speed at which the aircraft is controllable with the loss of the critical engine and the operating engine at takeoff power. V_{MC} is marked with a red line on the airspeed indicator and is determined during aircraft certification.

Review 11: Flight Characteristics of Single-Engine Operations

1. • P-factor
   • Torque
   • Accelerated slipstream
   • Spiraling slipstream

2. The "law of the lever" can be applied to single-engine operations by the formula, weight × arm = moment. The law of the lever helps the pilot understand the significance of rudder authority in multi-engine operations when you experience an engine failure. In this context, the law of the lever is commonly referred to as rudder authority. In single-engine operations, applied weight is measured in foot-pounds of rudder force. A moment is a force that causes something to rotate. When arm length or force is changed, the moment is altered accordingly. Greater moments equal greater rotating force and make the airplane more difficult to control; the opposite holds true with lesser moments making the aircraft easier to control.

3. The ability of the rudder to generate adequate moment under specific conditions via the law of the lever (or weight × arm).

4. P-factor is the result of a descending propeller blade having a higher angle of attack in the horizontal plane, or thrust. On the conventional twin, this descending blade is further from the CG of the aircraft on the right engine, as compared to on the left. This greater distance gives the right engine a larger moment compared to the descending blade of the left engine. When the left engine fails, the resulting roll and yaw imparted by the right engine is greater, compared to a right-engine failure and the moment from the left engine. This greater moment on the right engine makes the failure of the left engine critical, compared to a right-engine failure.

5. As a result of P-factor, the induced airflow behind the descending blade is greater that of the ascending blade. This produces more velocity and greater lift on the outer portion of the right wing and the inner portion of the left wing. The arms are correspondingly different, causing the moment to be greater for the right when the left engine is failed, making the left engine the critical one.

6. As the air spirals rearward from the left engine, it imparts a force on the rudder, contributing to a yaw to the left. On the right engine, this rearward spiraling air does not impart a force on the rudder. When a right engine is failed, this spiraling slipsteam works to counteract yawing tendencies, but when the left engine fails there is not additional help to counteract the yawing. This contributes to making the left engine critical.

7. As the third law of motion states, simply, for every action there is a reaction; the propeller blades turning to the right reacts with a yaw to the left. In the event of a left engine failure, this torque adds to the yaw inherent with an engine failure.

8. By definition, a counter-rotating aircraft does not have a critical engine: the loss of either engine will have the same aerodynamic effect on the aircraft.

Review 12: Single-Engine Aerodynamics and Operations

1. When using only rudder to counteract an engine failure, the pilot will have a dramatic increase in V_{MC} speed. Without bank and the helpful horizontal component of lift, rudder authority is diminished. Performance will also be impacted negatively due to the sideslip, but this is minimal compared to the V_{MC} increase.

2. Using only aileron to counteract an engine failure will result in a decrease in V_{MC} but a dramatic decrease in aircraft performance due to the large sideslip of the airplane and the corresponding drag.

3. Zero sideslip is a method of flying a multi-engine aircraft using both rudder and aileron deflection to achieve maximum performance while only increasing V_{MC} a few knots.

4. • Critical engine inoperative
  • No more than 5 degrees of bank
  • Maximum available takeoff power
  • Trimmed for takeoff
  • Flaps in the takeoff position
  • Landing gear retracted
  • Propeller controls in the recommended takeoff position
  • Most unfavorable weight (maximum takeoff weight)
  • Most unfavorable CG position
  • Out of ground effect
  • Maximum rudder force of 150 pounds to maintain control

5.

Certification Factor	Effect on V_{MC}	Effect on Performance
Critical engine inoperative	Increase	Decrease
No more than 5 degrees of bank	Decrease	Decrease
Maximum available takeoff power	Increase	Increase
Trimmed for takeoff	Increase	Negligible
Flaps in the takeoff position	Aircraft-specific	Flaps extended—Decrease Flaps retracted—Increase
Landing gear retracted	Increase	Increase
Propeller controls in the takeoff position	Increase	Increase
Maximum takeoff weight	Increase	Decrease
Most unfavorable CG	Increase	Increase
Out of ground effect	Increase	Decrease
Maximum rudder force of 150 pounds	Increase	Negligible

6. A V_{MC} demonstration will give the pilot a better understanding of how different configurations affect the aircraft's V_{MC} speed. It will also familiarize the pilot with the indications of a loss of directional control and the proper recovery techniques and procedures at safe altitudes.

7. As density altitude increases, power in a normally-aspirated engine will decrease. This reduction in power will cause a decrease in V_{MC} speed. At higher altitudes, stall may occur prior to V_{MC} [see Figure 12.4]; understanding this is key, so this can be practiced in flight with a certified flight instructor. Simulated loss of directional control—called a V_{MC} demo—is a maneuver practiced by multi-engine pilots to help them learn recovery techniques. A single-engine stall, however, is not practiced and may prove unrecoverable due to the characteristics of a multi-engine aircraft.

Section III Multi-Engine Operations

Review 13: Weight and Balance

1. *Takeoff Weight:* 3,796.78

Center of gravity: 88.57

Within limitations? No, the CG is forward of the forward CG envelope. The pilot will need to redistribute the weight to move the CG rearward.

Item	Weight (lbs)	Arm aft (inches)	Moment (in/lbs)
Basic empty weight	2,682.78	85.99	230,695.71
Pilot	220.00	80.50	17,710.00
Front passenger	200.00	80.50	16,100.00
Passenger 1	150.00	118.10	17,715.00
Passenger 2			
Baggage area (200 lbs. max.)	50.00	142.80	7,140.00
Fuel (108 gallons max)	510.0	95.00	48,450.00
Ramp weight	3,812.8	88.60	337,810.71
Fuel for runup (2.67 gallons)	-16.0	95.00	-1,520.00
Takeoff weight (3,800 lbs. max.)	**3,796.78**	**88.57**	336,290.71
Fuel use for trip		95.00	
Landing weight			

2. *Takeoff Weight:* 3,714.4

Center of gravity: 90.72

Within limitations? Yes. The CG falls well inside the envelope.

Item	Weight (lbs)	Arm aft (inches)	Moment (in/lbs)
Basic empty weight	2,682.63	85.89	230,398.03
Pilot	150.00	80.50	12,075.00
Front passenger			
Passenger 1	50.00	118.10	5,905.00
Passenger 2			
Baggage area (200 lbs. max.)	200.00	142.80	28,560.00
Fuel (108 gallons max)	648.0	95.00	61,560.00
Ramp weight	3,730.6	90.74	338,498.03
Fuel for runup (2.67 gallons)	-16.0	95.00	-1,520.00
Takeoff weight (3,800 lbs. max.)	**3,714.63**	**90.72**	336,978.03
Fuel use for trip		95.00	
Landing weight			

3. *Takeoff weight:* 7,361.56

Center of gravity: 153.14

Within limitations? Yes. The weight is below the maximum takeoff weight of 7,450 pounds and the CG fits well inside the envelope.

Item	Weight	Arm	Moment/100
Basic empty weight	5,213.56	152.70	7,961.27
Pilot	190	137.00	260.30
Seat 1	215	137.00	294.55
Seat 2	170	162.00	275.40
Seat 3	170	162.00	275.40
Seat 4	0	190.00	0.00
Seat 5	0	190.00	0.00
Seat 6	0	218.00	0.00
Nose	50	71.00	35.50
Wing lockers	15	186.00	27.90
Baggage A	10	266.00	26.60
Baggage B	10	282.00	28.20
Zero fuel weight	6,043.56	151.98	9,185.12
Fuel (main tanks)	600	152.00	912.00
Fuel (aux tanks)	456	164.00	747.84
Fuel (lockers)	312	164.00	511.68
Ramp weight	7,411.56	153.23	11,356.64
Taxi fuel	-50		-83.00
Takeoff weight	**7,361.56**	**153.14**	11,273.64
Fuel burn	666	152.00	1,012.32
Locker fuel burn	312	167.00	521.04
Landing weight	6,383.56	152.58	9,740.28

Review 14: Performance

1. *Accelerate/stop distance:* 2,800 ft

Takeoff ground roll distance: 1,500 ft

Takeoff distance over 50-ft obstacle: 2,500 ft

Obstacle speed: 78 KIAS

Climb performance—one engine operating (gear up): 80 fpm

2. *Landing distance:* 630 ft

Landing distance over 50-ft obstacle: 1,400 ft

Approach speed: 69 KIAS

3. *One engine inoperative service ceiling:* 5,000 ft

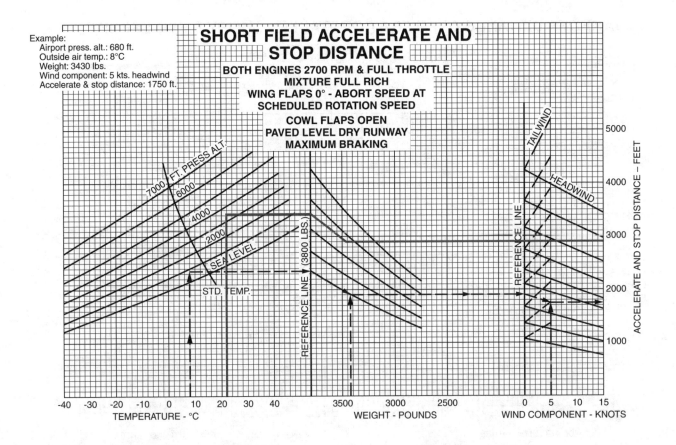

SHORT FIELD ACCELERATE AND STOP DISTANCE

BOTH ENGINES 2700 RPM & FULL THROTTLE
MIXTURE FULL RICH
WING FLAPS 0° - ABORT SPEED AT
SCHEDULED ROTATION SPEED
COWL FLAPS OPEN
PAVED LEVEL DRY RUNWAY
MAXIMUM BRAKING

Example:
Airport press. alt.: 680 ft.
Outside air temp.: 8°C
Weight: 3430 lbs.
Wind component: 5 kts. headwind
Accelerate & stop distance: 1750 ft.

CLIMB PERFORMANCE – ONE ENGINE OPERATING – GEAR UP

ASSOCIATED CONDITIONS:
Wing Flaps: 0°
Cowl Flaps:
  (Operating Engine): OPEN
  (Inoperative Engine): CLOSED
Landing Gear: UP

Mixture: FULL RICH
Prop:
  (Inoperative Engine): FEATHERED
Power: 2700 RPM
    FULL THROTTLE
Airspeed: 88 KIAS

NOTE
2° TO 3° BANK TOWARD
OPERATING ENGINE

EXAMPLE:
Outside Air Temp.: 8°C
Press Alt.: 1250 FT.
Weight: 3430
One Engine
  Inoperative Climb: 285 F.P.M.

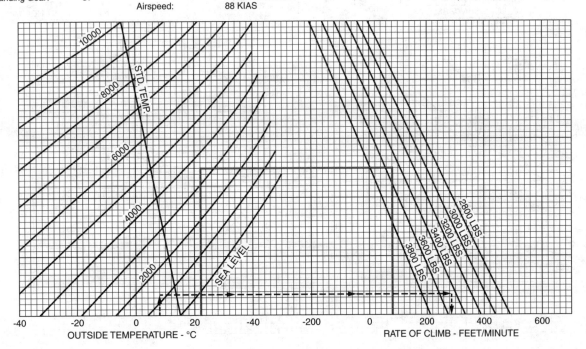

TAKEOFF DISTANCE OVER 50 FT OBSTACLE - SHORT FIELD EFFORT

ASSOCIATED CONDITIONS:
Wing Flaps: 0°
Cowl Flaps: OPEN
Power: 2700 RPM & FULL THROTTLE
BEFORE BRAKE RELEASE
Runway: PAVED, LEVEL & DRY

WEIGHT POUNDS	ROTATE SPEED KIAS	OBSTACLE SPEED KIAS
3800	70	82
3400	66	77
3000	62	72
2600	57	67

CAUTION

BEST ONE ENGINE INOPER-
ATIVE RATE OF CLIMB IS
LESS THAN 50 FPM IF T.O.
WT. IS IN THE SHADED AREA.

EXAMPLE:
O.A.T.: 8°C
Airport Pressure Altitude: 1250 FT
Weight: 3430 LBS
Wind Component: 6 KT HEADWIND
Takeoff Distance
Over 50 FT Obstacle: 1520 FT

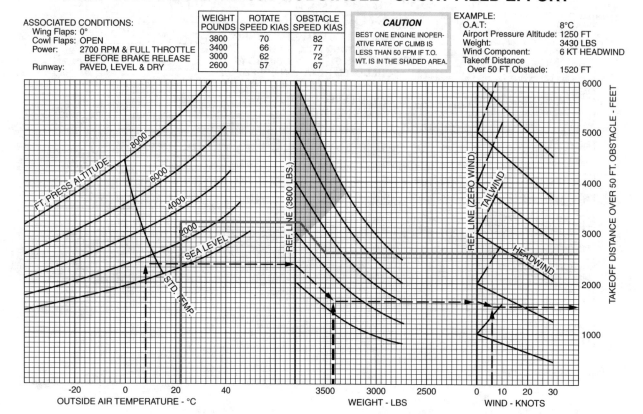

TAKEOFF GROUND ROLL - SHORT FIELD EFFORT

ASSOCIATED CONDITIONS:
Wing Flaps: 0°
Cowl Flaps: OPEN
Power: 2700 RPM & FULL THROTTLE
BEFORE BRAKE RELEASE
Runway: PAVED, LEVEL & DRY

WEIGHT POUNDS	ROTATE SPEED KIAS
3800	70
3400	66
3000	62
2600	57

CAUTION

BEST ONE ENGINE INOPER-
ATIVE RATE OF CLIMB IS
LESS THAN 50 FPM IF T.O.
WT. IS IN THE SHADED AREA.

EXAMPLE:
O.A.T.: 8°C
Airport Pressure Altitude: 1250 FT
Weight: 3430 LBS
Wind Component: 6 KT HEADWIND
Takeoff Ground Roll: 860 FT

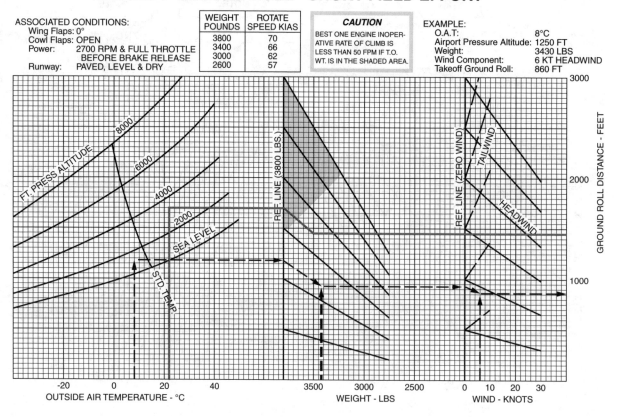

LANDING DISTANCE OVER 50 FT OBSTACLE - SHORT FIELD EFFORT

ASSOCIATED CONDITIONS:
Wing Flaps: 40°
Power: OFF
Cowl Flaps: AS REQUIRED
Runway: PAVED LEVEL & DRY
Touchdown: FULL STALL
Approach Speed: AS SCHEDULED

EXAMPLE:
O.A.T: 8°
Press. Alt.: 680 FT
Weight: 3107 LBS
Wind Component: 5 KT HEADWIND

Approach Speed: 68 KIAS
Total Landing Distance: 1238 FT

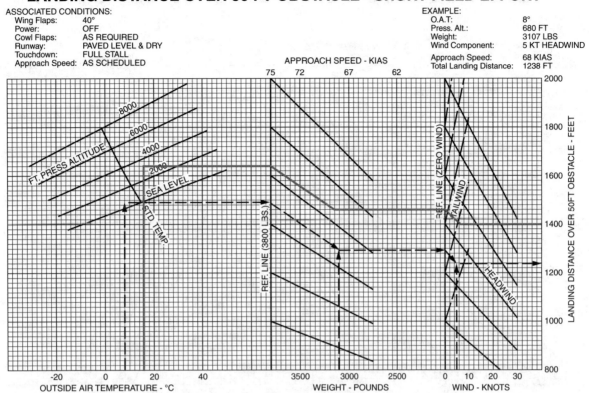

LANDING GROUND ROLL - SHORT FIELD EFFORT

ASSOCIATED CONDITIONS:
Wing Flaps: 40°
Power: OFF
Cowl Flaps: OPEN
Runway: PAVED LEVEL & DRY
Touchdown: FULL STALL

EXAMPLE:
O.A.T: 8°
Press. Alt.: 680 FT
Weight: 3107 LBS
Wind Component: 5 KT HEADWIND
Landing Ground Roll: 542 FT

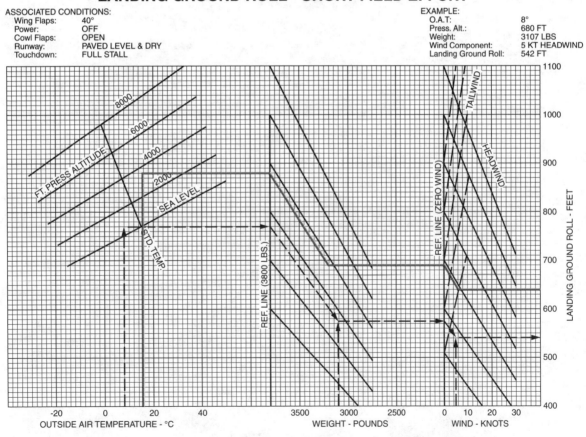

CLIMB PERFORMANCE – ONE ENGINE OPERATING – GEAR UP

ASSOCIATED CONDITIONS:

Wing Flaps:	0°	Mixture:	FULL RICH
Cowl Flaps:		Prop:	
(Operating Engine):	OPEN	(Inoperative Engine):	FEATHERED
(Inoperative Engine):	CLOSED	Power:	2700 RPM
Landing Gear:	UP		FULL THROTTLE
		Airspeed:	88 KIAS

NOTE
2° TO 3° BANK TOWARD
OPERATING ENGINE

EXAMPLE:

Outside Air Temp.:	8°C
Press Alt.:	1250 FT.
Weight:	3430
One Engine	
Inoperative Climb:	285 F.P.M.

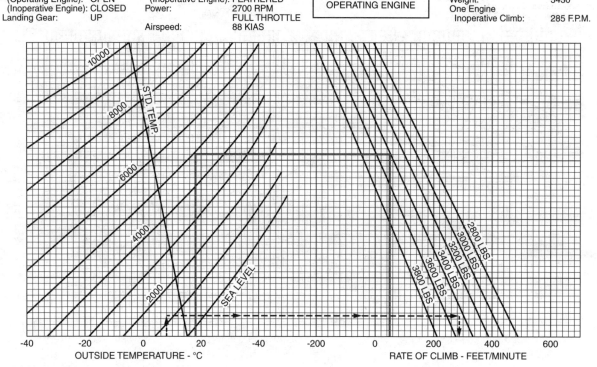

OUTSIDE TEMPERATURE - °C   RATE OF CLIMB - FEET/MINUTE

Review 15: Regulations

1. A carrier—pilot or operator—becomes a common carrier when it "holds out" to the public or a segment of the public and is willing to offer transportation to any person who wants it. There are four elements defining common carriage:

   1. Holding out

   2. Transporting persons or property

   3. From place to place

   4. For compensation

   If any of the above is not met, the operation is considered private carriage.

2. Holding out is a phrase used to describe advertising the availability of services. This can mean physically advertising—for example, via a newspaper or website—or it can mean showing a willingness to offer a service. The latter form of advertising is more indirect and difficult to characterize.

3. 1. Exchange of money (most likely)

   2. Exchange of products

   3. Exchange of services

   4. Flight time (logged or not)

   5. Goodwill or an expectation of goodwill

4. An equal exchange of services.

5. The carriage of passengers for hire on cross-country flight in excess of 50 NM or at night is prohibited.

6. 14 CFR Part 119 are regulations that apply to air carriers or commercial operators intending to operate in air commerce (to charge for services).

7. • Operations conducted under Part 91 subpart K—fractional ownership fleet operators (i.e., NetJets)
   • Student instruction—if you hold your instructor certificate
   • Nonstop commercial air tours (such as Grand Canyon tours)
   • Ferry or training flights
   • Crop dusting
   • Banner towing
   • Aerial photography or survey (commercial pilots cannot transport a photographer)
   • Fire fighting
   • Helicopter operations in construction or repair work (does apply to transportation to and from the site)
   • Powerline or pipeline patrol
   • Nonstop flights conducted within 25 SM of the airport of takeoff for the purpose of parachute jumping
   • Emergency mail service
   • Flying candidates for elections (rule refers to 14 CFR §91.321)

8. Dry lease—leasing only the airplane.

   Wet lease—leasing the airplane and pilot from the same source.

9. No, this is not a legal operation unless the FBO has a Part 135 certificate. To be legal under Part 91, the pilot and aircraft must come from separate sources.

10. Yes, you can legally fly for your neighbor and receive compensation, in this case Seattle Seahawks season tickets. This is considered private carriage since your neighbor owns the airplane and is compensating you to be the pilot.